THE
POLITICAL COMMUNITY

SEBASTIAN DE GRAZIA

THE
POLITICAL COMMUNITY

A STUDY OF ANOMIE

*That were to set an Anomy, and to
bring disorder, doubt and incertantie
over all.*—LAMBARDE, *Archeion* (1635)

THE UNIVERSITY OF CHICAGO PRESS
CHICAGO & LONDON

THE UNIVERSITY OF CHICAGO PRESS, CHICAGO & LONDON
The University of Toronto Press, Toronto 5, Canada

Soc

ACKNOWLEDGMENTS

I WISH to record a special indebtedness to Ralph Winfred Tyler for encouragement and help in the preparation of this study in political theory. I owe similar thanks to my colleagues W. Lloyd Warner, Renzo Sereno, Herman Finer, Wilhelm Pauck, Pendleton Herring, Lionel Blitsten, J. Gordon Hall, Fred Eggan, Harold D. Lasswell, Malcolm P. Sharp, Avery Leiserson, Robert Redfield, and to Charles E. Merriam. Grateful acknowledgment is made to the Social Science Research Committee of the University of Chicago for its support in the preparation of the book. For the tasks of editing, proofing, typing, and assembling the materials, my gratitude goes to Muriel Deutsch, B. J. Tullis, Yvonne Kustudick, and Gertrude Heitz. I wish also to express my affectionate appreciation for the help of my wife at each stage of the book.

Acknowledgments are gratefully made to the following publishers and authors for permission to reprint:

The Macmillan Company, for use of William B. Yeats, *Later Poems* (copyright, 1924); Stuart Chase, *The Nemesis of American Business* (copyright, 1939); M. Ostrogorski, *Democracy and the Party System* (copyright, 1910); Charles and Mary Beard, *America in Midpassage* (copyright, 1939); Perry Miller, *The New England Mind* (copyright, 1939); Robert Briffault, *The Mothers* (copyright, 1931); Harold R. G. Greaves, *The British Constitution* (copyright, 1938); and Miriam Beard, *The History of the Business Man* (copyright, 1938, by Miriam Beard Vagts).

Harcourt, Brace and Company, Inc., for use of James A. Farley, *Behind the Ballots;* C. G. Jung, *Modern Man in Search of a Soul;* Robert S. Lynd and Helen Merrell Lynd, *Middletown in Transition;* Virginia Woolf, *Mrs. Dalloway;* and Sinclair Lewis, *Babbitt* (copyright, 1922).

The Oxford University Press, for use of O. F. Raum, *Chaga Childhood;* Arnold J. Toynbee, *A Study of History; Nationalism;* A. M. Hocart, *Kingship;* Bronislaw Malinowski, *Foundations of Faith and Morals;* and Lucretius, *On the Nature of Things.*

Rinehart and Company, Inc., for use of R. M. MacIver, *Society;* Charles W. Ferguson, *Fifty Million Brothers;* and Erich Fromm, *Escape from Freedom.*

Harper and Brothers, Publishers, for use of Frank H. Knight and Thornton W. Merriam, *The Economic Order and Religion;* and J. B. Priestley, *Postscripts.*

v

Rand McNally and Company, for use of Mary Alice Jones, *Tell Me about God* (copyright, 1943).

Routledge and Kegan Paul, Ltd., for use of C. G. and B. Z. Seligman, *Pagan Tribes of the Nilotic Sudan;* and C. G. Jung; *Modern Man in Search of a Soul.*

The Ronald Press Company, for use of Therese Benedek, *Insight and Personality Adjustment* (copyright, 1946).

The W. W. Norton Company, Inc., for use of Otto Fenichel, *The Psychoanalytic Theory of the Neuroses* (copyright, 1945); and Karen Horney, *The Neurotic Personality of Our Time* (copyright, 1937).

Henry Holt and Company, Inc., for use of Henri de Man, *Joy in Work.*

Alfred A. Knopf, Inc., for use of Kingsley Martin, *The Magic of Monarchy.*

John Murray, for use of Derrick Sington and Arthur Weidenfeld, *The Goebbels Experiment.*

Dodd, Mead and Company, Inc., for use of H. C. Englebrecht, *The Revolt against War.*

Albert Whitman and Company, for use of Edward Everett Hale, *The Man without a Country.*

Longmans, Green and Company, Inc., for use of Quincy Wright, *The Causes of War and the Conditions of Peace.*

J. B. Lippincott Company, for use of Franz Alexander, *Our Age of Unreason.*

The Blakiston Company, for use of Roy R. Grinker and John P. Spiegel, *Men under Stress.*

The Principia Press, Inc., for use of Lauren J. Mills, *One Soul in Bodies Twain.*

Charles Scribner's Sons, for use of Dixon Wecter, *The Saga of American Society;* Max Weber, *The Protestant Ethic and the Spirit of Capitalism;* and Edmund Gosse, *Father and Son.*

The Commonwealth Fund, for use of James S. Plant, *Personality and the Cultural Pattern.*

The Muhlenberg Press, for use of *Little Visits with Jesus.*

Little, Brown and Company, for use of Erich Maria Remarque, *All Quiet on the Western Front.*

Prentice-Hall, Inc., for use of Theodore Abel, *Why Hitler Came to Power* (copyright, 1938).

The John Day Company, Inc., for use of Peter Drucker, *The End of Economic Man.*

Appleton-Century-Crofts, Inc., for use of Caroline B. Zachry, *Emotions and Conduct in Adolescence;* Ralph Linton, *The Study of Man;* Raymond T. Bye, *Principles of Economics;* and Walter Bagehot, *The English Constitution.*

Doubleday and Company, for use of Drew Pearson and Robert S. Allen, *The Nine Old Men* (copyright, 1936); and William L. Riordan, *Plunkitt of Tammany Hall* (copyright, 1905).

The Houghton Mifflin Company, for use of Frank H. Knight, *Risk, Uncertainty and Profit.*

Penguin Books, Ltd., for use of Charles Madge and Tom Harrisson, *Britain by Mass Observation.*

George Allen and Unwin, Ltd., for use of Carolyn E. Playne, *Society at War;* Harold R. G. Greaves, *The British Constitution;* and Max Weber, *The Protestant Ethic and the Spirit of Capitalism.*

The Hogarth Press, Ltd., for use of Rainer Maria Rilke, *Duino Elegies;* Sigmund Freud, *Civilization and Its Discontents;* and Virginia Woolf, *Mrs. Dalloway.*

Ivor Nicholson and Watson, Ltd., for use of H. V. Routh, *Money, Morals and Manners as Revealed in Modern Literature.*

John Gloag, for use of *Word Warfare* (published by Ivor Nicholson and Watson, Ltd., 1939).

E. P. Dutton, for use of Jean Jacques Rousseau, *Émile;* and E. Wight Bakke, *The Unemployed Man.*

The Orgone Institute Press, for use of Wilhelm Reich, *The Function of the Orgasm.*

William Heineman, Ltd., for use of J. B. Priestley, *Postscripts;* and Edmund Gosse, *Father and Son.*

James Nisbet and Company, Ltd., for use of E. Wight Bakke, *The Unemployed Man.*

Roy V. Peel, for use of *The Political Clubs of New York City* (published by G. P. Putnam's Sons).

Harper's Magazine, for use of "Man Out of Work" by Anonymous.

S DE G

UNIVERSITY OF CHICAGO

INTRODUCTION

THE Great Community, as the ancient Greeks understood well, the community which embraces all other communities, is the political community. Holding it together are systems of beliefs, flexible bands weaving through and around each member of the community, compacting it, allowing some stretch at times, coiling like a steel spring at others. The basic denominator of citizens is these belief-systems which express their ideas concerning their relationship to one another and to their rulers. Without them, without this fundament of commonness, no political community can be said to exist. The study of anomie is the study of the ideological factors that weaken or destroy the bonds of allegiance which make the political community. The rupture or twisting of these bonds affects the ties of all the lesser associations within the community in a graver manner than has been suspected.

It is high time that these facts are made known once again. For many long years now the importance to men of common belief-systems has been neglected. The cause is not hard to find, for in a sense the scholarly world has been offering prizes for the discovery of diversity and contradictions among the peoples of the world. In the nineteenth century a number of social philosophers found the idea of a distinction between the state and "society" attractive. The idea was attractive not only to themselves but to those who believed that the good life for everyone depended on freedom from many of the long-established ties of church and state. These latter men were the champions, wittingly or not, of an economic ideology whose path was blocked by the moral restraints of the political and religious community. The political community bore the frontal attack, an attack designed to reduce it to a collection of individual consumers who could act like the fictional unattached men in the theories of classical economics. But such a collection was not a community, it was a congeries; hence the preference for the term "society," which came to mean a body of men grouped together by something less than religious and political bonds. With this word before his eyes the social scientist, too, lost sight of the political community. He found himself encouraged to consider belief-systems as mere faiths, as the irrational elements of "society," sandbags in a vessel that needed speed, not ballast. What need had men of them? So when, as anthropologist, he made expeditions into primitive communities, he marveled at the rich variety of morals and manners—and let their universal function escape him. Breaking the news of primitive practices to a world that found them coarse and immoral became an infectious habit. A perverse joy seized the scholarly world.

One thing cannot be said: that the anthropologist doubted whether the rude peoples he found were communities. He did not. He knew they were. But in his reports to civilization his labors were heaviest in presenting differences and contrarieties. Meanwhile his efforts were having the indirect effect of doubling the burden of theologians and political philosophers, already hard put in the tide of swelling relativism. Had the scholarly explorer only told them that he had found the sense of community almost everywhere alive, their minds might have felt less oppressed. They could then have asked: What is it that makes a group of people a community? The answer is—their religious and political beliefs. And these beliefs fulfil a need common to man everywhere. Never mind their variety. There are many lands and diverse customs, but it is the same need in all men that brings them together. What this need is, is the problem that makes the pages of this book akin from cover to cover.

Today the great nations of the West neither bask in the sunlight of community nor shiver in the darkness of anarchy. They wander somewhere in the dusk of a "society." The fabric of their political and religious beliefs is pierced and rent by the intrusion of ideologies which are not fundamental, which are not universal, which need not stay to wreak confusion and play hob with men's souls. A collection of individual consumers men will never be. They could not if they wanted to. It goes against the grain. But neither are they Citizens or Believers. Instead, men stand today in this twilight zone of a "society," uneasy, distressed, feeling joined to their fellows only in war or crisis; and behind the inner doors of their mind they welcome war or crisis for the feeling of community it gives them. They stand as "individuals," which is all they can ever be in a society.

But the earth is parched with the aridity of the Individual. Never constant, always a sign of disorder, the notion of the individual has agitated the Western world since the deaths of Alexander and Aristotle. The world then, as now, wanted for men of station and purpose. Once more it needs the ideal of the Citizen, a man of duties and responsibilities, a man of position and significance, of religious and political beliefs, a man with status in the political community.

Modern political science, too, has had a tendency—here more largely due no doubt to the influence of Marxian theory—to consider beliefs only on a superficial plane. In part, also, this surface consideration is due to the fact that in restful epochs systems of beliefs behave like the blood's circulation—they run quiet and deep. How deep they are, how firmly imbedded in the personality, will be shown in the early chapters of this study. But if a threat disrupts an ideological system (if a wound, for that matter, breaks the skin), the vital psychological function of beliefs stands out in scarlet vividness. Out of disturbances in the reigning belief-systems anomie arises, a mental tension which in its moderate type reveals an intermittent apprehension in the adult of a danger before which he is helpless and which in its severe type mounts to an anxiety fraught with terrifying images of a menacing world.

In the social sciences problems have a way of spilling over one discipline onto another. The field would be awash were it not for the resistant dams that exist in the form of different terms for similar things in the political, sociological, and psychological areas. The concept of anomie which is introduced here is a good example of an idea that from the beginning has had difficulties in remaining within the confines of its birth. Its first important appearance occurred in 1893 in a book by Émile Durkheim entitled *De la division du travail social*. The division of labor was an idea developed by Adam Smith, the classical economist. But Émile Durkheim, who in his book associated the idea of anomie with the idea of the division of labor, was a great French sociologist. In other works Durkheim enriched the concept of anomie by relating it to certain social phenomena like suicide and certain economic phenomena like fluctuations in the business cycle. And when he came to the problem of a corrective for anomie, the sociologist had to turn this time to a political solution, guild socialism, or guild representation, using in addition, so it is said, some of the ideas of the political theorist, Pierre Joseph Proudhon.

Moreover, the overlapping of the concept "anomie" within the social sciences does not end with Durkheim. Both before and after and even during his lifetime, other men—philosophers, political scientists, economists, poets, sociologists, theologians, historians—were writing about the same problem. True, they did not call it anomie. Durkheim first named the phenomenon; and its diffusion as a term, even among social scientists, has not been wide. The sociologists themselves have not used the concept much in their writings, with the exception of those who were either disciples of Durkheim or commentators on his work. But the contributions of other writers will seem more clearly related, if, not the word "anomie" is kept in mind, but Durkheim's meaning of it as the disintegrated state of a society that possesses no body of common values or morals which effectively govern conduct.

Was not Plato arguing the necessity for a body of common values with moral authority when he proposed to fabricate a royal fable for his Republic? Joseph de Maistre in his *Considérations sur la France* was similarly engaged. Reason disintegrates, he insisted, Faith unites. Was not Marx lamenting the deterioration of a body of values of a bygone day in his Manifesto?

> The bourgeoisie . . . has put an end to all feudal, patriarchal, idyllic relations. It has pitilessly torn asunder . . . and has left no other bond between man and man than naked self-interest, than callous "cash payment." It has drowned the most heavenly ecstasies of religious fervor, of chivalrous enthusiasm, of philistine sentimentalism in the icy water of egotistical calculation. . . . The bourgeoisie has stripped of its halo every occupation hitherto honored and looked up to with reverent awe . . . has torn away from the family its sentimental veil.

Did not Nietzsche believe that he could create a new body of purposes for hopeless lives when he demanded that the world "turn toward the ideal of the most domineering, the most living, the most aggressive of men, toward him who has not merely reconciled and adjusted himself to things as they are and have been; but who wants more of them, just as they are . . . crying insatiably *da capo* not to his own life only, but to the whole scene and all the play''; when he shouted with the voice of Zarathustra, "I bring you a goal! Lo, I preach to you the Superman!" And John Dewey in *Freedom and Culture* soberly reminds his era that "a culture which permits science to destroy traditional values but which distrusts its power to create new ones is a culture which is destroying itself." He, too, like the others and like Durkheim, is speaking of the plight of a society without *solidarité*, an anomic society.

These men were concerned in large measure with the political organization of communities. They are political theorists, and by no means the only ones of their brethren, who have implicitly recognized the importance of anomie in the problem of political organization. Indeed, in this broad sense, anomie has been almost universally recognized as a growing malady of modern civilization as well as an outstanding curse of the so-called declining eras of other societies. Arnold J. Toynbee, the most recent surveyor of civilizations, unknowingly describes anomie when he searches for the common psychological factor in the breakdown and disintegration of all the civilized societies in the world's history. In the people of such communities, he finds

a painful consciousness of being "on the run" from forces of evil which have taken the offensive and established their ascendancy. The passive expression of this consciousness of continual and progressive moral defeat is a sense of drift. The routed soul is prostrated by a perception of its failure to control its environment; it comes to believe that the Universe, including the soul itself, is at the mercy of a power that is as irrational as it is invincible.

Subsequent chapters will clearly show that the historian is painting a picture of the animistic and hostile environment that distinguishes the more virulent form of anomie. They will also show that it is not necessary for a whole civilization to break down before one can observe in its component political units an ideological decay. In recent decades many persons were surprised at the ease with which modern states like Italy, Germany, and France crumbled from within. Although this study does not treat these twentieth-century events seriatim (only the case of Germany is specifically analyzed), it does present the generalizations which in their further application may make these crises in contemporary civilization less puzzling.

Surprisingly, for a problem of such antiquity and yet great moment, little systematic study has been given to anomie and its effect on the political community. Perhaps the recency of its isolation and diagnosis by Durkheim accounts for the lack of attention. Yet after his time, too, most speculation on the subject has been limited to vague ascriptions of such causes as the mobility of urban populations or the disillusion brought by science. It was the objective of this study to arrive at a theory of anomie and thus at a systematized set of new hypotheses on the causes and consequences of the disintegration of political belief-systems. Interest was centered on the relationships of belief-systems to one another, their psychological congruence or incongruence, superficiality or depth. And as the evolution of systems of beliefs from child to adult was delineated, a rather restricted meaning was attached to the term "belief-system." It refers to the ensemble of beliefs which men hold concerning activities that presumably contribute to their common welfare. As such, a belief-system inevitably contains the ideas of people about their relationship to one another and to their rulers. Clearly, the very aim of the study committed it to an intensive consideration of religious, political, and economic ideologies, including such contemporary representatives as Protestantism and Catholicism, democracy and fascism. This part of the task, it must be admitted, invited the dangers of prejudice. Therefore a continuing effort was made to maintain the spirit of dispassion.

The theory of the political community could not have been significantly furthered were it not for recent advances in the social sciences. Psychology and its closely related branches of psychiatry and psychoanalysis in particular have made far-reaching additions to knowledge in the last fifty years. The swiftly expanding body of facts and propositions in modern psychology proved to be the most useful lieutenant in this attack on the problem of anomie and the political community. "Politics uses the rest of the sciences," said Aristotle.

From almost any standpoint the consequences of anomie are

serious. Its presence throughout a community creates the most different kinds of reactions. It has caused the women of some primitive tribes to become barren; it has driven men insane; it has impelled masses of people toward the banners of new ideological movements. That anomie has existed in the United States and that it still exists in its attenuated form is shown in the chapters that follow. In later pages an effort is made to systematize the many consequences which emanate from anomie, an effort laying particular stress on its political manifestations in war, unemployment, and mass movements. Because of clear differences in precipitating conditions and in consequences, the forms of anomie fall into two types: a moderate form called simple anomie and a severe form called acute anomie. Simple anomie, the less dramatic order, should not be slighted. Its influence is pervasive; insidious, one might say, It affords a clear example of the interconnection of all aspects of the life of man as a political animal. Thus, scarcely an hour of the leisure time spent by the average person today would measure up to the standards of self-development and political education set by the most renowned philosopher of democracy, John Stuart Mill. Responsibility for this fact rests in no small part on the disorder of simple anomie. Even the milder form of anomie, then, can adversely affect the individual's chances for the growth of his potentialities, his use of the freedom offered by a democracy in that sphere which the French call *la vie privée*.

The spelling-out of anomie's many ramifications in mental disorder, war, political associations, and mass movements may lead the reader to suspect that contained in this book is an implicit suggestion that the elimination of anomie would remove most of the modern world's problems. Such a suspicion would be incorrect. But it is not far from true to say that until the problem of the anomic community is solved, the other great problems cannot be properly approached. The consequences of anomie are so serious that it would be hard for any *preventive* remedy to be more deadly than the disease. No remedy designed while anomie throughout a nation was at a fairly low level could be as radical as that which would probably be attempted when people were struggling to free themselves from fear of it at its height. Even for some time after its removal the terror of acute anomie lives on. Nothing shows this more clearly than the onward push of National Socialism after the German people regained a measure of solidarity or the first of the modern great wars that followed the French Revolution's quest for fraternity. If anomie can be stopped before reaching the acute stage and if the political community can be firmly established, then the real problem can be faced—to make of life a work of art. But until there is the solid ground of a political community beneath a man, he cannot reach, he can barely see, this goal.

The disrupting effect of a disturbance in belief-systems makes a re-evaluation of their function imperative. They perform for human ecology what instincts accomplish for some insect ecologies. Although systems of beliefs are transmitted culturally and not biologically, they are rooted in the prolonged biological infirmity of the human organism; and, as far as their universality is concerned, they might as well be transmitted through the genes. In many ways systems of beliefs may be likened to the social heredity of the species *Homo sapiens*. Disturbances in their transmission from generation to generation will wreck a human community just as surely as disturbances in the internal chemical balance of a variety of insects would throw their community into chaos. The *reason* for the behavior in an ant colony need not be apparent or rational, but it is rational in that their instinctive behavior makes possible their communal life.

The analogy of insect ecology is perhaps unfortunate. It encourages the propensity to consider faiths—political as well as religious—as irrational ideas. Yet the deference of people to authority which they can rarely empirically justify does not signify that their behavior is unreasonable. Regardless of whether persons are fully cognizant of the effects of their faith, a system of beliefs serves the conceivably rational function of keeping a community well knit and purposively organized. Recently, the philosopher Alfred North Whitehead cautioned against exaggerating the worth of conscious intellectual conceptions and dogmas as against unconscious processes. "Intellectual activity," he warned, "is apt to flourish at the expense of wisdom." Edmund Burke said the same thing long ago. People who hold beliefs are not unaware of their importance; they merely cannot speak out in defense of their wisdom. In discussing the function of systems of beliefs, Malinowski once remarked that "magic helps those who help themselves." It would be less unfair to primitive peoples if one forgot to make the usual invidious distinctions between magic, religion, superstition, and political faith. And it might be more accurate to say that "they help themselves who have common faith in their system of beliefs."

This is not the place to discuss the many implications which emerge from this study of the political community, but some of the distinctive features of the approach may be touched upon: (1) It demonstrates the close psychological connection and mutual support of religious and political ideologies and thus asks for a reopening of their joint study by political scientists. (2) It shifts the concentration of political theory away from economic classes and their antagonistic interests to the genuine political groupings of ruler and ruled. (3) Of these political groups, it studies primarily the ruled population, the people; and in its stress on their common need of a ruler, it lays aside the emphasis placed by modern élite theory on the methods by which a ruling class preserves its ascendancy, an emphasis which often seems to deny the possibility of a genuine need for leadership among the people. Had Ortega been more clear when he made his prediction in 1930—"Before long there will be heard throughout the planet a formidable cry, rising like the howling of innumerable dogs to the stars, asking for someone or something to take command, to impose an occupation, a duty"—had he been more clear, his words might not have received the treatment accorded Cassandra's. This study takes the oracular vagueness out of Ortega's prophecy and makes it one of impressive specificity. But Plato had spoken of the same thing when he used the simile of a rudderless ship to depict the chaos of a universe abandoned by God. More scholarly regard should be given to the central role of the ruler in the political ideology. Men will quietly abide in their systems of beliefs so long as they feel that all their values are assured by their ruling entity. In Walter Pater's language (he once defined life as a wandering to find home) they have found their home. Let their belief-systems fail them, thenceforth there is no quiet while they strive to achieve once more a confident interpretation of the world.

TABLE OF CONTENTS

PART I
THE UNIVERSALITY OF POLITICAL AND RELIGIOUS BELIEF-SYSTEMS

INTRODUCTION

THE self-styled lord of language, Oscar Wilde, once asserted that there were two great tragedies in life: one, not getting what we want; and the other, getting what we want. This is roughly the psychology that Émile Durkheim, probably the most influential French sociologist, used in explaining his concept, anomie.[1] In his book *Le Suicide*, published in 1897, he first noted the surprising fact that the suicide rate increased in approximately the same magnitude in both economic depression and prosperity. Although a peak of suicides might well be expected in the black days of poverty and unemployment, during prosperous eras people should be too happy, if one is to believe the utilitarian philosophers, to commit suicide. For this reason Durkheim doubted that the high suicide rate in depression was due to economic hardship. As support he could point also to the fact that the poorest countries had the lowest number of suicides for each one hundred thousand inhabitants. Perhaps some one factor was responsible for the twin peaks of the suicide curve.

Durkheim found the one factor in anomie:

In severe economic crises there occurs a lowering in the social scale, so to speak, a process that flings certain individuals abruptly into a position inferior to that which they had previously occupied. They must reduce their needs, restrain their wants, learn to control themselves even more than before. . . . But . . . this uncommon additional self-restraint cannot be completed in an instant. As a result, they are not adjusted to the condition thrust upon them; even the thought of it they find unbearable, and this is the source of sufferings which leads them to abandon a broken life even before they have had much real experience with it.

But results are not different if the disturbance originates in a sudden ease in power and wealth. Then, indeed, as the conditions of life are changed, the scale by which people's wants were controlled can no longer remain unchanged. . . . Its calibration is turned topsy-turvy; yet, on the other hand, no new graduation can be quickly improvised. . . . People no longer feel sure about what is possible and what is not, what is just and what is unjust, which claims or aspirations are legitimate and which go beyond measure. . . . Thus, the appetites of men, being no longer restrained by a public opinion, now bewildered and disoriented, do not know any more where the bounds are before which they ought to come to a halt. . . . The richer prize offered to them stimulates them, makes them more

3

exacting, more impatient of every rule, just at the time when the traditional rules have lost their authority. The state of rulelessness or *anomie* is thus further heightened by the fact that passions are less disciplined at the very moment when there is need of a stronger discipline. . . . How, under these conditions, could the will to live do other than languish?

To be satisfied, then, desires must have upper and lower limits imposed and met by the community. When no body of common values and sentiments exists, a person feels isolated or lost, without standards. He is sure of neither his place in the community nor what action he should perform; he cannot discover what his fellow-men value since they, too, are confused. In depression expectations are so frustrated and in unusual prosperity so satiated that in both cases a sense of confusion results, a loss of orientation, a sense of getting nowhere fast. This is anomie. It stands in contrast to *solidarité*, the expression Durkheim used to designate the perfect integration of a society with clear-cut values that define the status of each member of the community.

Perhaps it is inaccurate to speak, however figuratively, of Durkheim's psychology. In the first place, the faintest glimmerings of modern psychological methods crept out of the physiological laboratory and the psychiatric clinic only in the last quarter of the nineteenth century. Actually, the work of the classical psychologists, which was predominantly in the field of the perception of the special senses, would have had little bearing on Durkheim's labors. Sensory perception was probably too small a segment of experience to seem related to the large questions of the organization and disorganization of communities. Before the publication of *Le Suicide*, the psychoanalytic school of psychology, which grew out of the medical clinic, was wrapped in the mysteries of hypnosis. It was not until 1900 that Freud published his unsettling book on the interpretation of dreams, a book willing to deal with motives, larger units of human experience. Truly, psychology as it is known today was in a primitive stage at the time Émile Durkheim was writing about anomie.

Second, one looks in vain among his works for a definitive psychological picture of anomie. Being a sociologist, Durkheim was more properly concerned with depicting anomie as a sociological state. For him, anomie was most often the disordered condition of a society that possessed a weak *conscience collective*, the phrase he used to refer to the ensemble of beliefs and sentiments common to average citizens of the same community. If there are no shared rules or norms of conduct in a community, or if the goals defined by these rules are unattainable, as in depression or unusual prosperity, then men suffer. But a complete and concrete portrayal of their suffering is not to be found.

Without some description of anomie as it affects the individual, the task of applying modern psychological facts to the problem is almost insuperable. Happily, it is possible to piece together the puzzle, somewhat, by taking discontinuous sentences or phrases from *Le Suicide*. Also, the specific words and phrases in French that Durkheim repeatedly used—*un perpétuel état de mécontentement, tourments, déceptions répétées, inutilité, intolérable, désorientée, inquiétude douloureuse, malaisé, stérilité, désenchantement, douloureux*—help create the composite picture of anomie as it affects the individual. And after some study it becomes apparent that anomie as Durkheim conceived it in the subjective sense had three characteristics: a painful uneasiness or anxiety, a feeling of separation from the group or of isolation from group standards, a feeling of pointlessness or that no certain goals exist.

With this much as a basis, it should be possible to proceed to examine the subject of anomie in the light of more recent psychological discoveries. Durkheim contended that in the anomie of modern societies the "actions [of men] become ruleless (*déréglées*) and they suffer from this condition." The question now becomes: Why does man suffer from this condition? Why has mankind a need for rules or norms or beliefs? Why has the thwarting of this need resulted uniformly in anxiety? From Plato's royal fable to the present, almost everyone who has recognized mankind's need for common beliefs has done little more than respect it as natural and ultimate. There seems to have been general agreement on the answer that Emerson once gave. "Mankind," he said, "is born believing."

If the causes of anomie and its effects on the political community are to be uncovered, however, the need for beliefs cannot be regarded as irreducible. The genetic approach in psychology, which traces human needs from the birth of the individual organism, has met with notable success in explaining adult motivation and for this reason ought to be used here. Yet, every datum of mental growth recorded by this approach cannot possibly be described within the space of these pages. Furthermore, most of this sea of psychological data would prove to be irrelevant. An exploration, hence, should be made for only those facets of human development believed pertinent to anomie. Anomie is known to be associated in persons with an anxiety characterized by feelings of isolation and pointlessness and in communities with the breakdown or absence of common values or beliefs. These are the facts, then, which will serve as guides through the accumulation of material amassed by psychologist, psychoanalyst, and psychiatrist alike.

CHAPTER ONE

THE PRIMARY FUNCTION OF SYSTEMS OF BELIEF

Uniformities in Childhood Experience

THE helplessness of the human organism at birth and for some succeeding years is a biological fact with immense social importance.[1] Because of it, all humans reared by humans receive a number of like experiences. It would be a mistake to describe the effect of these experiences on the growing individual as the influence of heredity; for whenever infants have been isolated from human contact over long periods, they cannot be said to have had these experiences; and they certainly show corresponding personality differences. Rigorously speaking, the telltale signs of similar upbringing experiences are not attributable to heredity; yet, in seeming paradox, they almost invariably appear because of the hereditary makeup of man. The feebleness of the human infant thus necessitates a number of uniform cultural experiences. This chapter will probe several of these cultural events for their effect on the developing individual.

Soon after the baby is born his needs must be tended. At some times, in parts of the world, the practice has been completely to disregard, for one reason or another, certain categories of infants, for example, girl babies in densely populated China. But these creatures never live long enough to be socialized. If the infant is not given nutriment and air, some stimulation of the skin, and protection from excessive heat or cold, he quickly dies. The inability of the newborn infant to satisfy his recurring needs, then, results in a period of life when, if he is to survive, his wants must be attended to with little effort on his part. He is fed, cuddled, cleansed, by older persons whenever they think he needs such care.

The ready ministering of adults has an influence on the mental life of the infant. As long as the situation lasts, no sharp distinction can be made between the self and the external environment. In his short periods of wakefulness, the infant organism's needs are quickly gratified, tensions are transient, and the world and the self have no sharply drawn boundaries. This period in life has been called the autarchic stage since, if the infant has any mental life at all at the time, the feeling must exist that the means of satisfying himself are within himself. In this sense, life is similar to his previous parasitic attachment to his mother, and hardly more difficult. The abiding sense of comfort in the organism plus the limited sensory experience dispense with the necessity of making much distinction between the outside world and the self.[2]

Before long, however, an increasing number of discrepancies appear between needs and their gratification. The infant soon experiences delays in the resolution of tensions. He may have to cry for a few long minutes before anyone tends to him; as he reaches for an object, he may find his hand forced back. Some objects, such as the mother's breast, seem to appear whenever certain gestures or sounds, like crying or sucking movements, are made; other objects seem never to respond. Gradually, external reality is revealed in all grimness. Yet for a long time consciousness of self remains quite blurred. The infant claws his own face or jumps at the sound of his own voice. The small child of two who says, "You are a little girl, aren't you me?" has a rather dim realization of self and nonself. And the small boy who attempts to walk under a table and bumps his forehead on its top has not yet developed a picture of how far his entire body extends. Even at the age of five the child continues to confuse himself and his images with his surroundings.[3]

In the development of self-awareness there is one aspect of reality that takes a particularly long time to penetrate the child's mind—the distinction between animate and inanimate objects. During the infant's autarchic stage all feeling is thought to be shared by whatever parts of the surrounding environment he perceives. If the pangs of hunger are felt or the prick of an open safety pin, the whole perceptible world shares in the pain. He requires some time to learn that everything that happens to or inside his skin is felt by himself alone. So, when the infant finally realizes that some things are not part of himself, these things remain endowed with the property of feelings or life, as they were before. At this stage these feelings are no longer thought to be always identical with the feelings of the self. Those objects which satisfy the infant's wants on the performance of certain movements or sounds do appear to share his feelings; those that do not conform to his desires, since they are frustrating and have life, are hostile objects. In other words, when the split between the ego and the outer world occurs, nothing forces the infant to believe that the perceptible environment loses the life it once had as part of himself. Even when the child is much older, teaching him the difference between animate and inanimate objects is a hard task. The child of two or three years who has stumbled over a large stone can only with difficulty be dissuaded from the position that "the stone did it." You protest in vain, "But the stone didn't make you fall; it couldn't. It isn't alive. It can't move." A firm "It *did* move" is the likely and final reply. Moreover, the stone had undeniable intentions of tripping him. The child generally must pass through several well-defined stages before he begins to see external reality as the adults about him do. At first, all things are conscious. Later, only things that move, for example, a cart or bicycle, are alive. Then, objects that can move of their own accord, like the wind, are conscious. And, lastly, consciousness is more or less restricted to animals.[4]

As more and more of the outer world peels off the self, so to speak, more and more of it becomes accordingly nonconforming to the infant's wants and uncontrollable by his gestures and sounds. Increasingly less attention is given the growing child on the assumption that hardiness accompanies growth. The experiences of the Pilaga Indian child of the Argentine can serve as an illustration. As a baby he was the object of constant attention. At the first whimper he was nursed by his mother. He was frequently bathed, kept free of lice, and kissed over and over again by the mother, who would rub her mouth violently on the baby's in ecstatic pleasure. The first evidences of a change are the mother's less frequent mouth-rubbing and her delay in stopping her work to nurse the weeping baby. In order to gather in the crops of wild fruits, she must spend hours away from home. She often cannot take the child with her, for the distance she must travel with the double burden of baby and fruit would be too great. The baby is usually left with an old, feeble, and sometimes blind grandparent who can do little for him. A period of even greater suffering for the baby begins when he can walk a little, when he starts to explore the world outside the house. Here, alone, outside the circle of his family, the child is afraid. Larger children tear past at breakneck speed, screaming and tumbling about on the ground in horseplay. Strangers walk by. Without adult comfort the baby bursts into tears. During this period the Pilaga baby is almost continuously in tears. Not only is he frightened by contact with strangers, but his mother leaves him more and more alone as she goes about her work. Formerly she had left the baby alone for hours; now she leaves him alone for a whole day. He eats a little pounded corn or drinks a little honeyed water, but the baby gets hungry and by evening is so wrought up that when the tired mother comes home he cannot wait to be picked up but has a tantrum at her feet.[5]

At this age, then, things happen to the child. He is bumped, jostled, disturbed, or dropped. Periods of wakefulness lengthen. He feels the startling pain of loud noises, of thirst, or of bright sunlight in his eyes. All these sources of discomfort are observed in due course to emanate from outside the self. In the new outer world the main and consistent satisfiers, even though now sometimes tardy, prove to be his human attendants.[6] They are the ones who relieve the pain. They can control the environment so that it gratifies, rather than frustrates, the organism's reappearing needs.

A sketch of the first conception of the world that the child acquires, once he has passed through the time when the self and the environment were a unity, would depict the child as a feeble dweller in an environment made up of uncontrollable, animate, thwarting, and, hence, hostile objects. Within this world, however, there are certain figures—usually, but not always, the parents—who are able to control it, tame the hostile objects, make all things friendly by turning them to provide for the child's needs. In his "Third Elegy" Rainer Maria Rilke has been able to communicate poetically the vital role of these persons, a task demanding a memory nearly equal to the artistry:

Mother, you made him small, it was you that began him;
he was new to you, you arched over those new eyes
the friendly world, averting the one that was strange.
Where, oh, where, are the years when you simply displaced
for him, with your slender figure, the surging abyss?
You hid so much from him then; made the nightly-suspected room
harmless, and out of your heart full of refuge
mingled more human space with that of his nights.
Not in the darkness, no, but within your far nearer presence
you placed the light, and it shone as though out of friendship.
Nowhere a creak you could not explain with a smile,
as though you had long known *when* the floor would behave itself thus . . .
And he listened to you and was soothed. So much it availed,
gently, your coming.[7]

Out of the child's relations with such figures comes his disposition to acquire new systems of beliefs, new conceptions of the world.

The Centrality of Separation-Anxiety

Intentionally or not adults begin to describe their belief-systems to the child shortly after he acquires speech.[8] It appears, however, that a system of beliefs acquires major psychological function for the child only after he experiences certain shocks. In the history of the human organism it is possible to make out a series of such critical experiences. All originate in the inability of the human organism from infancy to adolescence to provide alone for its recurring biological needs.[9]

One type of anxiety serves as the prototype for the ensuing shocks. It occurs shortly after the infant links the gratification of his needs with the presence of discernible attendants. Then, given the inevitable absence of attendants and the equally inevitable onset of the needs of hunger and thirst and the like, the organism shows signs of extreme uneasiness, such as panicky screaming fits, which disappear only at the ministering presence of the returned attendants. Some of the physiological and psychological effects of this experience recur with every subsequent similar situation, for a salient characteristic of anxiety is its renewal properties. The anxieties of adulthood repeat the symptoms that appeared in adolescence, and the anxieties of adolescence in turn reactivate the pattern of anxiety of approximately the first three years of life.

Anxiety usually reveals itself in both physiological and psychological conditions. There may be disturbances of gastrointestinal activity (such as diarrhea, an urge to defecate, constipation, or sinking feelings in the pit of the stomach), vasomotor phenomena (for example, flushed or cold skin or cold sweat), and cardiac or respiratory irregularities (pounding heart, choking or gasping breath). Psychologically, there is a deep fear or terror without definite sense of cause, a mental anguish so intense as to be avoided at all costs.[10]

It was formerly thought that anxiety was rare or absent in infants or children. Numerous studies have demonstrated, however, that anxiety is an unavoidable and crucial part of childhood.[11] Its physiological side in children often appears in nausea, vomiting, abdominal pain or distress, trembling and pain in the joints. The particular anxiety that results from the absence of attending persons has several notable features. By this time the child has learned that his attendants whom he recognizes by sound and sight are the ones who gratify his needs with maximum dispatch. Automatically, then, all situations in which they are not perceived become dangerous. Thus anxiety may strike the child on being left alone or on being in the dark or on being approached by a stranger in place of one of his usual attendants. He cannot yet differentiate temporary absence from permanent loss. Teaching the child that "out-of-sight" does not mean "gone-forever" is a task of many difficulties. He wants his parents around at all times, and as his faculty of locomotion develops, he tries never to let them get out of view or hearing. Without them he is gripped by a debilitating terror that the source of *all* gratifications—which for the child is his adult attendants—is gone. A feeling of complete privation overwhelms him. Without these figures who nurture and sustain him, the whole conception of an orderly environment crumbles. The world around him suddenly becomes unmanageable, wild, alive, and menacing. Formerly benign objects, such as family friends, may only terrify him. Total extinction in isolation threatens the child. It may be possible to share in the experience of this anxiety by visualizing the panic of a small, lost child, his fear and distrust of everybody and everything, no matter how comforting or gentle would-be helpers try to be. The most descriptive name for this fundamental dread is separation-anxiety.[12]

In slightly later life the attendants upon occasion find it necessary to restrict the child's free expression of impulse in order to prepare him for a communal existence.[13] The type of activity restricted varies from culture to culture: The morals of many countries prohibit a child's striking his mother, yet in others, such as parts of modern Japan, there is no such prohibition. Some cultures abhor the exposure of certain areas of the body, while others select different areas for covering; some societies permit the child almost complete freedom in his toilet functions, and others surround him with the most complete regulation. But the study of ethnography reveals no community without a whole series of restrictions and taboos on the developing child.

The adults, who must transmit the moral traits of their particular culture to the child, attempt to educate the child by threats (or a partial carrying-out of threats) to withdraw from him the satisfying character of their relationship. Again, these threats may vary in expression from group to group. Some attendants may temporarily isolate the child, for example, by sending him to his room; others may threaten to beat him until the viscera issue from his mouth; some may proceed with dire forms of corporal punishment, while others may make mere movements of a mutilating nature. But all these actions are designed to secure conformity, and all arouse an anxiety in the organism similar in its effects to the previous experience of being left alone.[14]

To avoid this anguish, the child begins using movements and sounds that have the ability to restore a harmonious relationship with his attendants. These movements and sounds are unwittingly suggested by the adults themselves and accordingly will also differ by cultures. They generally include a number of forms of facial expression and physical contact, such as smiles, kissing, smelling, patting, stroking, rubbing, hugging, and so on; and certain vocal expressions, such as (in English) "I love you," "you're good," or others of a nonverbal character. Adults describe these gestures and sounds as "affectionate," and they not only make them toward the child but require them from him. In this way the child learns how to elicit signs from his attendants that carry the meaning of reassurance.

These favorable evaluations, obtained by abandoning disapproved activity and by making affectionate gestures, assure the dependent child that his needs will be taken care of. Since his earliest years the child will have associated these signs with the gratification of his most basic needs. And they come to signify the security of a place in the family, a complex emotion often described as a feeling of belonging.[15]

A third crisis occurs when the child learns through extra-familial contacts, through parental statements, through simple observation, that his attendants may not be forever capable of providing for his wants. They can die or fall sick or show fear. In the world of the child the adult attendants are omnipotent figures. It is not incorrect, in fact, to say that they attain towering proportions over the rest of the environment. Young children frequently represent their parents as being "bigger than the world." The child's lowly perspective sets his parents' heads up in the sky. Study after study has shown that adults are given, in the words of the child psychologist, Jean Piaget, the qualities of omniscience, omnipotence, omnipresence, omnitemporality, and omnimorality. Therefore, the revelation of the human limitations of adults in the family, especially when abrupt, involves a deprivational experience comparable to the anxious situations previously mentioned. Before this time the child believes that man made nature and organized it to suit his ends. It is thus a severe jolt to learn that irregular and unpredictable nature, with its death, accident, violence, and hunger, does not follow adult plans. No man, he learns, can control these terrible forces. An exemplary case is that of the child who was staggered to find his hitherto all-powerful father sobbing over the spectacle of the fruit orchard ravaged by a violent storm.[16] In periods of economic adversity, too, children are exposed earlier than they otherwise might be to the shaking experience of distraught parents worrying about the source of the family's means of sustenance. The question—who tells these terrible, arbitrary forces how to behave?—becomes important, together with its corollary—how does one propitiate these superbeings?[17] The exact point of the event in the child's development varies. Rural children in all probability experience it at an earlier age than urban children because they are relatively closer to the titanic forces of nature in the raw, such as droughts, locust plagues, and so on.[18] In cities the sometimes more subtle observation of the effects of economic, political, and military instabilities must first be made.

Belief-Systems in Orderly Succession

But whenever the chronological point of its occurrence, the third crisis is most interesting for the manner of its resolution. Previously, the critical situations were relieved by the ministering of human attendants or by securing favorable signs which guaranteed that ministering was forthcoming whenever needed. The shock of this disillusion, however, is cushioned by the prior provision of the anthropomorphic symbols in religious and political beliefs. The manner used by the Chaga community of East Africa to acquaint the child with personalized beliefs demonstrates the practice. Every morning the Chaga father takes his child into the yard. Up on the mountain the "silent observer" or "man of the sky" resides to watch over offspring. He observes the children like an eagle. To impress the reality of this continuous presence upon the child, the father each day holds his hand, prays to the deity, and spits toward the sky. He points to the child's shadow on the ground and calls it "the constant guardian." The connection between the shadow and the "silent observer" is also emphasized when the moon is full, or in the dark hut, when dancing flames on the hearth project the child's silhouette on the wall. Before his attention is drawn to the threatening shadow behind him, the child is made to dance round the fire. The father tells the child that the guardian protects the weak and comforts the child, warning him by omens. The deity rewards the good behavior of the child, after he has grown up, by causing crops to grow, cattle to thrive, and other ambitions to be fulfilled. This "man of heaven" is appealed to in extremities, especially when sacrifices to the ancestors in case of illness or barrenness have proved futile. When the family is in the depths of despair, the spirits of the right and of the left having proved impotent, he is remembered as a savior. Unlike the ancestors who live in the earth, his dwelling is made in the sky. Sacrifices are offered to him in the yard when the sun, with which he is identified in name, is in the zenith, whereas the ancestors receive their offerings in the dark hut or the dusky grove. To him alone are given the qualities of kindness, leniency, and justice. He is the final arbiter and the supreme judge receiving the complaints of the lowly and the downtrodden, a just and wise being. He is the controller of the affairs of men and ultimately he rewards the good and punishes the wicked irrespective of their earthly status.

All communities up to those of the present day transmit belief-systems containing similar superhuman entities to their youngest generation at the age when it apparently becomes capable of elementary abstraction. Yet until the child is aware of the limitations of attendants in providing for his satisfactions, he has great difficulty in comprehending deities in the adult sense. In response to questions about the origins of obvious topographic features of the environment, like lakes and mountains, children will answer that they do not know whether it was God or some men who made them; or they may report that they conceive God to be a chief of men or like any other man except that he makes his residence in the clouds and either he or else some men made the clouds. Once the relevant mortal proportions of human attendants have been discovered, however, the omnipotent qualities formerly attributed to them are shifted rather quickly to the anthropomorphic religious symbols.

At about the same time that this process is going on, the religious symbolism imparted by adults is joined by the personalized symbols of the political sphere—the kings, the chiefs, the presidents, the heroes, the leaders and fathers of countries. It should not be supposed that the phenomenon is part of the Western world alone. In somewhat different forms it occurs in every community, for there is no known community without at least a rudimentary political organization.

This point may be disputed. It is said, for example, that the lives of the Yurok Indians of northwest California, the Bantu peoples of British East Africa, or the Andaman Islanders of the Bay of Bengal have no political aspects. The work of most students on the origins of the state (for whom this point is controversial) is of little use here since their procedure is invariably to set up what they consider to be the distinctive features of the state (usually some institutionalized governmental organs such as law or armed forces) and then to proceed to trace the growth and appearance of these features. The question hinges, of course, on whether one wants to exclude informal leadership and controls or occasional coercion. As far as this investigation is concerned, no social organization is comprehensible apart from a political organization. The reasons for this will become apparent later in the book. It may help, however, to state preliminarily that, although the collection of people under question be composed only of groups of families, so long as there is any degree of communication, enterprise, or distribution among the families, political organization in the sense here intended must be present. Existing family contacts would break, members of different families would treat each other unmorally, agreements would evaporate, perhaps in the flare of violence, unless the rules of interfamily communication were made moral rules, that is, rules of good and evil. And the only way that they can become morals is by being made a matter of conscience in children. Once they are thus implanted, a community exists, for the ethicizing process requires (again, as will be later made clear) that conformity to the rules of interfamily behavior be demanded of children in the name of a person or anthropomorphism which can be only a personalized religious or political entity. Thus for the purposes of this study it is only necessary that the groups under consideration have a name to refer to their collective selves and common history; they will then have interfamily morals plus a pattern of subordination to persons, real or symbolic. In short, they will have a state.

Now in some areas the adults make constant and conscious efforts to imbue the child with political beliefs at the same time that religious beliefs are being imparted; in other places formal political indoctrination is delayed until after puberty. But in neither case is it possible to keep the child at this age from sharp experiences with the political beliefs of the community. The political education of the Chaga child illustrates the use of both the intentional and the unintentional ways of imparting political beliefs:

> From a very early age, the child hears about the chief. He and his henchmen are used, like the ancestors, as bogies and facilitators of conduct. Boys following

their father to the pasture, and girls walking behind their mothers to the market, are sure to meet the headman one day. They hear the parent greet him: *"Kocha mangi ya kikaro!"* (i.e., "Welcome, head of the district"), or: *"Kocha manawo!"* ("Welcome, his child," i.e., the chief's). They imitate these words and, as soon as he is out of earshot, ask about him. By and by they hear all that is worth knowing of him: the degree of his popularity, the manner of his appointment, his way of dealing with difficult situations, his favouritism or rectitude, his success or failure as the chief's political agent. The headman is invited to beer carousals and the children watch him being treated with consideration by their father. He is given a potful for himself, "in honour of the chief," as his privilege is justified. If the party is small, he gets at least a bigger calabash than the rest. Even greater deference is shown toward a councillor of the chief. He is solemnly greeted: *"Kocha mnjama o mangi!"* (i.e., "Welcome, privy councillor of the chief"). At drinking-bouts much fuss is made of him. . . . When a child sees the chief come along the path, it is at once struck by the size of his retinue, the reverential manner with which old and young rise at the roadside, the volley of greetings fired at him, and the murmur of comment which arises in wayside groups after the paladins have passed. Through stories, comments on events of the day, and definite instruction, children learn the vocabulary of honorary names used in addressing the chief. When the great moment of greeting him comes, the father whispers excitedly to his son: "Don't forget my teaching!" There follows a torrent of deferential terms, like *Njamombe* (owner of the cattle), *Simba* (lion), *Njofu* (elephant), *Kishamba-kya-uruka* (the great one of the country), *Samari*, (sceptre), *Msuri* (the rich), *Kilavo* (supper, as the chief is used to sending gifts of food in the evening), *Ruwa-lyako* (my god), and *Ruwa-lya-umbe* (god of the cattle, that is, the one from whom they come). By learning these names and their implications, by falling in with his father's attitude, and by observing that the honoured headmen and councillors are respectful towards their common master, the boy gains a standard for his own attitude.[19]

If political and religious beliefs everywhere call forth such behavior from adults, it is small wonder that the child universally receives profound experiences that root these beliefs forever in the feeling of terror of the uncontrollable and awe of the superhuman, the feeling of the *mysterium tremendum*,[20] of a power greater than that of his parents.

The Mutual Obligations of Ruler and Subjects

A survey of political belief-systems shows that adult subjects, with differing degrees of consciousness or explicitness, have always endowed their kings or tribal chiefs with a special capacity to control those aspects of the environment most important for the continued existence of the political community.[21] Which aspects the community regards as significant vary with its ways of gaining sustenance and thus depend in large part on the flora and fauna of the territory. If a political community lives by sedentary agriculture, its leaders will be those who apparently have a talent for controlling climatic and soil conditions; if it lives by the hunt, its leaders will be those who ostensibly have a talent for divining the movements of game and related phenomena; if predatory warfare sustains the tribe, victorious warriors are its leaders.[22]

Political authority accumulates in the hands of those who are believed to have outstanding skill in the most hazardous and fortuitous elements of provisioning the community. Success in extracting nutriment from the peculiar conditions of land, sea, and air is the supernatural quality of kings, be it called *mana* as in Polynesia, *iddhi* as in India, or *wakan, manitow,* or *orenda* as in Indian North America. The ancient Babylonians looked to their kings for abundance. In Fiji kings carried the title of *Sri,* which means both prosperity and food. In Polynesia the word *sau* signifies king, peace, and prosperity. Homeric mythology held kings responsible for the food supply. The Burgundians held their king responsible for the fortunes of war. Under the Roman Empire power over crops and prosperity became specially connected with the emperor. From the time of Augustus, Roman coins bore such inscriptions as "The Prosperity of Augustus," "The Yearly Increase of Augustus," and "The Welfare of Augustus." An interesting inscription is *Fortuna redux Caes. Aug.,* meaning the "returned prosperity of Augustus" and celebrating the fact that after his final triumph Augustus brought back the goddess Prosperity with him to Rome. His successors repeated the minting practice to show that Prosperity also followed their acts. The Malays have faith that their king possesses a personal influence over the works of nature, such as the growth of crops and the bearing of fruit trees. Drought, dearth, or defeat in war notified the Khazars of southern Russia that the natural powers of their king were on the wane. If rain was needed in India, the kings of old gave gifts, kept a fast, observed the commandments, and, entering their royal bedchamber, lay on wooden couches for seven days. Then it rained. Among the Trobriand Islanders the magic of rain and sunshine is vested in one person and one person only, that of the Paramount Chief of the District. From this magic he derives his political power and prestige. In later days the power of controlling the environment in these important respects is often thought to reside in European colonial officials sent down to govern. A British agent once reported that he was thanked on leaving a province for having given the people rain during his rule. To present the conclusion of A. M. Hocart, a keen anthropologist: "The invention of a man who did not work with his hands, but merely existed and acted on his environment at a distance, like the sun, was one of the most momentous in the history of man; it was nothing less than the invention of government."[23]

A common element of all religions, too, is a faith in the ability of their respective deities to control the environment. According to Bronislaw Malinowski:

> They are of the same substance as our belief in Providence. . . . The mythology, which assigns common parentage to a particular lineage of man with rain or the fertility of plants, an animal species or wind, established a common measure between man and the relevant aspects of his environment. It submits those forces of rain, weather, fertility, vegetation, and fauna, which man needs, yet cannot practically master, to a superadded, supernatural control. Whether we call this type of belief Totemism or Zoolatry, or the religion of Mana, or preanimism, they achieve one main end. They humanize the outer world; they put man in harmony with his environment and destiny; they give him an inkling of a working Providence in the surrounding Universe.[24]

As explained beforehand, they reassure by regulating the environment so that it will be friendly and fruitful, rather than hostile and harmful.

But before one can be sure that the world will be favorably disposed, one must be ready to conduct one's self in an affectionate and sacrificing manner. In religions, offerings must be made, faith or love must be unswerving, evil acts avoided, or ritual scrupulously carried out. In political ideologies, duties must be performed, loyalty must be unquestioning, treasonable acts shunned, or ceremonies observed. Violation of either the religious or the political precepts, like disobeying parental dictates, brings swift calamity. Some religions assign this punitive task to the same god that they cast in the affectionate role. Such a god was the Jahveh of the ancient Hebrews. Other religions divide the functions. Thus, in Zoroastrianism there is Ahriman as well as

Ormuzd, and in Christianity there is the Devil in addition to God. The less sophisticated peoples give a stock answer to the question of why they obey the customary norms. "The spirits (or gods) become angry and make things bad if we do not obey custom."[25] Punishment in the political sphere is, if anything, more immediate and tangible: the sword, the ax or noose, arrest, torture, expropriation, fine.

Thus the child, in addition to performing acts which obtain reassuring affectionate expressions from adults in the primary environment of the family, must now behave in ways designed to obtain similar expressions from figures which he rarely, if ever, sees. His behavior at this stage is not at all unlike his earlier ways. It is true that these new figures presumably have at heart the interest of a larger community, different from the family. But the point to note is the similarity of the child's adjustments to situations replete with anxiety. Having recognized that there are forces against which his human attendants have little power, having been previously told that there are deities or personages which can control the potentially damaging forces, the child behaves as he is told he should to obtain favorable expressions from the new figures. In religion, as in the family, certain types of behavior are prohibited and others called for. These are the religious commandments or norms. For the sake of the tribe or the nation, too, the child must abandon the thought of certain activity and, on the other hand, perform duties, positive acts of allegiance and loyalty. These are the political customs or the laws. Conformity, the child learns, brings assurance against the feeling of helpless fear now associated with the mention of catastrophe, starvation, and mortal wounds. Since the new figures rule the life-and-death aspects of the environment beyond the control of ordinary adults, they can guarantee that it will not be inimical. By behaving properly and affectionately toward them, the child can become a member of a bigger family, the larger community; he knows that he will always be provided for; he need no longer be anxious. Clearly, the child has resolved his anxiety through the acquisition of a new set of beliefs. Now the principal figures in his world include a number of superbeings who regulate the environment and require certain evidences of love and sacrifice from the child before they will see to it that the environment shines benevolently.

The division of labor between the political and religious figures poses no problem for the mind of the child. He is not much troubled by adult ranking of these rulers; whether, for instance, the king derives his power from the god or has it in essence. Each or any of them can provide security for the child and his attendants, and that fact alone suffices to relieve the gnawing worry. At this point the distinction between mortal and immortal life, which later often defines the spheres of influence of the sacred and secular personages, is not at all clear. But the personages themselves grow to assume so significant a role that it may be wise to use a special designation for them. Henceforth, the italicized word, *ruler*, will be used to denote the entity, tangible or intangible, which members of a community believe able to control those aspects of the environment most necessary for the commonweal.

The term *ruler* was chosen for its several advantages. It can convey the idea of ruling over subjects, as well as the hitherto neglected idea of ruling or regulating aspects of the material environment. It connotes the political realm which is the sense most necessary here, and yet, when italicized, it can remind the reader of its difference from common usage in also embracing religious and economic figures and intangible entities. In ordinary parlance the word may have an authoritarian connotation, but here it has none; for a person is not a *ruler*, no matter how powerful the forces at his command, unless the members of the community believe in his capacity and willingness to guide and provide for them. Nor has the word any relation to the manner of the *ruler*'s selection. His may be a hereditary or an elected succession; he may be, as will be seen, a feudal lord, a president, a prime minister, a god, or the personification of a nation. In every case, he is dependent on popular belief. Once that is gone, he too is gone. He lives or dies in the minds of his subjects.[26]

To go back now to the child's earliest *rulers*, his attendants, they have not yet sunk to an unimportant position in his conception of the world. In all probability his anxiety about their limitations originally came from them themselves, in a sort of sympathetic vibration. Their insecurity is his; his security is theirs.

The attendants still are the fundamental support for everyday life on earth. Childhood has a secure rock bottom in the family situation. It is the threat of the collapse of this support that brings on the next crisis.

Renascence in Adolescence

In members of the human species dramatic biological changes appear at an age in years that has great individual variation but is best set in the second decade of life. Communities in all times have interpreted the onset of these modifications to signify that the helplessness of the child is fast approaching an end. It is not difficult to understand why the changes are given this interpretation, for they seem most directly to affect the organism's productive and reproductive capacities. The sudden increases in height and weight; the growth of hair on face and body, of bones and muscles, of reproductive organs; the appearance of menstruation or fluid emissions—all point with striking effect to the fact that the adolescent is about ready to assume a full role in the community. With the proper tools and education the youth now should have the strength to obtain food, produce offspring, and fight an adult. Hence, the pubescent boy is made to feel that a loosening of his dependence on the family is necessary. Awareness of the family's intention to withdraw its support arouses the familiar anxiety of separation.[27]

Thus it happens that the final critical experience considered in this chapter appears in the years of adolescence. Unlike the others, this anxious period varies greatly in emotional intensity from one culture to another. To a large extent the variation depends on the typical mobility of persons within the community's hierarchy of status.[28] If mobility is slight, the culture can provide rituals which symbolically and educatively prepare the adolescent for the transition from the place in the family to the place in the community. The passage of youth in the feudal age through the learning and ceremonial stages of page, squire, and, finally, knight is an excellent example. The time, place, and ceremonies for the event vary from culture to culture and sex to sex. To prove that he can assume the new status, the youth may have to undergo ordeals, tests of skill and endurance, initiation into secret societies, change of dwellings, separation from the family, isolation in forest or desert, introduction to sexual practices, and decorations or mutilations.

If mobility is so intensive as to include freedom of occupational choice, there can be no fixed procedure for the adolescent's transition from dependence on the family to his position in the community. The three or four centuries after the end of the Roman Republic can be designated as an era with this type of mobility. Within six years a slave could become a freeman, within a generation or two an equestrian, a member of the *nobilitas*. In the management of state affairs could be found an influential class of freedmen and slaves as rich as the freeborn senatorial and equestrian classes. The imperial bureaucracy was chiefly staffed with slaves and freedmen of the emperors. The plebians had obtained many measures of equality with the patricians, and citizenship was granted to all subjects of the Empire except the *peregrini dediticii*, who in all likelihood were chiefly colonial serfs. During the reign of the Julii and Claudii, men could climb to the heights of public offices and even royalty through military action or public services, marriages or amours, commerce or swindling. The Italy of the fifteenth- and sixteenth-century Renaissance exhibited a similar degree of vertical mobility. In such times the individual has no set place awaiting his somewhat formal passing of tests. Adolescence passes with small ceremony, other than the marked change in attitude on the part of attendants, who at this time begin to view the youth with an air expectant of departure. Not only does it take longer to find a niche in such societies, but, once one is found, it may not be given formal recognition. For these reasons the length of the period of mental distress is usually much greater than the short, relatively tense arrival of ritual testing which is the usual event in cultures of low mobility.

In any case, receipt of a place in the community relieves the adolescent of this episode of separation-anxiety. In the great majority of cultures he does not acquire a new system of beliefs at this point. Rather, he occupies a new post in the political and religious ideologies already acquired. From the limited status of a child he has gone to the complete status of an adult in the tribe or the nation. Full member-status generally puts the individual in the position of being able to provide himself for his needs. Now he may hold property or marry or join the hunt or participate in ceremonies and council.

The *rulers* play a prominent part in this transition. More often than not, a ritual performance gives evidence that the adolescent's newly acquired ability to fend for himself is a direct gift from the political or religious personages. In a primitive warriors' tribe, the headman may hand him the necessary hunting and fighting paraphernalia—bow, arrows, spear, ax, and club— and give him a new name or new apparel, such as a belt or girdle. In the more literate society of the early Roman Republic, the adolescent laid aside his purple-bordered *toga praetexta*, received from the *pater familias* his pure white *toga virilis*, and then, on the feast of the Liberali, he was presented to the *Populus Romanus* assembled in the Forum. The ephebi of Athens, two years after the long hair of their childhood was cut short, were given their citizen names and presented by high figures of state with shield and spear and then sent to the temple of Agraulos to take the oath of allegiance. The political and religious personages may preside over the performance either by a symbolic representation, as when a public official grants the new status in the name of the state, or by an actual appearance, as when the feudal lord, surrounded by pomp and ceremony, knights the youth himself. Their beneficent presence results in a reaffirmation of the youth's faith in the reigning political and religious beliefs. After the anxiety of the family's withdrawal of support and the uncertainty of adolescent ordeals, the dispensation by the chiefs of a new place in society seems indeed blessed bounty.

To sum up: When supplemented by psychological and anthropological research, the clues to anomie left by Durkheim sufficed to call attention to four important situations of anxiety in the early history of the human organism: absence of attendants, withdrawal of affection by attendants, discovery of the limitations of attendants, and, lastly, partial abandonment by attendants. Because of the protracted inability of the newborn of the species to provide for its basic needs, all human beings can be said to have passed through these critical situations. In facing each of them the child reacts similarly because each revives separation-anxiety—the initial terror of helplessness felt in periods of isolation from the only sources of support. The relationship of anomie to separation-anxiety was further clarified by the realization that each of these crises commences with the deterioration of the child's system of beliefs about the world and terminates with the acquisition of a new or revised set of beliefs. Although the child is presented early in life with the ideational content of political and religious beliefs, he accepts them only after being confronted with the possibility of the loss of loving care and an orderly, gratifying world. Beliefs can perform their psychological function because they define the proper ways of obtaining protective assurance and they designate the beings of superior power, the environmental regulators, who alone can provide that assurance. The need for a body of moral beliefs can now be seen more fundamentally as a need for assurance that critical situations of certain helplessness will not recur. Thus, belief-systems serve as protection against the anxiety of separation provoked by such situations.

CHAPTER TWO

THE SERIES OF BELIEF-SYSTEMS
IN DEMOCRACY

THE materials of anthropology and ancient history may speak convincingly in conveying the idea that in the past certain uniform experiences produced uniform reactions in peoples everywhere. But when the moment comes for extending the idea into the present, the data seem to lose their eloquence, even though their logic has universal application. The unfamiliar frame of earlier and simpler societies gives their lives an unreal and almost fictional cast. Persons of bygone cultures well may have conformed to political and psychological laws, but not the practical people of today! Scholars sometimes contemplate the beliefs of primitives and ancients with a feeling of proud progress for their civilization. To see whether this sturdy impression has an equally sturdy foundation, the present chapter will treat parallel aspects of the ideologies that exist in the Western world today.

Needless to say, the choice of subject was not dictated by this consideration alone. The particular structure of beliefs in modern democracy reveals in clearest form a number of facts that are necessary to expand the theory of the political community. Here, then, is the more important objective to be pursued in this chapter. The anxious reactions of the child to a progression of all-important deprivations have already been adequately described. There is no reason now for reviewing these anxieties in the child of a more recent day, for his reactions are known. In truth, the most systematic study of the problem has been made by psychologists who worked with children of the present day. What remains to be done is to describe the beliefs with which the child of a modern democratic community fills the gap left by the serial disintegration of his earlier beliefs.

As was noted, before infants have learned the meaning of a rather large number of words, their knowledge of the world cannot vary much from culture to culture. Modern infants, no less than their primitive predecessors, must be given continuing care lest they expire. It happens that in the family of the Western world the mother is the infant's constant attendant, but long before the infant grows into a child her vigil over him begins of necessity and of choice to diminish. Separations will be as unavoidable for the modern child as is parental discipline.[1] One day, to take an extreme example, an American mother told her three-year-old girl that she was going out to buy a loaf of bread. Actually she had to go to the hospital for a week of medical care. The child watched at the window for her mother to come back, and, as hour after hour passed, she grew terrified. Later, in an attempt at pacification, she was taken past a huge building where she saw her mother in a bathrobe sitting at a window but could not speak with her. Even after the passage of many weeks, during which her mother had returned home in good health, the child could not sleep at night, fearing that her mother would go away again if she but closed her eyes. In this country the child's anxiety upon first being left at school by his parents is an almost nation-wide phenomenon.[2] Also, the child's frequent fear of being deserted by his parents is often exploited for disciplinary purposes. Parents warn the child that if he is not good they will go away and leave him. Some parents even wrap him up and say that they are going to give him away.

Thus the modern child, too, encounters separation-anxieties. Similarly, he learns that the best policy in vital matters is conformity to the parental figures who rule the world. Once at the verbal level, however, when he has a chance to associate words with adult attitudes and action, there is a chance for cultural variety in the details of supernatural beliefs that the child picks up.[3]

The Inevitability of Early Ideologies

It will be remembered that the impact of the political and religious climate to which the child is exposed gains full force as the limitations of his parents are discovered. In a remarkable autobiography, *Father and Son*, Edmund Gosse, the English literary historian of the late nineteenth century, describes the fashion in which he learned of his father's imperfections:

In consequence of hearing so much about an Omniscient God, a being of supernatural wisdom and penetration who was always with us, who made, in fact, a fourth in our company, I had come to think of Him, not without awe, but with absolute confidence. . . . I confused [my Father] in some sense with God; at all events I believed that my Father knew everything and saw everything. One morning in my sixth year, my Mother and I were alone in the morning-room, when my Father came in and announced some fact to us. I was standing on the rug, gazing at him, and when he made this statement, I remember turning quickly in embarrassment, and looking into the fire. The shock to me was as that of a thunderbolt, for what my Father had said *was not true.* My Mother and I, who had been present at the trifling incident, were aware that it had not happened exactly as it had been reported to him. My Mother gently told him so, and he accepted the correction. Nothing could possibly have been more trifling to my parents, but to me it meant an epoch. The shock was not caused by any suspicion that he was not telling the truth, as it appeared to him, but by the awful proof that he was not, as I had supposed, omniscient. . . . The theory that my Father was omniscient or infallible, was now dead and buried. . . . My Father, as a deity, as a natural force of immense prestige, fell in my eyes to a human level.

As chance would have it, a petty matter toppled Gosse's idol. Its triviality reminds one of the way boys forever pit their omnipotent parents (*in absentia*) against the equally powerful parents of their playmates. In rural areas, where half of the present generation of adults was reared, weather, floods, lightning, are the phenomena which preoccupy the child as well as the adults about him. The city child is more sheltered from climatic forces, which may signify nothing more to him than raincoats and overshoes. The Hopi Indians were probably thinking of the large percentage of white men in cities or in temperate zones when they insisted "that Jesus Christ might do for the modern Whites in a good climate, but that the Hopi gods had brought success [to the Indians] in the desert ever since the world began." Nevertheless, at some point early in the child's development, be he rural or urban, red or white, he discovers that his attendants can protect neither him nor themselves against the force of the elements, the ravages of the body, and the dangers that arise from man's relations with other men. Even the inferior position of his father to other men is a shocking revelation. One boy, for example, learned that when his father went mountaineering, someone else and not his father was acting as leader. He found the fact incredible and could scarcely be made to understand that his father was not always first.[4]

It thus makes little difference whether or not parents, leaders, or other transmitters of culture hand down to children an organized set of religious and political beliefs. If mothers ceased to tell their children of God, if churches were unknown, and if schools confined themselves to "the three R's," religions, earthly and celestial, would nevertheless be built. Thomas Hobbes left little to be uncovered by modern psychology in his analysis of the common need for religion:

> And this Feare of things invisible, is the naturall Seed of that, which every one in himself calleth Religion; and in them that worship, or feare that Power otherwise than they do, Superstition. . . .
>
> And first, it is peculiar to the nature of Man, to be inquisitive into the Causes of the Events they see, some more, some lesse; but all men so much, as to be curious in the search of the causes of their own good and evill fortune.
>
> Secondly, upon the sight of any thing that hath a Beginning, to think also it had a cause, which determined the same to begin, then when it did, rather than sooner or later.
>
> The two first, make Anxiety. For being assured that there be causes of all things that have arrived hitherto, or shall arrive hereafter; it is impossible for a man, who continually endeavoureth to secure himselfe against the evill he feares, and procure the good he desireth, not to be in a perpetuall solicitude of the time to come; So that every man, especially those that are over provident, are in an estate like to that of *Prometheus*. For as *Prometheus*, (which interpreted, is, *The prudent man*), was bound to the hill *Caucasus*, a place of large prospect, where, an Eagle feeding on his liver, devoured in the day, as much as was repayred in the night: So that man, which looks too far before him, in the care of future time, hath his heart all the day long, gnawed on by feare of death, poverty, or other calamity; and has no repose, nor pause of his anxiety, but in sleep.
>
> This perpetuall feare, always accompanying mankind in the ignorance of causes, as it were in the Dark, must needs have for object something. And therefore when there is nothing to be seen, there is nothing to accuse, either of their good, or evill fortune, but some *Power*, or Agent *Invisible:* In which sense perhaps it was, that some of the old Poets said, that the Gods were at first created by humane Feare.

Since mothers do tell their children of God, since faiths everywhere pass from parent to child, teacher to pupil, the content of beliefs becomes the more pressing concern in an analysis of the ideologies of the modern child.

Approximately one-half the population of the United States

belongs to an organized religion. For the children of this part of the population, membership in a church usually entails the following ceremonies: use of the Bible in the home; observance of the Sabbath; religious rites at births, marriages, and deaths; a short blessing of food before family meals; and prayers before retiring. The other half of the country is by no means wholly irreligious. The definition of a church member commonly used for statistical purposes underestimates not only the number of those who attend church, participate in other church activities, and claim affiliation, but also those who believe in supernatural beings. The people in this group generally shrink from the word "Godless." Many of them return to the fold of the church once they have become parents. If at no other time, most of them feel a compulsion to go to church on Easter or Christmas morning. And they want a clergyman when birth or death visits the family. These people, too, bequeath anthropomorphic deities to their children. What else could they prescribe for the insistent and at times even desperate questioning of the youngster?[5] They cannot follow what has been said to be the practice of philosophers—call the apex of their dialectical pyramid "God" because they have no idea what else to call it. Nor can they transmit some more fancy personalized concept of the deity, for example, God as a Cambridge mathematician. Jean Jacques Rousseau recognized these difficulties when he considered the problem of a religious education for his imaginary child, Émile:

The Incomprehensible embraces all, he gives its motion to the earth, and shapes the system of all creatures, but our eyes cannot see him nor can our hands search him out, he evades the efforts of our senses; we behold the work, but the workman is hidden from our eyes. It is no small matter to know that he exists, and when we have got so far, and when we ask, What is he? Where is he? our mind is overwhelmed, we lose ourselves, we know not what to think . . . every nation on the face of the earth, not even excepting the Jews, have made to themselves idols. We, ourselves, with our words, Spirit, Trinity, Persons, are for the most part quite anthropomorphic. . . . The ideas of creation, destruction, ubiquity, eternity, almighty power, those of the divine attributes—these are all ideas so confused and obscure that few men succeed in grasping them; yet there is nothing obscure about them to the common people, because they do not understand them in the least; how then should they present themselves in full force, that is to say in all their obscurity, to the young mind which is still occupied with the first working of the senses, and fails to realise anything but what it handles? In vain do the abysses of the Infinite open around us, a child does not know the meaning of fear; his weak eyes cannot gauge their depths. To children everything is infinite, they cannot assign limits to anything; not that their measure is so large, but because their understanding is so small. I have even noticed that they place the infinite rather below than above the dimensions known to them. They judge a distance to be immense rather by their feet than by their eyes; infinity is bounded for them, not so much by what they can see, but how far they can go. If you talk to them of the power of God, they will think he is nearly as strong as their father.

Rousseau seems to have had little knowledge of the fears of the very young child and believed him to live in blissful serenity. He therefore thought it possible to delay the child's religious education. He did not see the child's great need to know the ordering of the world about him. "But we need fear nothing of the sort for Émile who always declines to pay attention to what is beyond his reach, and listens with profound indifference to things he does not understand." Actually, some religious doctrines that appear in catechisms and the like, such as the aseity of God, are more easily understood by the child (understood in the sense of feeling them fully explained) than by more causally minded adults. For him, *deus causa sui,* God, unbegotten himself and the begetter of all things, is acceptable, because the child once thought that parents were the beginning and end of all things; nothing preceded them; they made everything. He even finds it hard to believe that anyone like his grandparents sired his father and mother, more readily believing that they, too, are his parents' children.[6]

Gradually, as was found in the last chapter, a transference of qualities from parents to *rulers* is effected. The following quotation from a life-history analyzed by the sociologist, Ernest W. Burgess, illustrates a beginning in the shift of prohibitions and punishment to the religious *ruler:*

"Mother and I were having lunch together. I said or did some naughty thing and my mother told me that God would see me. I said that I'd pull the blind down and then He couldn't see."

The girl's mother retorted, "Oh, but He sees everything. He can see through the blind."

"I looked up into the sky," said the girl. "In my imagination I saw an old gray-bearded man with human attributes."

The transition to *rulers* is also clearly seen in the children of Susan Isaacs' studies who believe, for example, that if they are naughty, "God will drown the world."[7]

Religious Training in the United States

For good or for evil, anthropomorphic beliefs cannot be stifled in the child. Outside the home, parental information finds support in the schools. It can be safely assumed that most of the regular members of organized religions in the United States send their children to Sunday schools. Many others send the children to Sunday school although they themselves do not attend church. The prevailing notion is that church and Sunday school are good influences on the child. About four-fifths of the churches in the country maintain Sunday schools, and some also support vacation and week-day church schools for children. Altogether, twelve million children under thirteen years of age are members of organized religions, and undoubtedly many more attend the Sunday schools.

What do they learn in these schools? A little pamphlet used as a basis for Protestant Sunday school lessons for nursery-school children contains on the last page "A Letter to Parents," which explains how parents, as well as teachers, should instruct their children:

All the lessons in this group tell of the heavenly Father's love and care for His children. The seven already used emphasized the heavenly Father's care in *providing* for His children. In this lesson and the lessons which follow, the heavenly Father's care in protecting His children is stressed.

Most little children have a natural sense of faith and trust. Unless parents have grossly abused the wonderful privilege that is theirs as parents, their children will have unbounded faith in the love and care of mother and daddy. The little child feels utterly safe in his daddy's arms, and so he will readily understand and accept the mother hen's care for her baby chicks. He will be happy in the thought that Jesus has promised that the heavenly Father will love and take care of him.

When you read or tell this story to your child, show him the picture on page three of this leaflet. Tell him, "Jesus said that the mother hen takes care of the baby chicks. I wonder who takes care of the little boy and girl?" Conclude your conversation with the assurance, "Jesus has said that the heavenly Father takes care of little boys and girls."[8]

A book entitled *Tell Me about God* and designed for much the same purpose may be cited with profit. Its nineteen chapter headings are: "The Bible Helps Us To Know God," "God Loves Us and Cares for Us," "God Helps Us Take Care of Ourselves," "God Is Always Near," "God Plans for Day and Night," "God Plans a Beautiful World," "God Plans Food for Us," "God Gives Us Water," "God Helps Us in Trouble," "God Wants Us To Help," "God Is Very Great," "God Made the Night," "God Wants Us To Talk with Him," "God Sent His Son," "God Wants Us To Help Each Other," "God Helps Us To Be Good," "God Forgives Us," "God Loves All His Children," and "Let Us Give Thanks to God."[9]

Even without going into the text, it is easy to see in these chapter headings the capacities once attached to attendants—omnipotence, environmental regulation, ministering affection, direction toward good conduct. This book closely represents the ideas contained not only in all Sunday-school textbooks but in the services of worship in Protestant schools of religion.[10] So similar are they in describing God's all-powerful character, his commandments to men, and his control of the universe that separate discussion is unnecessary. And lest it be thought that boys and girls listen and read but do not absorb these ideas, it should be mentioned that whenever they have been questioned carefully about their religious conceptions, their responses are strikingly like their stimuli. God has hands and feet and a face like a man; he exercises his divine office like a general and a lawmaker; he reveals himself and punishes wrongdoers through storms and earthquakes; he wants faith, love, and unquestioning obedience.

Elementary Catholic books and schools have no less of a religious orientation of this kind. The encyclical on education by Pope Pius XI laid down the policy for Catholic schools of every grade:

It is necessary that all the teaching and the whole organization of the school, and its teachers, syllabus and text books in every branch, be regulated by the Christian spirit, under the direction and maternal supervision of the Church; so that Religion may be in very truth the foundation and the crown of youth's entire training; and this in every grade of school, not only in the elementary but the intermediate and the higher institutions of learning as well. To use the words of Leo XIII: "It is necessary not only that religious instruction be given to the young at certain fixed times, but also that every other subject taught be permeated with Christian piety."

Thus, in Catholic education, all fields of learning are set in a religious perspective. And like the God of the Protestants, the Catholic God is omnipotent, a benevolent mover of the universe, and a demander of good conduct.

Formal and Informal Political Education

From the start, books for American children were religious in character. The earliest of all was *The Rule of the New-Creature*, published in 1682, followed closely by John Cotton's treatise, *Spiritual Milk for Boston Babes: Drawn Out of the Breasts of Both Testaments for Their Souls Nourishment*. But political education was not to lag far behind the religious. Originally printed in the seventeenth century, the first American primer went through several editions. A changing Frontispiece in each new edition dramatized American political history. The first extant copy pictures "George III" in royal raiment; the next edition displays "General Washington"; while the last hails the Father of His Country with the caption, "President of the United States of America." Undoubtedly, these wood engravings were designed to help the early American child learn his letters.

Not only in books but in many other phases of the early life of the modern child religious and political beliefs coexist. In the world of nation-states, the religious symbolism imparted by home and school is joined at almost every step by the personalized symbols of nationalism. The kings, the presidents, the nations, the heroes, and the fathers of countries cannot avoid mention in the modern household. It is not necessary for the child to encounter educational experiences as striking as that which one youngster met: "On passing every illumination during the night of the Jubilee [of Queen Victoria], my father, who was carrying me, smacked me 'to make me remember the day.' I was four and I *have* remembered."[11] The child in his burning search for authoritative or powerful persons absorbs all awesome references made by the adults or older children about him. The beginnings of a transition to political beliefs are discernible in the experience of a six-year-old English girl who was refused something she wanted on the ground that her father had no money. The following dialogue ensued:

The child: "Well, why don't you make some new money, Daddy?"
The father: "Oh no. Only the king can do that."
The child (crestfallen): "But, Daddy, aren't you a king?"

Policemen, too, become extremely important, for parents frequently refer to them as the ones who punish by "arrest" those who break the law. "What is the law?" asks the child.[12] The law, he may then be told, is something everyone must obey. Like the highly wrought and metaphysical notions of God, the idea that people make the laws through their representatives is something the child would find hard to digest, especially since those who make the laws must themselves obey them. He is like the seventeenth-century good citizen of Paris who, having heard it said that there was no king in Venice, was astounded and nearly died from laughter at the mere mention of so ridiculous an idea. It is much more understandable to the child that the king or Congress or the president makes the law; and if people are not good in thought and deed, they are punished.

Should this sort of questioning not occur, the child would nevertheless receive unintentional political education by hearing family remarks like, "The President is speaking tonight" or "Did you see the Prime Minister's picture in this morning's newspaper?" The political world of the child under five years of age is peopled with awe-inspiring chief executives, fantastic policemen, soldiers, firemen (for firemen control fires and save people), together with good people (law-abiding citizens), who are happy and content, and bad (law-breaking persons), who are jailed or hanged.[13]

Once in the elementary public schools, the attitudes of awe toward political concepts are reinforced with conduct. The pledge of allegiance to the flag is required in most public schools. The assembled singing of patriotic songs—"America," "The Star-spangled Banner," "America, the Beautiful," "Battle Hymn of the Republic," "Hail, Columbia," and "Yankee Doodle"—is rarely omitted from the curriculum. Since the words of these songs are familiar to all Americans, they need not be repeated here. The content of textbooks, which pupils are often made to recite aloud to develop their reading and speaking faculties, also requires little elaboration. Still it is worth while to stress that the deeds of the presidents of the United States are eulogized in elementary-school books, while the virtues therein held up for the child to acquire are those of the citizen who renders political service to his country by defending it in war or advancing it in peace.[14]

The nation thus becomes an expanded home. Conversely, Rousseau sometimes described the home as "that miniature fatherland." The parental superbeings instead are the chief executives, past and present, the founding fathers, and other national heroes. The methods for retaining their protection are embodied in the words "law" and "duty." The law makes known what conduct to avoid in order to keep the environment in harmony. The child is seeking a kind attendant behind phenomena. He finds it in the chief executive. For this reason, the discovery of the existence of law, clear and fixed, is a happy one. By obeying its rules, the child can retain the friendship of the political *rulers* and the ensuing enjoyment of a governed universe.[15] "Duty" is made up of the deeds one should perform for one's country out of love. Failure to follow law or duty invokes catastrophe—death or disgrace, the exile of a Benedict Arnold or the lonely misery of a man without a country. The identity of home and nation finds intense expression in the words of Philip Nolan, the "man without a country":

"Youngster, let that show you what it is to be without a family, without a home, and without a country. And if you are ever tempted to say a word or to do a thing that shall put a bar between you and your family, your home, and your country, pray God in his mercy to take you that instant home to His own heaven. Stick by your family, boy; write and send, and talk about it. Let it be nearer and nearer to your thought, the farther you have to travel from it; and rush back to it when you are free, as that poor black slave is doing now. And for your country, boy," and the words rattled in his throat, "and for that flag," and he pointed to the ship, "never dream a dream but of serving her as she bids you, though the service carry you through a thousand hells. No matter what happens to you, no matter who flatters you or who abuses you, never look at another flag, never let a night pass but you pray God to bless that flag. Remember, boy, that behind all these men you have to do with, behind officers, and government, and people even, there is the Country Herself, your Country, and that you belong to Her as you belong to your own mother. Stand by Her, boy, as you would stand by your mother, if those devils there had got hold of her today!"

I was frightened to death by his calm, hard passion; but I blundered out, that I would, by all that was holy, and that I had never thought of doing anything else. He hardly seemed to hear me; but he did, almost in a whisper, say: "Oh, if anybody had said so to me when I was of your age!"

The religious and political ideologies of the modern child do not change appreciably until adolescence. The cosmos is so well ordered by the protection of the home with its religious and political ceiling, that the child gives small heed to systems of belief. Questions and other attempts to verify his notions greatly decline.[16] It is not until adolescence, when a new crisis approaches, that the youth's ideologies meet an ordeal.

The Political Void in Adolescence

From the record of ancient and primitive societies it might be expected that at this time the secular and sacerdotal figures would take the leading role in ushering the youth into a new status. Certainly it is true that at the approximate age of puberty the major religions, Catholic, Jewish, and Protestant, use their ceremonies of confirmation to mark a new status in the religious community. But in the political orbit the rites of passage are conspicuously absent.

Perhaps the age of maturity—twenty-one years—the age of voting, brings the equivalence of the status-giving customs of the simpler societies. The possession of the vote does give the youth some additional influence, but there is no real ceremony. In states with permanent registration laws there is the necessity of affixing one's signature to governmental forms; other than this, there are no observances. The disuse in which a good share of youth lets its franchise fall wherever in the world it has it is well known. The remark of a new twenty-one-year-old gives proper weight to the part played by maturity ceremonies in bringing the electorate to the polls. When asked why he voted, he replied, "they said I was old enough. . . . That's the onliest reason."

The closest approximation appears to be the ritual of graduation from secondary school. Yet, only about one-fourth of the adolescent group emerges fully graduated from public secondary school. Even so, can the principal of a high school be conceived of as a political chief, or the paper diploma as the bow and spear or *toga virilis?* Where are the reaffirmations of allegiance to the political ideology? Wherein lies the individual's new status as a full member of the body politic? He finds himself instead in what has been feelingly called the "the floundering period." Apparently, then, graduation is solely what the word denotes: a graded step has been taken. The youth is now stamped with the label, "mentally and physically able," but in a society with freedom of occupational choice, the answer to "able for what and for whom?" is not quickly forthcoming.[17]

Emergence of an Economic Ideology

The gap between school and employment in the United States has been found to be nearly two years. For those who drop out of school before the age of sixteen, the average period before finding a permanent job, namely, any job lasting over eight months, is around three and one-half years. Graduated or not, almost one-half of all youth emerging from schools find no full-time employment for a year or more.[18] Obviously, the average youth encounters a period of prolonged idleness, of futile job-seeking, parental pressure, and lack of money. Many accept part-time or makeshift jobs; and all too often for their satisfaction these positions—farm work, seasonal selling, casual labor, messenger service—turn out to be the factors which shape their choice of a permanent occupation.

Surely, this unhappy span of months parallels the trial and ordeal of earlier and preliterate societies. Only one thing will make the youth less miserable, will relieve him of parental strictures, enable him to "stay out late," buy him clothes or a car, and give him the money to "date" girls. Plainly and simply—a job. The job is everything. Without it, complete frustration. The jobless youth is sans income, sans status, sans sex partner, sans everything. He knows this, for he has had it pounded into him subtly and directly, consciously and unconsciously; he was being groomed by education and by training for the assumption of some task favorably regarded by the community. In the last year of school more and more frequently the question was asked of him, "What are you going to do when you get out of school?"

The trepidation the adolescent feels about going out into the world is typified in the following letter of a boy in his last year of high school:

Whenever I think of looking for a job I break out into cold perspiration and I visualize how I will look for a job and fail to get one. I never get myself to think that it will be easy to get a job. In this feeling am I normal, that this is the feeling that every one gets when he goes out into the unknown or is it a mental quirk brought on by a sort of inferiority complex? I am pretty sure that I am not inferior to the boys and girls of my age, but I can't explain this feeling in any other way.[19]

No matter how few the persons who wander through modern life without ever obtaining a permanent position in the economy, their number is in sharp contrast to that of primitive communities where no one fails his adolescent tests and finds himself without a niche in communal life. The rebuffs the youth gets from trying to "land a job" reinforce the threat of isolation which he feels at the thought of leaving the home. The adolescent needs to be told only a few times, "Sorry, we can't use you," to believe that the world has no use for what he has to offer. "Jobs play the biggest part in your life and they're so uncertain. When you've looked and looked, you get the feeling that nobody has any use for you. It takes away your self-confidence." Thus the revived conception of a hostile environment begins to affect adolescents. Their anxiety makes them extremists. They seek for solutions and their desperate single-mindedness borders on radicalism. The adolescent attraction toward political extremisms and the poles of fundamentalism and atheism is a familiar observation. In crime, as in conversion, adolescence is a crucial period. The peak of the age curve of crime fluctuates around late adolescence, and writings on juvenile delinquency, popular and scientific, are legion.

The life of crime, however, is a career adopted by relatively few. Eventually most adolescents get jobs. The fever of the prolonged period of dangling between school and vocation is drowned in a wave of relief. Who or what has given the young man surcease? In the preliterate societies and at times even in Athens and Rome the answer was the political *rulers* who either personally or symbolically participated in presenting him with his new status. But, as just noted, in the modern Western world this does not happen. The youth does not feel he owes his new job to the government but to an entity he may never see, the businessman.

This construct is the godhead of a new ideology first met as a subsidiary set of beliefs which suddenly zooms to importance in early adolescence. The child under ten years of age is scarcely aware of its existence. The businessman as a household hero, even while in the guise of a captain of industry, has never rivaled the political figures of monarchs and presidents. Not long ago a radio spokesman for industry, W. J. Cameron, recognized this fact and uttered his hope for a change in the following preoration:

Carlyle and Emerson spoke to their generation of the Hero. . . . Their heroes were Prophets, Poets, Men of Letters, Warrior-Kings. . . . Never, never could the hero be a manufacturer . . . an agriculturist, a builder of railways, an inventor. . . . While this was in process, another race of heroes was being born not of books but of experience's vital touch. . . . A view of life is forming that will include the industrial world among the finer arts of human service.

Perhaps in the future, but not in this generation. The great dramas and fairy tales in the traditions of the Western world are made of the stuff of kings, not businessmen.

In all textbooks of elementary schools America's heroes are political leaders. An ordinary history schoolbook devotes two-thirds of its discussions of personalities to statesmen and military men and fills in the remainder with scientists, inventors, and philanthropists. From his secondary-school education the youth is likely to remember only Thomas Edison as a nonpolitical hero, and to remember him as a scientist or an inventor, not as a businessman. But when the matter of "After school, what?" approaches, when news columns of the newspapers are scanned incidentally to the "Help Wanted" advertisements, then knowledge of the source of jobs becomes vital, then the promptings of vague memory or of press editorials teach that the economic system of the United States is free enterprise, that it regulates itself by a law of supply and demand, that it had therefore better not be interfered with, that some persons of foresight, enterprise, and stick-to-itiveness—called businessmen—are the ones who provide employment for the millions of Americans.[20] And suddenly the young man has a new conception of the world. The businessman gives him his means of support and gratification, his status, his protection against separation-anxiety, and receives in return his loyalty and gratitude and work in the prescribed manner.

Such are the systems of belief typical of the child and youth in the democracies of the West. In the account given of the crisis of modern adolescence it was stated that the job is the distinctive mark of status. The job, and the businessman too, however, are not entities of political or religious ideologies but of the economic process. For the first time, then, in this tracing of the roots of anomie, a way of life is encountered which presents a new ideology at adolescence, instead of reinforcing the existing political and religious traditions already long in existence.

The political and religious status systems have seldom challenged the validity of one another's claims to providing for the commonweal in their respective spheres of the here-and-now and the hereafter. There have been notable conflicts over the margins of the secular and sacred areas. Yet even the poles of theocracy and "whoever rules, his is the religion" represent disagreement only over whether the religious or the political status system shall be the higher ranking. In the chronicles of mankind rarely has the religious system cast doubt on the political system's claim that there is much to render unto Caesar. And rarely has the state branded all religion with the mark, *religio illicita!* A symbiotic relationship of the two primary status systems is the usual historical finding. To quote once more from the anthropologist Hocart:

> In the earliest records known, man appears to us worshipping gods and their earthly representatives, namely kings.
>
> We have no right, in the present state of our knowledge, to assert that the worship of gods preceded that of kings; we do not know. Perhaps there never were any gods without kings, or kings without gods. When we have discovered the origin of divine kingship we shall know, but at present we only know that when history begins there are kings, the representatives of gods.[21]

But what of the intrusion of these fundamentally economic concepts? Can three ideologies live in harmony within the mind?[22] And is it only because of the metaphysical division of life into mortal and immortal that religion and politics thrive side by side, rendering mutual support? Now that he has a job, the youth of modern democracy, whose career line was pursued from childhood through adolescence, is rid of debilitating worry. Where is his anomie? Is it simply *une maladie imaginaire*, a product of jaded romantic writers imbued with a pessimism persuasive enough to infect sober social scientists? Or is the youth's surcease momentary? Turned adult, does he feel the impact of these questions?

THE THEORY OF ANOMIE: I. CAUSES

INTRODUCTION

"A MAN cannot serve two masters." So advises a venerable religious saying which has comforted countless men wavering in a welter of loyalties. Whence comes its power to wring a sympathetic response from the human spirit? The child or the youth, even in the present day, has a handful of gods. True it may be that in immature manner he often confuses their qualities with the earliest attributes of his attendants; but though he blur and merge them, they are none the fewer. What is involved is still only one master for each system of beliefs, the father or mother for the family system, the god for the religious, and the chief for the political system of beliefs. But it can be shown that even within a single system of beliefs several superbeings may coexist. In fact, strict monotheism is an extremely rare occurrence. The cosmology of the Hopi Indians, for example, maintains a sun god and a sky god, an earth goddess and a corn mother. Furthermore, it has already been observed that some religious ideologies assign a different god to the functions of protection and chastisement, to good and to evil. The Greek and Roman pagan religions constitute excellent examples of numerous *rulers* coinhabiting one system of beliefs, each tending to his respective sphere or function. The difficulties Christianity has had in settling the question of the Trinity illustrate the problems of establishing a true monotheism. To speak precisely, most religions are monolatrous—they worship one god above others.

When the missionary brings his religion to the heathen, the same question of a plurality of religious *rulers* often arises. Some of the more practical proselytizers, in areas where Christians are dominant in a military sense, show considerable skill in handling the problem. They will call in a number of persons of authority and ask them, "Who is your main deity?" Upon being informed, they will say, "All right, he is God. From now on do not pay so much attention to the lesser lights."[1] Whether or not some such conversation occurs, if a new superbeing performing functions similar to the old is forcibly introduced, the newly converted will merely feel that the old god is the same in everything but name. In this fashion, no personality crisis results. Apparently, then, man can have many gods. In line with the thesis that systems of beliefs reproduce in certain respects the family setting, any single system of beliefs can contain only one supreme god although many smaller deities may exist within the divine family.[2] This appears to be the historical case; no known ideology maintains a board or committee of omnipotent *rulers*. But taken together at any given moment in the life of man, the gods (even counting master-gods alone) are plural, at the very least two, the political and the religious.[3]

CHAPTER III

CONFLICT BETWEEN BELIEF-SYSTEMS

IN ORDER that the next step be made in the right direction, two considerations should be brought to mind: First, separation-anxiety, which was found to resemble closely Durkheim's discrete description of anomie, follows upon the disintegration of the child or youth's ideologies. Second, ideologies are not made of one piece but of a number of integrated parts, a *system* of beliefs, as they usually have been referred to here. Now that it has been ascertained that a plurality of *rulers* in itself does not break down the reigning ideologies, the search for ideological disintegration should be made in another part of a system of beliefs.

Toward the close of chapter i two analytical categories were in process of formation—*rulers* and the methods for securing their ministrations. It is the latter area of beliefs that remains to be investigated. And, for the purpose of expediting discussion, the standards of conduct which, according to any given belief-system, the *rulers* require of believers in order to regulate the environment for their benefit will henceforth be called "directives."[1]

The term "directives," like the term *ruler*, refers to people's beliefs. They are ways people believe they must act to avoid trouble, fear, and anxiety. From the positive side they are formulas for salvation or for success or for the good life. As the earlier chapters showed, the human being almost from its beginnings is showered with prohibitions, directions, and threats. Conformity to these "thou shalt's" and "thou shalt not's" becomes virtue and brings happiness, whereas disobedience becomes evil and brings grief. Thus these directives embody the community's ideas of good and bad. Little have social scientists realized that these moral ideas are a community's ways of trying to regulate the environment through their *rulers* and are, thus, ways of avoiding anxiety. The point will be further discussed in chapter v, but at this time it should be recalled that parents first direct the child in the name of their own authority; and later, using words like "law," "duty," and "sin," they demand similar behavior in the name of political and religious *rulers*. Violation of these injunctions becomes associated with immediate and terrible punishment, with the withdrawal of parental affection and support, and with the dreaded anxiety of separation. Conformity, on the other hand, brings peace and security. To illustrate now a clash in directives and its results, an extreme example will be used—the religious practice of head-hunting.[2]

Had anyone visited Eddystone Island in Tasmania before the advent of the Christians, he would have found that the taking of heads was a central part of the religious directives. Human heads were believed necessary for the reaching and conciliating of deities, including ancestral ghosts. Canoe-building, funerals, horticulture, and pig-breeding were among the events that involved the offering or hunting of heads. When the white man stopped this bloody practice, he cut the roots of the religious life of the natives. They no longer knew how to propitiate their gods. Their religion was undermined. The directives given them in exchange —love thy neighbor and call on thy god by prayer—were incomprehensible. To follow the new directives was to violate the old. They grew apathetic, indifferent to work and the future, and at the same time so proficient in abortion that the tribe was committing suicide by depopulation.[3]

A similar demoralization has followed whenever head-hunting or human sacrifice has been forcibly prevented by Christians— in Malaysia, in Indonesia, among the Incas and the scalp-hunting American Indians, and in Formosa. With typical interchange of religious and political ideologies, the possession of heads or scalps was a symbol of success and power. Sometimes the heads of persons taken in this world would become the servants of their possessor in the next. Among the Naga, the girls unrelentingly taunted the young men, refusing to consider them as matrimonial prospects until they were shown some heads. Every love in one village culminated in the loss of someone's head in another. On the island of Kiwai, houses in the process of construction had to be blessed by smearing parts of them with human blood. "Put post—kill bushman; make on-top-house—kill bushman; put on thatch—kill bushman."[4]

Under such circumstances it is clear that a man cannot have two masters. To obey one is to disobey the other. Uneasiness must result, for the conciliation of *rulers* is not a trifling matter. One cannot say, "Today I'll obey god X and take several heads for an offering; tomorrow, under conditions Y (no enemy bushmen about), I'll follow god Z and recite fifteen decades of Ave Marias." An analysis of modern systems of beliefs may provide further instruction in this matter of conflicting ways of obeying *rulers*, those supreme beings who are believed to hold in their hands the powers of punishment and provision.

Co-operative–Competitive Directives

In the broad analyses of belief-systems presented in the earlier chapters no conflicts were apparent among the directives of family, state, and religion. All required obedience to the precepts of the *rulers*. But none stops there. They go on to prescribe relations among men. Of the Ten Commandments, for example, four pertain to man's relation to God and six to man's relation to man. The major commands of these belief-systems emphasize love not only for the deities but also for the members of the community, be they the brothers of the family, the believers of the religion, or the citizens of the state. "Blood is thicker than water"; "Love thy neighbor"; *E pluribus unum*. As was seen, systems of beliefs are made in the image of an idealized home, and there one loves and obeys one's parents, loves the remaining members of the family, and treats all other persons as outsiders.[5] In truth, ideologies can be called brotherhood religions and their believers brethren.

Without proceeding to directives other than those regulating the relations of community members, a conflict with the belief-system of business or capitalism is already obvious. The way to win status there requires a different treatment of men. The directive of the business ideology concerning human relations is competition—rivalry among men for monetary acquisition. In the pursuit of this end, men are to be bound, swayed, or guided by no other consideration, sentiment, objective, or norm.[6]

Competition is opposed to sentiment, in exchange. Whenever any eco-
nomical agent does or forbears anything under the influence of any sentiment
other than the desire of giving the least and gaining the most he can in exchange, be that sentiment, patriotism, or gratitude, or charity, or vanity, leading him to do any otherwise than self interest would prompt, in that case, also,
the rule of competition is departed from: another rule is for the time sub-
stituted.[7]

The inability to maintain competition in the face of sentiment
makes it absolutely necessary to diminish the number of affiliations persons have with one another and leads to the oft-charged
impersonality of capitalist economics. Competition specifically
requires the reversal of the famous first ethic of Kant—men should
be treated as ends and not means—and of the even older saying—
man is the measure of all things. According to the competitive
directive one is supposed to vie with other men for the end of
pecuniary gain, a way of existence that the economic historian
Tawney disrespectfully called "the life of snatching to hoard."
The brotherliness of religious sects like the Quakers or the Baptists in Colonial America, for example, made it necessary at first
for them strictly to exempt all commercial agreements among
brethren.

Fully recognizing the impersonal ideal of a competitive system,
the economist Frank H. Knight, in attempting to study the
essential features of exchange relations, made the following
fictitious assumption about its necessary human relations:

Every member of the society is to act as an individual only, in entire independence of all other persons. To complete his independence he must be free
from social wants, prejudices, preferences, or repulsions, or any values which
are not completely manifested in market dealing. Exchange of finished goods
is the only form of relation between individuals, or at least there is no other
form which influences economic conduct. And in exchanges between individuals, no interests of persons not parties to the exchange are to be concerned,
either for good or for ill.[8]

Since one cannot have emotional ties with one's neighbors, the
distinction in laissez faire ideology between home and outside,
between family and stranger, countryman and foreigner, believer
and heretic, is obliterated. Everyone gets treated in the same way
—competitively. In straight contradiction with the preferential
directive of family, religion, and state, the doctrine of free trade

admits of no favorites. The extraordinary character of this attitude was more apparent in the mid-eighteenth century when statements like David Hume's prayer "for the flourishing commerce of Germany, Spain, Italy, and even France itself" shocked the patriotic Englishman. The conflict of the political ideology with the impersonalism of the competitive directive is seen most clearly in the early stages of any political crisis that involves the danger of military action. Then the economic system of beliefs must retreat before the charge of selling to the enemy. The same clash is also part of all tariff versus free trade controversies and of the difficulties laissez faire countries have in planning the strategy of long-run national defense.

Following on the heels of the competitive directive and its accompanying impersonality is the so-called "rationalism" of capitalism.[9] If one is not tied to people by sentiment, it is easy to be rational and detached about them. Like any other object they can be considered as part of a chain of ways and means to the end of economic acquisition. In efflux of time, rationalism permeates the entire culture. Not only business management and accounting but science (including social science and psychology, the objective studies of man) thrives under such nourishment. Eventually the most holy or tabooed areas of man's previous life come under scrutiny. Art and the church, too, must submit to a weighing on a scale graduated in degrees of economic gain.

The position of the poor in the capitalist system of beliefs neatly combines the three doctrines of competition, impersonalism, and rationalism. Obviously, the poor are poor because by being idle or unemployed they violate the competitive directive. They are out of the struggle. Not charity but a deaf ear should be turned to them, for idleness is wickedness. It is impossible that an idle man can be a good man. What is more, to be rational about it, alms to the prolific poverty-stricken simply enables them to produce more poor for posterity. Hence, "the rich do not in reality possess the *power* of finding employment and maintenance for the poor." Thus spoke Malthus, unwittingly in the process of giving economics the name of the "dismal science."

It must be made clear that in the economic belief-system there is no conflict with the political, religious, and familial directive of love and faith for *rulers*. Nor is there any clash with the end of the betterment of the community. The common good is the pledge of all ideologies. Despite all appearances, competition in its final working out was not supposed to be harmful to one's neighbor. In its beginnings the capitalist belief-system advanced the thesis that self-love (the early term for the competitive attitude) was the best guide for social love. What became known as the paradox of Bernard de Mandeville—private vices ultimately redound to the public benefit—remains to this day a provocative poem:

> Thus every part was full of Vice,
> Yet the whole Mass a Paradise;
>
> . . . .
>
> Such were the Blessings of that State;
> Their crimes conspir'd to make them Great:
> And Virtue, who from Politicks
> Had learn'd a Thousand Cunning Tricks,
> Was, by their happy Influence,
> Made Friends with Vice: And ever since,
> The worst of all the Multitude
> Did something for the Common Good.
>
> . . . .
>
> This, as in Musick Harmony,
> Made Jarrings in the main agree;
> Parties directly opposite,
> Assist each other, as 'twere for Spight;
>
> . . . .
>
> Thus Vice nurs'd Ingenuity,
> Which joyn'd with Time and Industry,
> Had carry'd Life's Conveniencies,
> It's real Pleasures, Comforts, Ease,
> To such a Height, the very Poor
> Liv'd better than the Rich before,
> And nothing could be added more.

Adam Smith expressed the same idea somewhat later, in more prosaic fashion:

Every individual is continually exerting himself to find out the most advantageous employment for whatever capital he can command. It is his own advantage, indeed, and not that of the society, which he has in view. But the study of his own advantage naturally, or rather necessarily, leads him to prefer that employment which is most advantageous to society. . . . He generally, indeed, neither intends to promote the public interest nor knows how much he is promoting it. . . . By pursuing his own interest he frequently promotes that of the society more effectually than when he really intends to promote it. I have never known much good done by those who affected to trade for the public good. It is an affectation, indeed, not very common among merchants, and very few words need be employed in dissuading them from it.

Freedom for the play of self-love was the germinal idea of competition. In the writings of David Ricardo competition was but an abstract part of the economic ideology. In the writings of Bastiat it takes the form of slogans, "Competition is Liberty" and "Liberty is Harmony." Real impetus, however, came from *The Origin of Species*. The doctrine of the struggle for existence, originally a phrase of Malthus, became the new order not only of the economic sphere but of the entire universe.

Charles Darwin had another important effect on the embryonic system of beliefs of capitalism. The physiocrats thought that the harmony of self-love and social love was part of God's scheme for the world. This was implicit in their resounding maxim: *Laissez faire et laissez passer, le monde va de lui-même.* Let things alone —let them go, they advised; the world will take care of itself. For Bastiat, competition was the estimable decree of a wise providence. For Blackstone, "The Creator . . . has been pleased so to contrive the constitution and frame of humanity that we should want no other prompter to enquire after . . . but only our self-love, that universal principle of action." Adam Smith, too, spoke of the trader's being led to promote the public good by "an invisible hand." Even the philosophical school of deism wrote of a capitalized "Nature." With the ideal of the survival of the fittest, a new class of supermen was introduced—those who reached the top in the competitive struggle for existence. If competition was the God-ordained or Natural order of the cosmos, the victors were the élite, worthy of respect and authority. Thus, economic Darwinism helped to move the religious deity one step away from the economic world, making it even more a *causa remota*, and placed in closer contact the new businessman.[10]

There can be no doubt that the competitive directive exists today. The maxim "competition is the life of trade" holds greater sway over the minds of men than in the days of the physiocrats or of Hume, Smith, and Ricardo. The United States is considered the flourishing embodiment of the competitive system. Here it is never surprising to pick up a newspaper or turn on the radio to learn from some prominent figure that competition is the life-blood of American industry.[11] Nor does practice seem to differ much from philosophy. A book on economics thus describes the workings of the competitive process:

> The worker sells his labor. In doing so, skilled workers compete with un-skilled, and men compete with women for employment. All of them may compete with machines which are possible substitutes for their labor. The owners of different kinds of machines or tools compete with each other for the patronage of manufacturers. . . .
> Rival salesmen besiege the potential buyer and endeavor to demonstrate the superiority of their wares. Expensive advertising campaigns endeavor to persuade the consumer to eat more dairy products in the face of equally enticing appeals to eat more fruit, while railroads and steamship lines issue alluring booklets designed to attract vacation travelers to use their respective facilities. Sometimes the struggle becomes more sinister, as business men resort to cut-throat competition, brute force, and underhand methods to drive their rivals from the field. Or the competition may be quite passive, the parties to it even unaware that they are rivals. But it is there none the less.[12]

Statements by factory workers also support the prevalence of competition in workaday reality: "There are plenty of guys around to fill the foremen's jobs. That's the trouble. The only good jobs are the foremen's, and there is only one in a hundred of those. Usually you have to wait for him to die, and then you compete against ninety-nine others for it." Nor are the professional classes exempt from the same feeling. Said a frank lawyer, "Now take me, I'm always fighting some guy to make a buck, and when I make it, he don't get it."[13]

So penetrating has been the competitive doctrine that it is difficult for most Americans to believe that life can be otherwise organized. But in most noncapitalist societies, a different attitude toward fellow-men prevails. An Azande native takes water in his mouth, blows it near him, and addresses his god thus:

> Father, as I am here,
> I have not stolen the goods of another,
> I have not taken the goods of another without recompense,
> I have not set my heart after the goods of another,
> All men are good in my eyes.[14]

Among all communities living by the co-operative directive, live-lihood rather than gain is the object of economic activity. Within the group, brotherly support whenever there is distress is part of the moral standards; *noblesse oblige* is a fully co-operative prin-ciple expressed in interest-free credit, liberal hospitality, and support; and men may be obliged to give services to fellow or chief without remuneration other than sustenance:

> To primitive man all men are either tribal brothers or strangers, and the lat-ter term is equivalent in primitive society to "enemy"; there is no middle status between those two opposite relations. If a man, not being by birth a tribal brother, is admitted into the community, if he is found to be well-disposed, if he is regarded with good will or affection or admiration—if, in short, he is not an enemy—he must needs be a tribal brother. Hence the sacredness of hospi-tality in all primitive sentiment; a man who has been admitted into the relation of guest is necessarily to be regarded and treated as a tribal brother.[16]

If trade or commerce exists, the other parties to the exchange are usually outsiders to whom a different code of morality applies. The admonition *caveat emptor*, for instance, originally warned the buyer of the Middle Ages to beware of outside-the-law, market-place dealings. Henry Maine has given a classic description of noncapitalistic trade in his *Village Communities in the East and West:*

> In order to understand what a market originally was, you must try to pic-ture to yourselves a territory occupied by village-communities. . . . But at sev-eral points, points probably where the domains of two or three villages con-verged, there appear to have been spaces of what we should now call neutral ground. These were the Markets. They were probably the only places at which the members of the different primitive groups met for any purpose except war-fare, and the persons who came to them were doubtless at first persons spe-cially empowered to exchange the produce and manufactures of one little vil-lage-community for those of another. . . . But, besides the notion of neutrality, another idea was anciently associated with markets. This was the idea of sharp practice and hard bargaining.
>
> What is the real origin of the feeling that it is not creditable to drive a hard bargain with a near relative or friend? It can hardly be that there is any rule of morality to forbid it. The feeling seems to me to bear the traces of the old no-tion that men united in natural groups do not deal with one another on prin-ciples of trade. The only natural group in which men are now joined is the family; and the only bond of union resembling that of the family is that which men create for themselves by friendship.

The general proposition which is the basis of Political Economy, made its first approach to truth under the only circumstances which admitted of men meeting at arm's length, not as members of the same group, but as strangers. Gradually the assumption of the right to get the best price has penetrated into the interior of these groups, but it is never completely received so long as the bond of connection between man and man is assumed to be that of family or clan-connection.

In contemporary democratic countries, then, there is a clear-cut conflict of the belief-system of family, state, and religion with the capitalist ideology in respect to their directive concerning treatment of members of the community. One is tempted to say that the injunction "Love thy neighbor" meets head-on with the instruction "Shove thy neighbor." What has been frequently described as the battle of "Commerce against Christ" refers in major part to this conflict in directives.

Even the most static religions, however, are not built of granite. Not only do they guide or resist the forces of their times, they also yield to pressure. It has been possible in the preceding chapters to speak of religion in the democratic countries as though the *Corpus Christianum* were one and undivided. This convenient practice now will have to be abandoned. The religious revolt against the universal Catholic church of Rome, which began with John Wycliffe, over a hundred years before Martin Luther, carried well into the seventeenth century past the breakup of the feudal manor into the formation of the industrial city. Out of the turmoil and dislocations came new turns and stresses in the growth of the Protestant religions.

Two great changes appeared as part of all Protestant denominations except the Church of England—a new indictment of idolatry of the flesh and a rejection of all human intermediaries between God and man.[16] These deviations from the practice of Catholicism did not countermand the fundamental directive of "Love thy neighbor." Nevertheless, through their contribution to impersonalism and rationalism, they did affect the relationships among members of the community. Without excessive exaggeration, it might be said that from these doctrines a rule of conduct emanated: "Trust no man, not even yourself. Only God should be your confidant. Let no one—not priest, nor saint, nor Virgin—intercede with him for you." Emotional or sensual relations with humans were anathema, since they not only were of no use toward salvation but also promoted "sentimental illusions and idolatrous superstitions." In their prized "rediscovery of the Gospels" the Protestants found especially unexplored meanings in the words of Paul.

The Calvinists and Puritans, for whom the only allowable social activity was activity for the greater glory of God, went a step farther. Real love of mankind was impractical for them without severity, rather than leniency, toward man. Suffering inflicted on human beings was thought to be conducive to the religious improvement of the sufferers. Their rigorous inner view took on an outer austerity. Even the "seasonable cheerfulness" to which they limited themselves seldom occurred without the jarring recollection that all is vanity. Living was not a sociable business. Those who took life gaily were soon to meet their reckoning. But those who held even their closest friends in deep distrust were on the righteous path, though "much deadness of heart" were their mortal lot.[17]

The removal of intermediaries between God and man had the additional influence of increasing men's reliance on the rational set of mind. The Protestant now was dependent on the Holy Writ. Every Christian was a priest and teacher. From the time of Luther's translation of the Bible the entire Protestant tradition, inscribed in 1646 in the Westminster Confession, was that the means of salvation were open to everyone through the writings of the Scriptures. Yet, to be able to understand the word of God, it was necessary to be able also to *interpret* the Bible and to extend its authority to the interpretations. "Whatsoever is drawn out of the Scripture by just consequence and deduction is as well the word of God, as that which is an express commandment or example in Scripture." With this premise, the conception of writing down ideas—agreements, covenants, pacts, constitutions—accords most wholeheartedly, as it does with the ability to reason from (to rationalize) written ideas and, above all, with the ability to read and write. The following passage shows the central portion of rationalism in the ideology of the Puritan:

We know nothing of God but by putting some Logical Notion upon him. All things are conveyed to us in a Logical Way, and bear some stamp of reason upon them, or else we should know nothing of them. Hence God, to fit his discovery of himself to our manner of entertaining it, takes the Rational or Logical Arguments upon himself, admits of a Distinction or a Description, utters Sentences or Actions about himself, speaks of himself as if he were an Effect & had Causes; a Subject & had Adjuncts. . . . And this tells us how useful & necessary reason is to Faith; it being an instrument which is used to convey the discoveries of God unto it; and therefore Faith doth not relinquish or cast off reason; for there is nothing in Religion contrary to it, tho' there are many things that do transcend, and must captivate it.[18]

The American Puritans took so well to reason and logic that they had to be warned against using the dialectic against the Scripture itself. That such rationalism had an effect on the faith of succeeding generations in constitutions, mass education, and rationalistic enterprise cannot be denied.

Much like the business belief-system, the roads of impersonalism and rationalism in religion led into a workhouse for the poor. "The new medicine for poverty" discovered by the Protestants was well documented for England by Richard Tawney in his *Religion and the Rise of Capitalism.* In the United States some of the most trenchant criticism came in the mid-nineteenth century from a Presbyterian, Stephen Colwell of Philadelphia. He denounced the Protestants for their concentration on the successful to the neglect of the religious welfare of the poor. The gospel was being sent to the heathen of far-off lands, while the heathen at home were untended. Protestants, he charged, persisted in rationalizing human sufferings as the penalties of idleness, diseases, or other causes that were not in great measure the fault of the victims themselves. In their selective reading of the New Testament they had overlooked the "imperative injunctions of brotherly kindness."

Today only with difficulty and by indirect methods can the Protestant attitude toward destitution be appraised.[19] If it is true that Protestantism forgot that "blessed are the poor," if it is true that Protestantism gave beggary and pauperism the evil connotations they presently possess, no longer is the view so strongly put forth. Preachers now seldom recommend harsh measures for the poor and idle. Their influence is on the more positive side of encouraging the virtues that favor a methodical application to work, the problem next in line of presentation.

But before proceeding to a new problem, a brief comment is needed on the significance of the resemblance of the Protestant religion to the capitalist ideology. No thesis is advanced here that a cause-and-effect relation exists between the growth of Protestantism and the birth of modern industrialism.[20] Nor should any inference be drawn that the Catholic church shunned great wealth. Dante's words live today to point a shaming finger at the apostasy of "the she-wolf of Rome who after her meal is hungrier than before." It is clear, however, that the systems of belief which issued from the Reformation, as distinct from Catholicism, contain elements which correspond to integral parts of the basic capitalist directive of competition. Concretely, Protestant religious education, more than the Catholic, teaches the child and the adult to consider other persons impersonally and rationally, a view which makes the demands of the economic directive on the individual seem less conflicting.[21]

Activist-Quietist Directives

The possibility that important differences between the directives of Catholicism and Protestantism may exist suggests the second discontinuity in modern systems of belief. A central directive in the business ideology is what may be called for lack of a better term "activism" or "externalization"—continuous and regular action upon the material (the nonhuman) environment, the work ethic of present democracies.

A word of comment on the term "activism." In literary or philosophic usage it is generally employed as one-half of the dichotomy, activism-quietism. In religious writings the contrast of *vita contemplativa, vita activa* is often used with similar meaning. "Quietism" itself is not too felicitous a term. "Nonactivism," which was avoided because of its awkwardness, would be closer in meaning. If one keeps in mind, however, that by quietism is not meant passivism, that quietism is simply the absence of an activist directive, and that quietism can be considered somewhere in the middle of a continuum whose poles are "activism" and "passivism," the meaning here intended may be more easily grasped.

In the ensuing discussion of the activist or "work directive," of work as a formula for salvation, a separation of the economic and religious contributions to the doctrine would require too much duplication. Continuously woven through the Reformation and the Industrial Revolution, they are inextricably of one piece; for religion in this case plays no subsidiary role but is at least the equal of economic conditions of life in giving form and meaning to the activist directive. Hence, unlike the treatment of the previous competitive–co-operative conflict in directives, this subject will be treated as a unified development in both the business and Protestant ideologies.

In one way or another, the religions of the Reformation all sanctified work.[22] By the late eighteenth century the directives of both the Protestant and the capitalist systems of belief included a powerful ethic of labor.[23] Prior recognition goes to Martin Luther, whose work doctrines broke a pattern as old as the Greco-Roman world. At his hands, labor acquired an unknown dignity,[24] for work to him was a way of serving God, be it in a most menial task or in the most respected profession. The world for Luther was made uncomfortable for man because of his sins; as in the medieval tradition, work is the penalty of the Fall of man, the *remedium peccati*. Since God made the world this way, there was no use in attempting to pervert his plans. One can only show one's self in obedience to his scheme of things by following one's calling, whatever it may be. The religious hue which the German word *Beruf*, or calling, acquired through Luther's usage spread into all Protestant countries and into their translations of the Bible.

The one best way to serve God is to do the work of one's divinely assigned station in life. But do it! All who can, must work. Infants and invalids alone are excused. All idleness, beggary, lives of ease from interest on loans, should cease. Gambling, drinking, and general idleness should be eradicated, for men thereby not only neglect their work but unfit their bodies for it. Therefore all holidays save Sunday should be eliminated. Worship of God and man's everyday work are the same. To work is to pray. No priestly concurrence is needed to decide which vocation is good. "A cobbler, a smith, a farmer, each has the work of his trade, and yet they are all alike consecrated priests and bishops."[25]

Even the soldier can be saved. *Sola fides!* was the famous slogan proclaiming to men that salvation through faith was all that was necessary. And what better way to express that faith than through the services of work![26] Thus Luther placed a scepter in the horny hands of labor.

There is another doctrine of work in Protestantism, different in some respect from that bequeathed by Luther. The early Calvinists had a way of writing and speaking of the *majorem gloriam Dei*. The world for them was corrupt and rotten and had to be transformed for the greater glory of God. Lutheranism suffered the world, but Calvinism wanted to master and reshape it by untiring work into a Holy Community. To establish the Kingdom of God on earth, all men, even the rich, must work. "If thou beest a man that lives without a calling, though thou hast two thousands to spend, yet if thou hast no calling, tending to publique good, thou art an uncleane beast," spoke John Cotton. "God sent you not unto this world as unto a Playhouse, but a Workhouse."[27] To please God, this work must be unflagging, disciplined, and regular. Only in this way could the Calvinist gain an iota of assurance that he possessed the *certitudo salutis*, that salvation was his lot, that he was one of the elect.

While man was for Luther a vessel of the Lord who showed by work his faith in God's scheme of things, for Calvin, man was a tool of the Lord that must remold the earth into a mirror of divine majesty. This distinction is important, for in the former instance the ideal is one of passive acceptance of a God-ordained station in a relatively static occupational system, while in the latter, the ideal of conscious and systematic attempts to build the Holy Community makes it a duty continuously to review, purify, change, and intensify one's vocation. For the early Calvinists the secular world and its inhabitants were solely the means, not ends with value in themselves.

John Calvin added still another element—of utmost importance for the modern form of labor—that work is also the antidote for anxiety over salvation, for fears of damnation, the *decretum horribile*. Intense activity alone makes religious doubts evaporate and brings the conviction of God's grace. Thomas Carlyle, bred of Scottish Calvinism, sounds the battle cry of activism in *Sartor*

resartus: "Produce! Produce! Were it but the pitifullest infinitesi-
mal fraction of a product, produce it in God's name! 'Tis the
utmost thou has in thee: out with it, then. Up, up. Whatsoever
thy hand findeth to do, do it with thy whole might. Work while
it is called today; for the night cometh . . . wherein . . . no man
can work."

Perhaps only one more religious work ethic needs discussion
—that of John Wesley and the eighteenth-century Methodist revival. A difference in it requires noting. Whereas in Lutheranism
and Calvinism work in itself was sanctified, in the writings and
preachings of Wesley the *fruits of work* were the signs of salvation.
Early Methodism developed three commands: gain all you can,
save all you can, and give all you can. Although the first of the
three received the greatest stress in practice, the use of what is
gained is the central part of Wesley's small body of theology.
"Render unto God, not a tenth, not a third, not a half, but all
that is God's, be it more or less; by employing all on yourself,
your household, the household of faith, and all mankind, in such
manner that you may give a good account of your stewardship."
Luther, with his agricultural notion of labor, had thought that
work itself brings one closer to his neighbor and thereby adds to
one's love for fellow-men. Wesley, living in a later age, an age of decreasing agricultural occupations, held that through the *gains* of
work one can best help steer mankind to the path of perfect
Christianity. "God," he wrote, "has commited to our charge that
precious talent, which contains all the rest—money; indeed it is
unspeakably precious, if we are wise and faithful stewards of it;
if we employ every part of it for such purposes as our blessed Lord
has commanded us to do." In order to gain, save, and give, strict
application to work, methodical, Methodistical, application was
enjoined: "So far am I from either causing or encouraging idleness, that an idle person, known to be such, is not suffered to remain in any of our societies; we drive him out, as we would a
thief or a murderer. 'To show all possible diligence' . . . is one
of our standing rules; and one, concerning the observance of
which we continually make the strictest inquiry."

The most far-reaching of the several types of work ethic probably belonged to Calvin. In the many forms which Calvinism as-

sumed and in the many sects that it infiltrated, the anxiety-alleviating function of the work directive was clearest. Nevertheless, as was seen in the first chapter, any new directive, once it has been in existence long enough to be inculcated in young children, serves the function of staving off anxiety. Thus, the different work ethics of all those Reformation sects that lived for more than a generation utilized work as a protection against the anxiety of alienation from God.

So well did the directive of work in a calling fit in with the demand of labor-saving inventions for more manpower that by the mid-eighteenth century it was an identical part of both the prevailing religious and economic systems of belief.[28] More and more often it was quoted in either context or in both. Not yet was it possible to speak widely of "work for work's sake," but to advocate unremitting application to the material environment with reference only to the end of monetary accumulation was not merely possible but proper. The secular element is so prominent in Poor Richard's sayings that one would never guess, had not Benjamin Franklin recalled the fact in his old age, that they were profoundly influenced by John Cotton's "Essays To Do Good."

Unless one retains a historical perspective, it is easy to miss the fact that the new work directive was a revolutionary change. Before the Reformation, men could openly curse life because work wrought under the sun was grievous unto them. The Greeks had a word for it—*ponos*—which has the same root as the Latin *poena*, sorrow. To them, work was little less than a curse. Xenophon taught and many believed that work was the painful price the gods charged for the means of subsistence. Hesiod of Boeotia, whom the Greeks called their greatest poet after Homer, is one of the few persons who can be found to speak in praise of work. But he speaks more in defense than in praise. His cry, "Work is no shame," protests against an existing attitude. Ultimately this champion of the peasant falls back, like Xenophon, on the theory that work is a necessity imposed by divine intervention. "But the immortal gods," he complains, "have placed sweat before success." The tension in the work of the ancient Greek was not comparable with that of today. Yet his labor, all told—public and private, mental and physical—was prodigious. No one who has seen the products of his infertile land and machineless economy can doubt it for a moment. But unemployment, not work, remained his ideal. "What is dearest to man's heart," declared Euripides for all his fellow-citizens, "is leisure." Their word for unemployment, *scholê*, meant "leisure," and their word for business was the negative *ascholia*, meaning "lack of leisure." The classic Greek did do hard or manual work, often alongside apprentice or slave. He shirked that kind of work less than work that afforded him no leisure. Above all he hated sustained or monotonous work, which he never tolerated if there were a way out. For him, work was not a means of salvation.[29]

Passing quickly over the Romans, who, like the Greeks, considered work for the most part a necessary evil, one finds the early Christians with but a few, relatively small innovations which they drew from the Talmud. "If man does not find his food like animals and birds but must earn it, that is due to sin." God imposed work on man as a penalty for the original sin committed by his forefathers in the earthly Paradise. The Reformers were fond of quoting Paul's statement that "if any would not work, neither should he eat" as spiritual fuel for their burning demands for work, but they seldom added his other words, "and having food and raiment let us therefore be content." To Augustine as to all other Fathers of the church, the urge which drives man to acquisition beyond the needs of simple sustenance was anathema, the *auri sacra fames*. Only on work as a means to goods which can be shared with the poor, for "the sweet uses of charity," does there appear in early Christianity the slightest light of divine blessing. Even so, he who is busy in many activities will perforce sin often and can hardly be saved. Therefore (and this doctrine became the bulwark of the medieval Catholic position) inactivity and idle contemplation are ways of avoiding sin.

All in all, Catholicism, as a system of beliefs, came to regard work as expiation for Adams' fall, as charity toward brothers, and (in the monasteries only) as purification through humility, again with the connotation of atonement. And throughout the Greco-Roman world winds the thread of a notion that labor, work on or with material objects, was far beneath pure contemplation or passive meditation on political or divine subjects. For Aristotle "perfect happiness is contemplative activity." The ideal of Aquinas was the introspective soul striving to become more perfect. In the same quiescent spirit Archimedes thought his actual inventions poor things, "mere amusements and accessories," contaminating pure ideas with matter. Pure science, not applied science, earned the respect of the Greek. And so it was with the Christian Fathers—not manual labor, but religious and intellectual meditation; not work, for the pope, the priest, the noble, the rich man, do not work. They simply lead a life of good or evil. Those few who escape the curse of work bear the mark of special divine favor. The rest must bear the scourge of original sin. The absence of the activist directive in the church continued up to contemporary Catholicism. It is therefore in the Catholic and not in the Protestant religion that a conflict exists with the work directive of the capitalist ideology. The worker in the Protestant and capitalist view is blessed; in the Catholic he labors under a curse.[30]

Naturally, the prevalence of this work sentiment among the people of Europe caused earliest employers of labor much grief. How to get persons into mill, mine, and factory—and keep them there!—were big problems. The peasant or the craftsman looked to his work to provide him with a livelihood. Production in the Middle Ages was for use, for use by human beings whose consumption was not great. Work was slow, its pace was governed by the length of time needed to produce a serviceable commodity by a man who wanted to get enough goods to live on and a little more. In the Bavarian mining industry of the sixteenth century, out of a total of 203 days, in one case, only 123 were working days; out of 161 days, in another instance, 99 were days of labor; in a third, only 193 out of 287 were working days. The proportion of holidays to working days was high, too, compared to modern standards. In order to increase agricultural production, the employer sometimes resorted to raising the piece rates of his workmen. But again and again production merely dropped off. A man working for one mark per acre, whose usual output was two and one-half acres, mowed only two acres when the rate was raised to one and one-quarter marks. He put to himself the question: how much must I work in order to earn the two and one-half marks that took care of my needs before? Not, how much more can I make at this new rate if I work until nightfall? In addition, raises in wages often resulted in absenteeism. These "paradoxes" can be seen today among preliterate peoples in Africa and Latin America. In Tehuantepec, the Zapotec Indians were said to work half as well at a daily rate of 50 centavos as at 25. The same complaint that employers in the waning of the Middle Ages made about their hired help is now heard on all sides from white overseers of colored labor—"They don't want to work. They're lazy."

In the United States the religious progeny of the men whose work ethic has been examined—Luther, Calvin, and Wesley—have always comprised the bulk of the population.[31] With no great exaggeration, André Siegfried, the French political scientist and economist, remarked of America: "Protestantism is the only national religion, and to ignore that fact is to view the country from a false angle."[32] What can be seen in American history, then, of the activist directive?

Although the greater vigor of the Puritan colonists over Catholics in French North America was observed early in American history, evidence of the activistic bent is more or less nonexistent until the huge sale (for those days) of Benjamin Franklin's *The Way of Wealth*. As he reports in his *Autobiography:*

I endeavor'd to make it both entertaining and useful, and it accordingly came to be in such demand, that I reap'd considerable profit from it, vending annually near ten thousand. And observing that it was generally read, scarce any neighborhood in the province being without it, I consider'd it as a proper vehicle for conveying instruction among the common people, who bought scarcely any other books; I therefore filled all the little spaces that occurr'd between the remarkable days in the calendar with proverbial sentences, chiefly such as inculcated industry and frugality, as the means of procuring wealth, and thereby securing virtue. . . . These proverbs . . . I assembled and form'd into a connected discourse prefix'd to the Almanack of 1757, as the harangue of a wise old man.

The point here is not so much the text of Franklin's works, which has been subjected to pertinent analysis by Werner Sombart and Max Weber, as the fact that it was a best-seller in the mid-eighteenth century. But in order to give the flavor of Franklin's writings on the theme of industry, some of the axiomatic outpourings of Poor Richard which are not to be found in the works of the preceding scholars can be extracted from *The Way to Wealth* and sampled here:

Sloth, like Rust, consumes faster than Labour wears; while the used Key is always bright.

The sleeping Fox catches no Poultry.

There will be sleeping enough in the Grave.

Lost Time is never found again; and what we call Time enough always proves little enough.

Drive thy Business, let not that drive thee.

He that hath a Trade hath an Estate; and he that hath a Calling, hath an Office of Profit and Honour.

Industry pays Debts, while Despair encreaseth them.

God gives all Things to Industry.

One to-day is worth two To-morrows.

Be ashamed to catch yourself idle.

Trouble springs from Idleness, and grievous Toil from needless Ease.

The sales of *The Way to Wealth* did not stop at national boundaries, but copies became familiar to the world in short order. Seventy editions of it have been printed in English, fifty-six in French, eleven in German, and nine in Italian. It has been translated into Danish, Swedish, Spanish, Welsh, Polish, Gaelic, Russian, Bohemian, Catalan, Dutch, Chinese, modern Greek, and phonetic writing. It has been printed four hundred times or more and is still popular.

As one passes to the nineteenth century, the evidences for activistic behavior swell to profusion. From the host of observers of varying perspicacity, one alone, but one of unquestioned competence, will suffice—Alexis de Tocqueville, gentleman and French scholar:

It is strange to see with what feverish ardour the Americans pursue their own welfare; and to watch the vague dread that constantly torments them lest they should not have chosen the shortest path which may lead to it.

A native of the United States clings to this world's goods as if he were certain never to die; and he is so hasty in grasping at all within his reach, that one would suppose he was constantly afraid of not living long enough to enjoy them. He clutches everything, he holds nothing fast, but soon loosens his grasp to pursue fresh gratifications.

In the United States a man builds a house to spend his latter years in it, and he sells it before the roof is on: he plants a garden, and lets it just as the trees are coming into bearing: he brings a field into tillage, and leaves other men to gather the crops: he embraces a profession, and gives it up: he settles in a place, which he soon afterward leaves, to carry his changeable longings elsewhere. If his private affairs leave him any leisure, he instantly plunges into a vortex of politics; and if at the end of a year of unremitting labor he finds he has a few days' vacation, his eager curiosity whirls him over the vast extent of the United States, and he will travel fifteen hundred miles in a few days, to shake off his happiness. Death at length overtakes him, but it is before he is weary of his bootless chase of that complete felicity which is for ever on the wing.[33]

After the Civil War and into the twentieth century, with the expansion of commerce and manufacturing, the energy and drive of American existence became more noticeable. Lord Bryce, in 1880, noted that "life is very tense in America . . . a tension which appears to be increasing rather than decreasing." In 1906 H. G. Wells's "first impression" was one of "headlong hurry." The home town of Babbitt "promoted" itself with the motto "Zip, Zoom, Zowie with Zenith," and the qualifications for success in those days of the twenties were found in the "live-wire" or "go-getter," with plenty of "push" and "drive," words which were consigned to limbo with the rapid turnover of jargon that now characterizes an age of radio and film. Today, the trade talk of the advertising and entertainment "industries" has supplanted the language of the salesman. And the ideal type of Sinclair Lewis is outstripped by Sammy, the upstart film producer, "the frantic marathoner of life . . . sprinting out of his mother's womb, turning life into a race in which the only rules are fight for the rail, and elbow on the turn, and the only finish-line is death." Despite the frills of expression, the qualifications for success remain Franklin's "industry."

Meanwhile, the more prosaic man in American business life —the office worker, the self-proprietor, the plant worker, the larger-scale retailer—*Homo faber*—works hard at his job. Business, it may be remembered, stems from the word "busy" and means the state of being busy. Whatever there is to be busy about is no longer a conscious religious goal. The modern man seems impelled by the thought that business must go on in order somehow to keep not only body and soul together but the world in shape.[34] With it he hopes to conquer all men's ills—unhappiness, disease, poverty, old age, time itself. At the risk of excessive quotation, the modern philosophical view of life described by Frank Knight must be presented:

> Its ideal is action. . . . Life is pictured as an effort; and while effort is justified by good results, these are not expected ever to be satisfying. The experienced reward is more the joy of pursuit than of possession . . . man is committed —"doomed," from the standpoint of the quietistic ideal—to strive toward goals which recede more rapidly than he as an individual, or even society, advances toward them. Thus life is finally . . . a sort of labor of Sisyphus.[35]

The American businessman and his activistic methods have become the model for the world. It is in America that the phenomenon of the "Tired Businessman" first appeared. The strength of business directives in the United States has been greater than in any other existing nation. It has been said that the slogan of the modern civilization of labor is "Work!" and that the *dementia Americana* is "hurry-up-itis." Sombart put it somewhat differently in saying that, while precapitalist man was a natural man who stood firm on two legs, modern man runs on all fours.[36] If that abstraction known as medieval man could stand outside a factory or office building at 8:00 or 8:45 o'clock on some Monday morning, he would watch in bewilderment as the streams of persons, mostly strangers to each other, poured in from all sides, punching time clocks and hastening to desks to remain sheltered (or cabined) for hours, moving materials or shuffling papers.[37] Why do they come? he might ask, for his sympathies would certainly lie with the American hobo refrain:

> O, why don't you work like other men do?
> How the hell can I work when the sky's so blue?

In the course of delineating the development and existence of the two great conflicts in directives, co-operation versus competition and activism versus quietism, it has been unfortunately necessary to use historical materials and to trace the relationships of ideas which often date from ages when the methods of investigation of modern social science were unknown. For that reason, the impression may linger that a convincing description of the economic ideology held by the present-day individual is lacking. Therefore, the second study of "Middletown" (actually Muncie, Indiana) will be used as evidence of what detailed sociological study can contribute to knowledge of the business system of beliefs. In the light of its years of painstaking work, the staff of the project compiled the town's credo:

By and large Middletown believes:

That one should be hard-working and persevering. "Hard work is the key to success."

That a man owes it to himself, to his family, and to society to "succeed."

That social welfare, in Middletown and elsewhere, is the result of two factors working together—the natural law of progress and the individual law of initiative, hard work, and thrift—and therefore:

That any interference with either of the two is undesirable. "The Lord helps him who helps himself."

That society should not coddle the man who does not work hard and save, for if a man does not "get on" it is his own fault.

That "the strongest and best should survive, for that is the law of nature, after all."

That economic conditions are the result of a natural order which cannot be changed by man-made laws.

That every man for himself is the right and necessary law of the business world, "tempered, of course, with judgment and fair dealing."

That competition is what makes progress and has made the United States great.

That ordinarily any man willing to work can get a job.

That a man "really gets what is coming to him in the United States."

That "any man who is willing to work hard and to be thrifty and improve his spare time can get to the top. That's the American way, and it's as true as it ever was."

That it is a man's own fault if he is dependent in old age.

That the captains of industry are social benefactors because they create employment. "Where'd all our jobs be if it wasn't for them?"

That capital is simply the accumulated savings of these people with foresight.

That if you "make it too easy" for the unemployed and people like that they will impose on you.

That leisure is a fine thing, but work comes first.

That "all of us hope we'll get to the place sometime where we can work less and have more time to play."

But that it is wrong for a man to retire when he is still able to work. "What will he do with all his time?"

That having a hobby is "all very well if a person has time for that sort of thing and it doesn't interfere with his job."

That leisure should be spent in wholesomely "worth-while" things and not be just idle or frivolous.

That because of "poor, weak human nature" there will always be some people too lazy to work, too spendthrift to save, too short-sighted to plan. "Doesn't the Bible prove this when it says, 'The poor ye have always with you'?"

That charity will always be necessary. "For you wouldn't let a dog starve."

That idleness and thriftlessness are only encouraged by making charity too easy.

That it "undermines a man's character" for him to get what he doesn't earn.[38]

Simple Anomie

These, then, are the conflicts in directives. In the democratic nations of today rules of conduct laid down in early childhood and partially deposited in the depths of conscience must frequently be broken in order to conform to the more immediate and tangible economic directives. Briefly and theoretically, the effect of these directive conflicts in the Catholic or Protestant is intermittent apprehension. Whenever one directive is consistently disobeyed for another, a feeling of confusion arises. Which is right? Am I doing right in doing this? How do I know that I am?[39] This is not the kind of unnecessary indecision that makes a man hesitate over adding a scarf to his apparel on a cool, windy day or over choosing from a menu of equally delectable dishes. The whole substructure of beliefs which unobtrusively support him from one day of life through the next is at stake. Nor can the feeling be easily put in words. He does not add that confusion about the means brings doubt about the end and, ultimately, distrust of the reigning *rulers*, who have laid down the entire program. But such is the tenor of the uncertainty that afflicts the individual in those moods of doubt following an act of his that violates a directive or an act of another that hits home. Such action, given or received, brings not mere expectation, but apprehension, of anxiety. The person fears an indefinite but impending danger situation. Upon being asked, he cannot say, in the words of the spiritual, "sometimes I feel like a motherless child" and that it is the old dread of helplessness which he fearfully anticipates whenever he finds it impossible to follow, untroubled, the several systems of belief that sustain him and give his life purpose and station.[40] It required the genius of Goethe to enable Faust to cry out, "Two souls, alas, dwell in my breast apart!" This intermittent apprehension in the adult, the psychological result of a conflict between systems of belief, should be called simple anomie.

It is not the result of planlessness or rulelessness, as its linguistic and Durkheimian origins imply. This discovery is a reward for not proceeding on the assumption that what seemed to be anarchy was in fact anarchy. Durkheim saw chaos because he *felt* chaos about him. Without bringing a historical or cultural perspective to bear on the problem, it is easy to fall into the error of presuming that man naturally feels uncomfortable when pursuing unreachable ends. When Durkheim spoke of the ill effects of "illimitable desires," he failed to realize that the establishment of illimitable desires in man is itself the result of a well-developed system of beliefs. It is not the natural result of man's freedom from all restraining rules or norms of behavior. Far from being natural to man, it took a long time to groom him for the mere idea of illimitable acquisition. To be the very model of the indefatigable entrepreneur it was necessary that a man drink in activism with his porridge or count among his predecessors a person who, with Cotton Mather, read a little of Calvin each night "to sweeten his mouth." Nor is anomie the evil outcome of too many ideologies. The Japanese, in addition to their emperor, had eight hundred ancestral deities. Man can have many gods and subgods and many ways of reaching or propitiating them. Simple anomie is, instead, the result of a clash between belief-systems or, more precisely, a conflict between the *directives* of belief-systems.

The lone individual has one way of meeting persistent anomic tension. He can try to reassure himself that the broken course of the directives he follows is correct, and to be sure of that he must seek some signs of approval or affection either from the powerful figures who plot the way or from the members of his community who run the same stumbling gamut of beliefs. Crude though the chart of action may be, this was the course he followed before whenever he needed to know how to please the supreme beings on whom he depended. And this was the course that always succeeded.

CHAPTER FOUR

DETERIORATION OF BELIEF-SYSTEMS

Acute Anomie

AS YET the only conflicts analyzed have been those occurring between different belief-systems. By an extended historical analysis going back beyond the Industrial Revolution into the Reformation and making contrasts with other civilizations and ways of life, two significant conflicts in present-day directives were uncovered—one between the co-operative ethic of political and religious belief-systems and the competitive ethic of the economic ideology, and the other (and somewhat less important) between the activist or work ethic of the economic and Protestant belief-systems and the quietist ethic of Catholicism. The next problem in forming the theory of anomie is to probe the effect of a conflict within a single ideology or, more properly, the deterioration of a system of beliefs.

Whereas conflict between ideologies chiefly implicates the directives, conflict within an ideology revolves about the position of the *ruler*.[1] In a sense the problem of the deterioration of belief-systems is the problem of the "mortalization" of deities. By tracing the growth of ideologies from the time of the child's earliest education, it was learned that the supreme figure in any system of beliefs is committed by the believers in that system to providing for them in a manner similar in some respects to parental care for the child. Accordingly, one finds that the deterioration of beliefs follows fast on any revelation that the reigning *ruler* is either unable or unwilling to perform his commitments. Inability, of course, signifies mortality, human frailty; and unwillingness discloses, to use a religious phrase, false gods, deities who have not the care of their flock uppermost in mind.

The unexpected crumbling of old idols should have an effect on adults similar to the shock of the child upon discovering the limitations of his attendants. Remove the stanchion and the whole system of beliefs collapses. The role of the *ruler* is crucial. Again the world seems at once alive and dangerous. "Chaos, cosmos, cosmos, chaos," chants the poet; for the environment is leaderless and hence uncontrollable. God's not in his heaven; man's all alone in the world. Now he can be truly called direction-less, rudderless, ruleless. The source of directives is gone. This is acute anomie, the disappearance of order and rules, through the degeneration of the *ruler*. Anxiety grips the individual.

Obviously such terror cannot be long endured. It was possible in the previous chapter to show the theoretical existence of sim-ple anomie by pointing to conflicts between systems of belief. Such conflicts result in simple anomie, the apprehension of sepa-ration-anxiety, a mental distress that can persist over long peri-ods of time, as long, in fact, as conflicts between beliefs stand. But an ideology divided within itself cannot stand. Once de-teriorating forces appear, a system of beliefs must either quickly solidify or disintegrate. If it disintegrates, the result is acute anomie, not the mere apprehension but the actual attack of anxiety. Thus this type of ideological disturbance, at once more violent and more ephemeral, can be illustrated only by discrete historical instances.

Separation of Ruler from Community

The eminent political scientist, Gaetano Mosca, once made the following important generalization after noting certain sim-ilar phenomena among the feudal Poles, Irish, English, and Rus-sians: When the elementary needs of life are to an extent satis-fied, what mostly contributes to creating and maintaining fric-tion between rulers and subjects is not so much difference in possession of material goods as membership in two different en-vironments. To take from Mosca's book, *The Ruling Class*, one example, the Polish nobles in the Middle Ages levied almost all the produce of their serfs, beat them, chose the most buxom of their daughters for their households, and otherwise "exploited" them. Yet the peasants never rebelled and "suffered the very bread to be snatched from their mouths that their lord might buy horses and costly weapons for hunting and for sabering Turks and Russians." All this, so long as he remained with them, spoke their language, swore the same oaths, ate the same kind of food, wore the same style of clothes, exhibited the same manners or lack of them, had the same rustic superstitions. But from the time when he adopted the French ruffled dress and minced speech, gave luxurious balls after the manner of Versailles and tried to dance the minuet, "peasantry and nobility became two peoples apart." The serfs grew reluctant to support him, revolted periodically and viciously, despite the fact that part of their lord's newly acquired French education was a "more humane" treatment of his subjects—allowing them a greater share of the crops, namely, a higher standard of living, and less arbitrary treatment. This example illustrates a string of circumstances which convinced the members of the community (in this case, the serfs) that the lord to whom they paid homage no longer made their commonweal his primary concern. In other words, they felt that he had deserted them and that they could no longer rely on him to protect them from enemies, defend their faith, and represent them to God.[2]

The Mortality of Rulers

So much at present for the conviction among believers that their leader is unwilling or uninterested in providing for them. The next facet of the problem, which concerns the conviction that the supreme entity in the ideology is *unable* to provide for the community, can be illustrated by the quite common primitive practice of systematic regicide. It is now well established that in numerous parts of the world kings were killed by their people in fact or by proxy or in effigy. At first blush the practice seems in contradiction to the theory here expounded of the great power of *rulers*. To see them publicly executed does not seem to demonstrate that their subjects believe them omnipotent. But once heed is taken of the time of death of these kings, the apparent contradiction is resolved. They die at the hands of their subjects either on the expiration of a set term or whenever disaster strikes the kingdom. Now it has not been the contention of this study that *rulers* are all-powerful (except in the eyes of the child) but instead that their subjects believe that they are able to control the aspects of the world of most importance to the community. Assuredly drought or dearth is disastrous for communities that live by agriculture. Those citizens of the medieval kingdom of southern Russia, the Khazars, who relied on their kings to regulate such matters, killed them if they failed. Among the Shilluk of the White Nile the custom of putting their divine kings to death at the first sign of infirmity or old age prevailed into the twentieth century. They believed that, should the king be allowed to become ill or senile, the cattle, too, would sicken and die, the crops would rot in the field, and men would be increasingly stricken with diseases; so with the Dinka tribes of the White Nile and their rainmaker, whose *natural* death would provoke a calamity. The warlike Zulus understandably put the king to death as soon as he began to have wrinkles or gray hair.

The key to the puzzling practice of killing kings at the end of a fixed term is again the idea that he will be no longer equal to performing his superhuman duties. According to the ethnologist Frazer, who reported these strange events, so important are the rulership powers that some peoples believe it unsafe to wait until the *ruler* shows signs of declining strength and prefer to dispatch him while in full vigor after a few years of supremacy. Even Sparta and Athens had ceremonies that apparently symbolized the death or deposition of the king after a set term.

In these cases of traditional regicide the elements of reasonableness in the act seem to overshadow the hatred which subjects might be expected to bear for a god with clay feet. Rather than be put in the terrible position of a people with a man-god who is unable to provide for them, they prefer systematically to kill their kings in the belief that each new *ruler* will really possess the superhuman, though temporary, powers. For to be rulerless is to be ruleless, to be ruleless is to be anomic. They must make sure that no acute anomie can exist in that treacherous span of time between *"Le roi est mort!"* and *"Vive le roi!"*

PART III

THREE IMPLICATIONS OF THE
THEORY OF CAUSES

INTRODUCTION

TO PROCEED, three implications of the theory of the causes of anomie just presented demand examination. The first is that the function which systems of belief perform in the mind of the child and youth should continue to an important extent in the adult. Should this be true, the symptoms of simple anomie ought to be observable in the United States, since it has been shown that in that country marked conflicts between systems of belief exist. And, third, acute anomie also should be observable in certain periods in the recent history of America.

If the genetic approach employed in chapters iii and iv is to be at all fruitful, there should be evidence to show that adult ideologies reflect the pattern and circumstances of childhood indoctrination in significant ways. Unless "the Child is father of the Man," there would have been no point in using the developmental method. Although several studies, chiefly psychoanalytic and psychiatric, have called attention to the fact that the highest political and religious figures are "parentalized," they have aroused academic resentment by loosely describing those figures as father-substitutes, for example, or father-surrogates, without specifying the extent of the parental relation. Critics have pointed out with forceful logic, "A man is not a child." Precisely! Yet, the present problem is a little broader. Not the supreme personages alone but the complete body of the ideology which encases them must be given an adult context.

CHAPTER FIVE

PERSISTENCE OF THE FUNCTION
OF IDEOLOGIES

IF ANY single phrase could describe the relation of systems of beliefs to the person, it should be *in loco domus*, for an ideology gives a person (as Josiah Royce said) "a sense of being at home in the universe." In the light of the historical circumstances surrounding the serial acquisition of ideologies, this ought not to be surprising. The configuration of beliefs which is an ideology will always express a system of relationships that parallels the family system of relationships in many respects.

All systems of belief describe (1) certain activities which the *rulers* are obliged to perform for the benefit of members of the community, (2) certain activities and attitudes which the members owe the *ruler*, and (3) a time and place for these activities. The action of *rulers* toward community members can be grouped under the headings of punishment and administration, the latter word denoting activities of both a directing and a provisioning order. The activities of members for the community's welfare are directed and their needs are provided for by regulation of the essential part of the environment. In the home the parent performs these functions for the children; in adult religion the churches not only instruct that God's will and commandments must be done and that the wages of sin is punishment but, further, that "God's relation to man is that of Father" and that "God is omnipotent" and that "God controls the universe through his personal presence and power." In the mind of the Middletowner, "God exists and runs the universe."[1]

In this book, the actions which members of communities owe the *rulers* have been designated "directives." In brief generalization for all ideologies, they are three: filial love, faith, and conformity to directions.[2] In the family the child bears love for his parents, which he is taught to show by affectionate gestures and a tabooed avoidance of aggressive thoughts and movements. He likewise has faith in their morality, their reason, and their permanent strength. And in "the important things" he does what he is told. In the Christian religion worship conveys the idea of love for God, and church rites are its ceremonial expressions. Blasphemy becomes the utterance of hateful thoughts, while faith generally measures firmness of conviction concerning the entire system of beliefs. Thus, the people of Middletown thought the interviewer was joking when he asked whether they were "Christians." And the Puerto Ricans of Comerío "made the sign of the cross as much as to say: 'God protect me from ever thinking such a thing.' " "He that believeth on the Son of God hath everlasting life." Therefore, "we never question such things" is the answer of the faithful everywhere. And the deserts of the blasphemer or the infidel, though varied, are uniformly just and sure.

Malinowski in the *Foundations of Faith and Morals* well summed up this conception of religious ideologies.

> I am my tribesman's brother, or my clansman's totemic kinsman, because we are all descended from the same being whom we worship in our ceremonies, to whom we sacrifice, and to whom we pray. We have only to change the word *descended* into *created* in order to pass to those religions which maintain as a fundamental principle the brotherhood of man, because he owes his existence to a Creator whom he addresses as "Our Father which art in Heaven." The conception of the Church as a big family is rooted in the very nature of religion.

In all ideologies that are transmitted to children at an early age, one inevitably finds the explicit command to regard and treat members of the community as brothers, for to introduce a directive that clashed with the brotherly ethic of the family would make children suffer intolerable conflicts and anxiety. This exceedingly important injunction of brotherly love, in addition to assuming consanguinity, demands a ban on serious violence, equality in receipt of the protection of the *ruler*'s regulation of the environment, and preferential treatment of members. That parents ban severe violence and give equal protection to their children, while demanding preferential consideration for family members, is obvious. In adult Christianity, too, all believers are brethren, deserve love and kindness from each other, and are equal before God (though superior to the heathen) as recipients of providence. The fact that all believers are equal before the *ruler* is the true meaning of equality as a necessary doctrine in both religious and political belief-systems. A religion that did not contain the ethic of brotherly equality before its god would expose its members to continuous anxiety over salvation and therefore would not be performing its principal psychological function. The doctrines of original Calvinism, for example, restricting salvation, as it did, to a minority which was itself unconscious of its election, could not last long without some modification like that of the Arminian reaction in Holland. In like fashion, the exclusiveness of salvation in early Christianity was broadened by the Mariolatry and worship of the saints in the medieval church.

Finally, a system of beliefs has a more or less determinate locus where intercourse among *rulers* and members takes place now or at some time in the future. The need of the human organism for shelter from the elements usually succeeds in building up the stereotype of home as a haven. In Christianity the common abode of God and believers will be heaven, the Kingdom of God.[3]

The Relationship of Citizens

The question now remains: Can the family pattern of relationships be seen also in the political systems of belief?[4] Like membership in the family and in the medieval church, membership in the state is involuntary. Consanguinity is implied not only in the notion of *pater patriae* (applied in the United States to George Washington and the Founding Fathers) but also in the open acceptance among tribes and nations of some form of the blood brotherhood. Primitives have their covenant of blood, a union of persons through blood-sharing, in a common life approved by the divine *ruler;*[5] modern nations have their right of blood, the *jus sanguinis*, a universal practice among the existing states of the world. The feeling of a national blood relationship accounts in no small degree for the difficulty that nations have in assimilating persons from different races. People link obvious difference in color to difference in blood. "Columbia's true sons" may be fat and thin, tall and short, blue-eyed and brown, fair and dark, or long-headed and round, for these are among the present limits of visible hereditary variation in the progeny of the American family; but the black man or the yellow man is a stranger to the white man's family. Because he never could have been born in it, he is of different blood and cannot possibly have the same blood-brotherhood relationship. Blood is an ancient symbol which always has had and has yet today an intensely emotional meaning. The speed with which Americans in World War II infringed the civil liberties of some sixty thousand legal citizens of the yellow race is a case in point, as is also the popular stir in the same period over the question of the establishment of separate Red Cross blood banks for Negro and white American soldiers. Miscegenation must precede assimilation in the body politic.[6]

The rich man, the poor, the bright and the dull, the skilled and the unskilled, the young and the old—all belong to the nation. Complete equality is the rule. As part of a study, Americans were once asked what they believed were the requisites of a citizen. The composite answer was nearly a complete blank. There were none.[7] A person is born a citizen. Aristotle in the *Politics* was forced to come to a similar conclusion in his analysis of Greek citizenship. He began the subject with the ordinary sense of the term. "In common use they define a citizen to be one who is sprung from citizens on both sides, not on the father's or the mother's only." Probing further, he wondered:

how the first [ancestors] of the family could prove themselves citizens, according to this popular and careless definition. Gorgias of Leontium, partly entertaining the same doubt, and partly in jest, says, that as a mortar is made by a mortar-maker, so a citizen is made by a citizen-maker.

But after a diffuse consideration of some exceptions to the practice, he decided:

It is through want of citizens regularly born that they [the exceptional states] admit such [other persons as citizens]: for these laws are always made in consequence of a scarcity of inhabitants; so, as their numbers increase, they first deprive the children of a male or female slave of this privilege, next the child of a freewoman, and last of all, they will admit none but those whose fathers and mothers were both free.

Behold! Aristotle returns to his starting-point. If the individual falls within the particular theory of blood relationship held by

the community, he is a citizen, true-born. Nothing changes this
status except he be found a traitor or a blasphemer.[8] It is the im-
mutability of a citizen's status that makes the person feel secure
in the political ideology. Come what may, he belongs. The old
jinni, Mark Hanna, once expressed his feelings on the subject
with typical vigor. "I won't have an American abused," he
barked in the State Department, "and I don't give a damn if
he has a jail record and ain't got a cent. You get those Swiss to let
him loose." Family status suggests itself as the perfect analogy
and recalls the accounts of mothers of incorrigible delinquents
pleading before the judge with the words, "But he's my boy!"[9]
Preferential treatment, co-operation, and *no fighting* are the
watchwords of national brothers which motivate behavior that
protects nationals through wide-flung embassies or sends planes
halfway across the globe to the rescue of imperiled countrymen.
If *E pluribus unum* is the motto of the United States in the un-
changing words of an obsolete language, "We must all hang together" is the patriot's language in the history book, while the
sentiment of the man in the street or the road is "We Americans
must stick together."

The Power of Administration for the Commonwealth

Further reflection on the characteristics of political belief-
systems will easily reveal their conformity to the rest of the
family pattern. As for the parent, so for the state, force is the
ultima ratio. Indeed, some scholars have found it easiest to distinguish the state from other associations by defining it in terms
of its monopoly of violence, its punitive function. Max Weber, for
instance, declared, "The State is an association that claims the
monopoly of the legitimate use of violence, and cannot be defined in
any other manner." Only the anarchists have proclaimed that
the punitive function of the state is not essential, but they, of
course, also wished to abolish the state. In Machiavelli's words,
when the question comes before the ruler "whether it is better to
be loved more than feared, or feared more than loved, the reply
is that one ought both to be feared and loved." And, as is often
the case with Machiavelli, his deceptively simple language lays
bare the complexity of the human mind. People want their *ruler*

to be strong and powerful, to have an awful strength. How else could he protect and provide for them and punish evildoers? It is only when people cease to believe in their leader's capacity or willingness to provide for them that they wish to deprive him of power. But then by definition he is not their *ruler*, and they usually have in mind a true *ruler* who is not in the seat of formal power. Accordingly, the *ruler* is one who is both loved and feared, one who seems to have the strength both to control the environment and to strike fear into the hearts of the unrighteous.

Actually it is not open physical force alone that the subject fears. He has that fear, certainly, but it is reinforced by a chain of fears leading all the way back to childhood until it reaches the fear of separation-anxiety. The moral standards of a religion or the laws of a nation-state or the taboos of a primitive community rest on the commands, prohibitions, and rewards of the guardians of childhood. Violation of directives not only arouses the fear of the punitive power of the *ruler* but automatically touches off the anxiety connected with the withdrawal of parental affection. What therefore prevents a wholesale flouting of morals or laws at each opportunity of escaping undetected is the unrecognized influence of separation-anxiety. Through the intensive probing of psychiatric interviews the result of violating directives is most clearly seen. The person who, while engaged in a theft, suddenly "saw" his father looking at him sadly or the person who "heard" his mother weeping as he paid a visit to a house of prostitution or the one who in his dreams "could not escape the searching glance of a hovering searchlight," one of many symbolic variants of the parental "evil eye"—each of these could be cited in illustration. If most people are honest and loyal and good, it is not because they have been given proof that being dishonest, traitorous, and evil does not pay. In *The Mind and Society* Vilfredo Pareto, the Italian political scientist, made a large collection of cases which showed individuals and communities throughout history imputing a cause-and-effect relationship between their following of directives and their good fortune or their disobeying of directives and their bad fortune—and they assumed this relationship without the smallest shred of evidence![10] For the observance of directives in adult life is not based on proof of cause and effect but rests instead on a cause-and-effect relationship established in childhood, where evil acts were followed almost inevitably by evil consequences. The sequence works in reverse, too, from effect to cause. Let Fate strike a blow at a person today, and, just like his predecessors in the days of the *hubris* of the ancient Greeks or the *fortuna* of the Renaissance Italians, he will stop and, with incipient guilt in mind, worry whether he is not being punished for breaking some moral code.

That theory of law is correct, then, which resolves it into a command of the lawgiver, an obligation thereupon imposed on the subject, and a sanction threatened for disobedience.[11] Add to this a reward, promised for conformity. Directives are, one must remember, formulas for salvation. If they are faithfully followed, the *ruler* is committed to manage the environment so that his subjects can enjoy life without fear for their common safety and well-being. Political leadership, therefore, means more than the mere instillation of fear. It also means administering and directing. In the modern nation-state, the political *ruler* is supposed to provide for the common welfare by controlling the environment so as to bring prosperity. Before the United States had long been a separate nation, Benjamin Franklin located the source of its well-being in the religious *ruler*. "The Divine Being seems to have manifested His approbation . . . by the remarkable prosperity with which He has been pleased to favor the whole country." Within the space of a few years the sequence of a wave of prosperity following the ratification of the Constitution led the people of the country to infer a causal connection and laid the foundation for its subsequent personification in the Supreme Court personnel. Nearly a century later, Disraeli, former prime minister of England, wrote to Queen Victoria in a mood of rueful humor at his own expense: "I always feel that I did not bring your Majesty good fortune, and there must be something unlucky in a Minister who had to encounter six bad harvests. Certainly I might say, with a greater man, 'I was defeated by the elements.' " By that time England was in the advanced stages of the Industrial Revolution, and the contemporary analysis of A. M. Hocart would have been almost as applicable then as now:

Meteorological promises are scarcely worth making nowadays: we are no longer an agricultural population, and only worry about the weather in so far as it affects cricket or tennis. Besides we know too much about winds and rain to expect a government to control them. Unfortunately we know too little about human nature to recognize the limitations of a government in the matter of commerce and industry. Poor crops therefore no longer decide the fate of kings in Europe, but bad trade may overturn a government. It is the good old idea of supernatural efficacy confined by the progress of industry and of physics to trade. It is the righteousness of kings put into commission and industrialized.[12]

One of the best examples of the belief in the *ruler*'s ability to produce prosperity appeared in the first election following the stock-market crash in October, 1929. As the *Times* of London worded it:

This promise of uninterrupted prosperity . . . gave Mr. Hoover his great majority. . . . And we can see, now that the depression has come, that if Mr. Smith had been elected the Democratic Party would have been well-nigh ruined. The American people would have been told, and would have believed, that a Democratic administration spelt business failure.

"The people do not understand," said the *Times* a few years later, "that they are expecting their rulers to perform miracles."[13] You could no more have convinced them that they were expecting miracles of their rulers than you could have convinced Africans of the helplessness of the royal rainmaker. The extent to which people pinned responsibility for the depression on Herbert Hoover can be gauged by the remark current immediately after the 1932 election: "Even if the Democrats had nominated Andy Gump, he would have been elected."

The Political Conduct of Subjects

The *rulers* have their duty, then, of regulating the environment whether for rain, shine, or prosperity. *Divinité oblige.* But, in return, believers in a political ideology have obligations to the *ruler.* David Hume once wondered at the "implicit submission with which men resign their own sentiments and passions to those of their rulers." Obedience to law is undeniably part of the citizen's debt to the *ruler.* "He that keepeth the law, happy is he" (Prov. 29:18).

At the time that Hume made his statement on submission, Englishmen knew that their rulers were the king and Parliament. If a man had to submit to being deprived of a cow, he was likely to blame an act of Parliament for it. That the political system of beliefs can exact obedience to directives involving jeopardy of life and limb has often been cited as evidence of its immense power. As the patriot of today looks on the row upon row of white crosses inscribed with his native language's version of *Mort pour la patrie*, he cannot easily express for what or for whom his countrymen made the supreme sacrifice. In the waning years of the feudal system, two centuries or more before Hume, a supporter of the Stuarts might have answered, "The King! May God save him!" for the divine right of kings had been proclaimed by James I:

> Kings are justly called gods; for they exercise a manner of resemblance of divine power upon earth. For if you will consider the attributes of God, you shall see how to create or destroy, make or unmake at His pleasure, to give life or send death, to judge all and to be accountable for none. And the like power have kings. They make and unmake their subjects; they have power of raising up and casting down; of life and death; judges over all their subjects and in all cases, yet accountable to none but God.

By backtracking still another two centuries, historical research was able to reconstruct with no small artistry the following startled reply of Richard de Beauchamp, Earl of Warwick, to his chaplain: "A Frenchman! Where did you pick up that expression? Are these Burgundians and Bretons and Picards and Gascons beginning to call themselves Frenchmen, just as our fellows are beginning to call themselves Englishmen? They actually talk of France and England as their countries. *Theirs*, if you please!"[14]

What is it that modern patriots consider theirs? What or whom do they obey and love?

One of the first to evaluate the psychological function of the British monarchy was Walter Bagehot. After the republicanism of the American and French revolutions had been revitalized in the antimonarchical attacks of James Mill and Jeremy Bentham, he pointed out that to attack the crown as superfluous was not only inaccurate but irrelevant, for although the queen may have been merely a symbol, that very symbol was the only "comprehensible element for the vacant many" and thereby helped to retain the loyalty of "the labourers of Somersetshire." Yet, while the liquidation of the monarchy might have had disorganizing effects in the illiterate sections of the British Empire, its existence was a target for the impersonal and anti-idolatrous elements in the new Protestant and business ideologies. The forces that changed God into Providence or Nature were not unrelated to those that provoked Thomas Jefferson's attacks on the trappings of political office. "For heaven's sake," was his advice to the new Supreme Court, "discard the monstrous wig which makes the English judges look like rats peeping through bunches of oakum." But no political organization can thrive without the cohesive force of love, faith, and obedience for an anthropomorphic entity. The cry of "idolatry" is a characteristic weapon of those who wish to decentralize or break up the authority of the existing regime. Just as descendants of the early Christian iconoclasts became the image-worshipers of the church, so the posterity of the anti-idolatrous Protestants turned to the idols of the nation.[15]

If Thomas Jefferson could walk across the plaza, through the massive Corinthian columns of the present home of the Supreme Court, and enter the great bronze doors over which the brow and beard of Chief Justice Hughes are carved in Dorset marble, his unbelieving eyes would witness the unfolding of a dramatic spectacle:

From those who are fortunate enough to obtain seats comes a buzz of expectant whispers. . . . In the audience are such notables as. . . . The stage is a long dais of carefully polished mahogany. The curtain is of red velvet, just beyond. And as the hands of the great gold clock, suspended above, come together at noon, a hushed silence falls over the throng. Behind the velvet curtains nine [men] . . . stand abreast, gowned in black. In front of them is a little boy in knee breeches. At a nod from the leading man,—a bearded gentleman of stately mien—the boy pushes a buzzer and the Nine Old Men advance abreast through the curtains.

The Audience rises.

"The Honorable, the Chief Justice and the Associate Justices of the Supreme Court!" calls the court crier.

The justices take their seats; the Supreme Court of the United States, most powerful judicial body in the world, is now in session. . . .

After the session, the shade of Jefferson might wander quietly through the

four elaborately designed courts, each sixty-four feet square and each featuring a fountain splashing rhythmically in the center. Then . . . a reading room with seven adjacent nooks, all adorned with paneled and pilastered work, the ceiling finished in color and gilt. The floors of the offices were finished in American quartered white oak, the corridors in Alabama white marble, and around the corridors were pillars of marble dug from the Sienna quarries of Italy, with a base and floor border of Levanto marble and rare marble panels of Brochi Sanguine.[16]

Having completed his tour of inspection, Jefferson might join another departed spirit, Huey Long (a strange bedfellow, indeed, for the Virginian!) in sighing, "Nine Million Dollars! A million dollars apiece for Nine Old Men. And they used to be glad to sit in one room."

The disappearance of the divine monarch made necessary the personification of the nation.[17] Whenever the political functions of the *ruler* are ideologically vested in a group, as in a democracy or in an oligarchy, the personification of the common term for the group as a whole or of the name of the area which it inhabits, is a likelihood. This process which at first hearing sounds like a feat of transubstantiation is not foreign to human minds. *Vox populi, vox Dei*, was a transposition of the Middle Ages. Jeremy Bentham understood the process as "the personification of fictions":

Amongst all the instruments of delusion employed for reconciling the people to the dominion of the one and the few, is the device of employing for the designation of persons, and classes of persons, instead of the ordinary and appropriate denominations, the names of so many abstract fictitious entities, contrived for the purpose. Take the following examples:

Instead of Kings, or the King—the *Crown* and the *Throne*.
Instead of a Churchman—the *Church*, and sometimes the *Altar*.
Instead of Lawyers—the *Law*.
Instead of Judges, or a Judge—the *Court*.
Instead of Rich men, or the Rich—*Property*.

Of this device, the object and effect is, that any unpleasant idea that in the mind of the hearer or reader might happen to stand associated with the idea of the person or the class, is disengaged from it: and in the stead of the more or less obnoxious individual or individuals, the object presented is a creature of the fancy, by the idea of which, as in poetry, the imagination is tickled—a phantom which, by means of the power with which the individual or class is clothed, is constituted an object of respect and veneration.[18]

In the development of modern republicanism, the nineteenth century saw the personality of the nation being first propagated by littérateurs and historians and later accepted by almost everyone, so that today, people talk and fight about nations exactly as if they were supreme individuals. The anthropomorphic representation of nations by word or by drawing, as in newspaper cartoons of Uncle Sam and John Bull, is practiced around the world. The scholars of *Nationalism* of the British Royal Institute of International Affairs believe that

to picture the nation as a society of individuals which is at once something different from those individuals, yet has no existence apart from them is a recondite idea of which only the more cultured and sophisticated citizens are likely to be capable. The approach of the ordinary man to the highly complex problems of his political environment is more straightforward. Any abstract object of thought tends to be pictured as a person—partly because the ordinary man wants something which can easily be grasped on account of its familiarity (and persons are more familiar to him than abstract ideas), partly because his attitude is primarily determined by emotion, and emotion is most naturally directed to a person. Just as religions personify their gods, so does patriotism or nationalism (which, as has been suggested, is in many ways a secularized form of religion) tend to personify the idea of the nation to which it is directed. The nation is pictured as possessing all the attributes of an ideal person.[19]

Nevertheless, complexity is only a part, and at that a small part, of the reason for the existence of the anthropomorphic nation. Why should ordinary adults who can master the intricacies of the automobile and other mechanical gadgets fumble with the word "nation"? At this juncture it becomes necessary to recall the historic function of an ideology, that to set the world aright there must be a regulator who bestrides the world like a Colossus, bringing order out of chaos. One can imagine a public opinion poll interviewer accosting a man on the curbstone to say, "Excuse me, Mister, but do you think that in many ways you feel toward your country as you did, when you were a child, toward your father or mother?" The interviewer would not be surprised to hear: "No, I don't. My country is just all the people in it like myself." Narrowly skirting the temptation to ask just who are they who are "like myself," the questioner would then ask, "Do you think that America has ever been guilty of wrongdoing?" Upon receiving a negative response, he will then press forward, "Well, *you* can do wrong, can't you? And if the nation is made up of people like you, why can't *it* do wrong?" Without knowing it, the imaginary interviewer is following the argument of Beatrice

Webb. "I do not quite understand the democratic theory that by multiplying ignorant opinions indefinitely you produce wisdom." It is the illogic of personal faith in the People that led Pareto to shout it down as "poppycock!"[20] much as it had led Hamilton to counter: "Your people, sir, is a great Beastie."

In republics, then, one finds the Nation to be the *ruler*. Along with it, varying in usage from one period to another, exist certain anthropomorphic synonyms—the People, the Public, or Public Opinion—of which the first, *le nouveau dieu politique: le Peuple*, is encountered most frequently today.[21] But if it be granted that the nation is personified, the form of the picture in the mind should be ascertained, at least in shadowy outline. The Study Group of the Royal Institute of International Affairs thought that the anthropomorphism was an "ideal person," but it is possible to be more specific. Since, as has been seen and will be further shown, the political system of beliefs describes relationships which resemble a home or family prototype, the *ruler* of the political ideology will have many of the attributes of attendants in childhood.[22] It is not surprising, then, to hear Lord Bryce, who most certainly could give a clear and precise definition of public opinion, yet speak of it in America as "an Oriental despot" before which men tremble, "like the Eastern slave who says, 'I hear and obey!'"

To remember Hobbes's epochal introduction:

> That great Leviathan called a Common-Wealth, or State . . . is but an Artificiall Man; though of greater stature and strength than the Naturall, for whose protection and defence it was intended; and in which, the Sovereignty is an Artificiall *Soul*, as giving life and motion to the whole body.

To see the words of Jacques Bénigne Bossuet, theologian and royal tutor:

> Human association demands that men love the land that they inhabit together, or that they regard it as their mother and nurse. . . . Truly, men feel themselves bound by something of great strength when they believe that the same land which bore and nourished them while they were alive will receive them to her bosom when they are dead.[23]

Or to hear a man of political action, like Parnell, say: "You would never have got young men to sacrifice themselves for so unlucky a country as Ireland, only that they pictured her as a woman."[24] Nor is it surprising to note that in poetical or oratorical expression the images of attendants as the nation are no less pronounced:

> Citizens, it is I [the Great Mother, *la Patrie*] that undertakes to protect your personal safety, your peace, your property: What wilt thou give me in return for constant benefit? If it happens that I am in peril, if unnatural children torment my bosom . . . wouldst thou abandon me in these stormy moments for the price of my invariable protection? . . . No! . . . There are times when I would command the sacrifice . . . even of thy life which I have so steadily protected.[25]

As these quotations partially illustrate, the words—father, mother, earth, land, king, queen, country, home—are locked in an etymological vise. Least of all should it be surprising to find that the profile of attendants is sharpened and brought into focus in the intensive scrutiny of the individual in the psychological clinic or in the extensive observation of the group by anthropological expeditions. The psychiatrist need not say to his client that "your *ruler* has the attributes of your attendants"; the person in the course of clinical visits soon discovers that he has been acting toward his country, for example, as though it were his parent. He himself can see the parallelism of attitudes.

Only in rare circumstances—when he is certain that no part of his political system of beliefs will be challenged or threatened—can the ordinary person discuss *his* nation as a simple abstraction.[26] Nevertheless, the filial love and loyalty which persons have for political *rulers* is not easy to capture and record; interviewers do not roam the streets asking, "Do you love your country?" Such emotion generally reveals itself among believers in the respectful tones employed whenever it is necessary to discuss ideological matters. Hence, it usually requires an outsider to notice the depth of such devotion. American tourists in Britain seldom fail to remark the reverence in which the English hold the king (in limited monarchies it is the crown to which such emotions perennially adhere). In like manner, Englishmen (as well as others) are astounded at the love Americans bear for America. Thus, Tocqueville: "It is impossible to conceive a more troublesome or more garrulous patriotism." Thus, Bryce: "Nowhere does the individual associate himself more constantly and directly with the greatness of his country." Thus, Ostrogorski: "In the

United States that cult [of the fetish-like worship of country] found its dogmatic formula in the cry: 'Our country, right or wrong.' " And thus the Middletowner: "The American democratic form of government is the final and ideal form of government. . . . The Constitution should not be fundamentally changed. . . . The Americans are the freest people in the world. . . . America will always be the land of opportunity and the greatest and richest country in the world."

The faith in *rulers* can also be seen in the cases of blasphemy or sacrilege that occasionally crop up. One cold night in London, early in December, 1936, a journalist remarked to a friend, as they came out of a cinema, that the King might abdicate. "Hush, sir; hush!" said a shocked voice behind him. It had only been three hundred and twenty years before that incident that another king, James I, had said: "As it is atheism and blasphemy to dispute what God can do, so it is presumption and high contempt in a subject to dispute what a king can do or to say that a king cannot do this or that"; and when Victoria had been dead for over a generation, angry readers were known to renounce the pleasure of perusing their favorite newspaper because it was insufficiently respectful to the Queen Mother. In fact, no journalist ever dared to attribute a fault to the king of England or even to refer to the character of any royal person "except in the whispered undertones of worshippers in a sacred place."[27]

A year seldom goes by in the United States without a case of lèse majesté. Perhaps once a year someone somewhere refuses to lift his hat to the passing flag or to perform other aspects of the political ritual, and the affair develops into a national *cause célèbre*. The trials and tribulations of Jehovah's Witnesses are a recent case in point.

An additional aspect of filial faith and love for the nation should be broached. To the child, the parents have empirical qualities of supremacy, inaccessibility, or freedom from interference. Certainly it is true that his attendants need not suffer any of his whims or wishes unless they so choose. An analogy can be found in the distinctive doctrine of national sovereignty. The state claims aspects of both internal and external sovereignty; for example, it may not be sued by ordinary mortals without its consent or interfered with by other states. In the classical sentence of Bodin: "Sovereignty is supremacy over citizens as well as subjects, and a power unrestrained by law." And, most important, persons *want* their nation to be "free from external control, and sufficiently strong to maintain that freedom," for, somehow, "this is felt to be necessary to its happiness and well-being."[28]

Still the nation is not only a personified entity corresponding in its imputed attributes and alleged activities to childhood attendants but is also a place of protection where the dangers of the world raging outside cannot enter. The two connotations of the nation, as person and place, frequently shift and merge, as the foregoing quotation of Joseph Barrère illustrated. But the sense of home as "the homeland" predominates in those ideologies in which a mortal person, rather than an institution, assumes the ruling role. It was with this meaning that one of the earliest students of political psychology rather crudely said, "The love of our country is little more, in many cases, than the love of an ass for his manger."[29] Home, as the place where the way of life of a system of beliefs is known and followed, and where the resultant freedom from separation-anxiety is secure, retains throughout life a unique sentiment which later extends over the terrain and climate and people of a national area, the fatherland or the mother-country or the native soil. The lack of this warm deep affection for a place is satirized in the clipped phrase, *ubi bene, ibi patria*. It is perhaps no coincidence that the American, John Howard Payne, whose mother died when he was thirteen years old, who spent most of his life as a wanderer over Europe, and who died as the United States' consul at Tunis—it is perhaps no coincidence that his claim to immortality is the writing of "Home, Sweet Home." Nor is it a coincidence that the melody of the song is an old Sicilian air that Payne picked up while traveling in Italy. There are cases on record of whole tribes, transplanted for their material betterment to different lands, being afflicted with the severest nostalgia. A political community without a territorial base is a rarity.[30]

The Complex of Rulers in a Republic

With apparent indiscrimination, discussion proceeded in this chapter to equate the *ruler* of the political system to the Nation, the People, the King, Parliament, the Prime Minister, or the President. The result may have been quite unedifying. The pattern of political personification in modern democracies, however, is not simple. Anyone or anything consistently standing in an administering and punitive relationship to the community is liable to attract to himself the popular beliefs and emotions that hedge a king. Over any period of time, that entity which the members of the community believe to be performing activities of the most necessary kind, namely, regulating the environment for the commonweal on this earth, that person or institution will be the political *ruler*. In a republic with a chief executive, a legislature, and a supreme court, the nation for long periods of time receives credit for this activity; and the three branches stand in the position of assistants or departmental principals, each handling one of the *ruler*'s functions as customarily divided. The attention of the community is sometimes fixed, however, on one or another of these branches at a time when its activity seems crucial. For many Americans the Supreme Court of the United States was in such a situation during the constitutional crisis of 1937. Parliament had such a position with English lawyers in the days when it was a fundamental principle with them that "Parliament can do everything but make a woman a man and a man a woman." The chief executive in the United States, for the greater part of the period from 1932 to 1945, for example, attained that role. In these intervals each branch, for the time being and for large groups, became the *ruler*.

In the Introduction to Part II it was noted that if *rulers* of different ideologies lay down the same directives, people exposed to the ideologies come to believe that the different *rulers* are one and the same. Similarly, the complex of *rulers* in a republic easily and often changes from a mixture to a compound. Should one of the government branches be a high court, its possibility of assuming alone the mantle of the *ruler* would be greater than the legislature's. The qualities of age, wisdom, impartiality, inaccessibility, and irrevocability associated with the upholders of the highest law can smoothly blend the Supreme Court into the image of the "Lord of Law," as the *ruler* is called in some communities.[31] On the other hand, a legislative body has weaknesses in this respect—

its numbers, its publicized internal disagreements, and sectional interests.[32] The greatest potentiality among governmental branches rests in the office of the chief executive, where lie the punitive (police and army) and the administering (policy-making and executing) powers. In addition to these advantages the incumbent is singular and alone has an unequivocal interest in the welfare of the whole political community. His acts can be justified only *pro bono publico*. The one brick lacking in the structure of the presidency is *complete* legislative or policy-making power.[33] But this brick is not the cornerstone. In the Great Depression, for instance, the charge was sometimes heard that the Congress had abdicated in favor of the president. During crises a plenary power accrues to the chief executive, and all the ingredients of the *ruler* are compounded in that one figure.[34]

To the question which opened this chapter—in what degree do adult ideologies reflect the pattern of childhood indoctrination?—it now can be said that, just as systems of belief function in adults as in the child, so do the ideological attitudes and emotions of adults resemble the child's. Attitudes and emotions, however, not behavior. There is a time when the youth is told to be a man—to do a man's work, to give a man's worship, to live a man's life. Thus it is that while the feeling of love which the child bears for his attendants may be the same as an adult's for the nation, the ways each one uses to express his sentiment may differ. The same relationship characterizes the attitude of obedience and the other sentiments which crystallize around the belief-systems of home and nation. Does this mean that the behavior of the child in the one case bears no relation to that of the adult toward the nation? Assuredly not. Were that the case, the study of attitudes and emotions would be less rewarding. The behavior of both child and adult is often similar, especially in the expression of love and faith. A child may throw his arms about his parent and bestow a kiss. The adult rests content with lavishing affection on the symbols of the nation. The throngs of women who kissed the Liberty Bell at its many stopping places on the way from Philadelphia to the San Francisco Exposition, the men who kissed the Constitution in its resting place or dropped on their knees before it, the persons who kissed the native soil on their return from abroad—all were performing symbolic actions which might never have occurred to the child until he had been taught the adult manner of devotion; but the similarities are obvious. In the behavior of obedience, too, many resemblances can be seen. A man may no longer obey the commands of his biological parents, but he obeys the commands of the nation as he obeyed his earliest *rulers*. Yet there is a radical change in the standard of performance demanded. The child obeys in the matter of household chores and the inhibition of certain impulses. He does certain things and does not do certain others. Similarly for the grownup. But *he* has acquired a more fully developed nervous system, a longer memory, a language, dexterity of hand and mind, skills common to most adults in the community. These he places at the service of his nation.

The differences in behavior are not so great, however, that one should forget Goethe's observation, "Man never knows how anthropomorphic he is." When speaking of the persistence of the function of ideologies—and not of the rapid turnover of cells in the living organism—one can say that the Child lives in the Man. The husk harmonizes with the core. The man can staunch a wound better than the child or plant a seed or deal with other men. He can do all those feats that impress the child so greatly. Yet he is one with the child before the mysteries of the universe. He applies all his increased knowledge and skill to these mysteries. So far, they remain. Strife, death, the elements, bodily decay, can plunge him and his loved ones into pain, darkness, and the anxiety of total oblivion. When he will not be awed or terrified or helpless before these problems, perhaps he will let loose his systems of beliefs. Until then, the husk must harmonize with the core.

To the thinking mind of the adult, the child does not know what really to dread. The man therefore laughs at the child's fear of what is not dreadful. Yet though his way of life be more intricate, the man is not free from a like fear. Give the child the security of home about him; give the man the orderliness of the world and its denizens. All the good in his earthly life will be seen as reward for his knowledge and following of the law of God and nation. To be freed of separation-anxiety is the citizen's bliss.

CHAPTER SIX

SIMPLE ANOMIE IN MODERN DEMOCRACY

ENOUGH has been said to show that systems of belief operate to give adults what Bagehot once named "a feeling of confidence in the universe." The impending task is the observation of simple anomie in the United States. Although it calls for a large number of quotations from observers, the objective ought not to be too difficult. To start, a case of literary parallelism should be presented. Upon comparison the writings of two different authors living over a generation apart and treating diverse subjects show striking similarities, of which a few are here given:

A native of the United States . . . clutches everything, he holds nothing fast, but soon loosens his grasp to pursue fresh gratifications.

If men, passionately bent upon physical gratifications, desire eagerly, they are also easily discouraged. . . . Men who have toiled to acquire a *competence* can hardly live after they have lost it.

The equality [men] desire . . . perpetually retires from before them, yet without hiding itself from their sight, and on retiring draws them on. At every moment they think they are about to grasp it; it escapes at every moment from their hold. They are near enough to see its charms, but too far off to enjoy them; and before they have fully tasted its delights, they die.

They thirst for novelty, for unknown delights, for nameless sensations, which nevertheless lose their savor as soon as they are experienced.

The man who always expected everything from the future, who has lived with his eyes riveted on what is to come, has nothing in his past to fortify him against the tribulations of the present. . . . Let the slightest reverse occur, and [these] men are powerless to bear it.

But one does not progress when one is moving toward no goal, or, what comes to the same thing, when the goal toward which one is moving is infinitely far away. If one's distance from the goal remains always the same, despite the distance one has gone, the result is the same as if one were running on a treadmill.

Many scanty fortunes spring up: those who possess them have a sufficient share of physical gratifications to conceive a taste for these pleasures—not enough to satisfy it. They never procure them without exertion, and they never indulge in them without apprehension. They are therefore always straining to pursue or to retain gratifications so delightful, so imperfect, so fugitive.

To these causes must be attributed that strange melancholy which oftentimes will haunt the inhabitants of democratic countries in the midst of their abundance, and that disgust at life which sometimes seizes upon them in the midst of calm and easy circumstances.

Complaints are made in France that the number of suicides increases; in America suicide is rare, but insanity is said to be more common than anywhere else. These are different symptoms of the same disease.

An unquenchable thirst is a perpetually renewed agony. . . . Overexcited ambitions always go beyond the results achieved, whatever these may be, for they are not warned to go no further. Thus nothing can appease them and all this excitement sustains itself perpetually without leading to any satisfaction.

Because prosperity has increased, desires are inflamed. . . . [But] Fatigue alone suffices to produce disillusionment, for it is difficult in the long run to avoid feeling the futility of a chase without end. . . . It is the most fortunate who suffer most from anomie.

How, under these conditions, could the will to live do other than languish? . . . Under these circumstances, one holds onto life only by an extremely slender thread, which may snap at any moment. . . . Such conditions lead to those abrupt rises in the suicide curves.

The reader should be reminded that the author of the column on the left is Tocqueville; the writer of the right-hand column, of course, is Durkheim. Tocqueville wrote of America in 1831, Durkheim of anomie in 1897. Whether the sociologist culled passages from Tocqueville or whether he merely retained and later rephrased the ideas is unimportant. Plagiarism is not the issue. The interesting thing is that Durkheim's description of the symptoms of anomie may have been derived from Tocqueville's analysis of the behavior of Americans.[1]

To move on more systematically, one can find in modern American life protests against the competitive and activist directives and, better, actual descriptions of simple anomie. From the literary elements in modern democracies many instances of the latter type have been aesthetically recorded. Among American poets, T. S. Eliot (although now an English citizen) should be placed foremost for works like *The Waste Land*, "The Love Song of J. Alfred Prufrock," and *Ash Wednesday*. Many of the works of Conrad Aiken and Ezra Pound also have an indisputable pertinence. Although not enjoying Eliot's *succès d'estime*, Pound in point of time, at least, should precede him; Eliot's *Waste Land* bore the dedication, "To Ezra Pound, *il miglior fabbro*." In the ranks of the novelists, F. Scott Fitzgerald and his disciple, John O'Hara, and also William Faulkner deserve to be singled out for their descriptions of *la vie anomique*. The pivotal role of belongingness in *The Hairy Ape* gives Eugene O'Neill predominance among American playwrights. As a stylistic device, the introduction of masks in his *The Great God Brown* had relevance, too, playing (in contrast to its Sicilian prototype) a depersonalizing role that hid the speakers' inner conflicts.

Some of the other new literary techniques ought not to be overlooked since they were often utilized to convey the uncomfortable sense of interminable flux in modern life where uncertainty is the only certainty. The stream-of-consciousness style, an invention of William James to which Sigmund Freud contributed a few patents, found ready employers here and abroad. Gertrude Stein, a pupil of James, was one of the important early innovators and, moreover, the author of the sobriquet, "the lost generation," the generation without umbilical cord. The winding subtleties of Proust's *A la recherche du temps perdu*, the isolatedness of Auden's *The Double Man*, the passions of D. H. Lawrence's *Aaron's Rod*, the fragility of Virginia Woolf's *To the Lighthouse*, the intellectualities of Huxley's *Point Counter Point*, and the sophistication of Isherwood's *The Memorial*—all condemn a world and a civilization, all portray central characters sick with disillusion and vacillancy. In each of these works the moral lesson and the anomic feeling are obvious. Who can escape the futility of the directionless "hero" in his efforts to communicate with the *Castle* of Franz Kafka, or who can suppress his sympathy when the robots themselves in Karel Čapek's *R.U.R.* revolt against their rational and impersonal treatment? Even the labyrinthian sleep-life of H. C. Earwicker ("Here Comes Everybody") registered in *Finnegans Wake* was apparently chosen for description by Joyce because he saw no standards for the selection of any one side of a man's biography; hence, the dream world of just one night's sleep. Thomas Mann, too, can be included, for his *Magic Mountain* is redolent of utopia, an escape from a disordered world, although in style he rejected the "cult of unintelligibility." As an eminent literary critic, G. A. Borgese, put it: unlike the others who dived deep in those waters, Mann "did not drink of them, he swam over them chin up, inspecting them with a captivated but uncaptured eye."

Not as much can be said for the cube, the cone, and the cylinder in abstract art, for the many-phased Picasso, or for other painters—Leger, Chirico, Rouault, Matisse, Braque—and, in general, the cubist, Dadaist, or surrealist genre. In music, also, the attempts to depict artistically the confusion of norms and the hustle and bustle of the contemporary era led to a search for colorful instruments, new rhythms, and new tonalities. The mechanist, the futurist, and the atonal schools are commendable examples. All the while, abreast of pen and brush, the flowing comment of modern art criticism brims with significant titles—*The Melody of Chaos*, "Weltschmerz," "Expectancy of Doom"—vague, yet indicative of anomie.

These last few pages, however, mean to do nothing more than pick out a strain which runs through much of present-day art and letters. An intensive political analysis of literature cannot be attempted here. Literature is faceted like diamonds. New insight strikes the eye of the beholder with each new glance. Artists are therefore suspect in social science. Their observations are too personal and particularized, their lives too far removed from the common lot, their symbolism too rich and individualized, to permit a prosaic rendition. Their inconsistencies become the hobgoblins of the scientific mind. Sociologists, on the other hand, can agree on the meaning of a term like "impersonalism," for example, and concur in its prevalence in modern society. Yet, though they try to steer clear of the good or evil consequences of the cultural traits they analyze, their dislike at times faintly emerges.

One would never suspect that bright yellow gold, the gold of philosophers and kings, of adventure and crime, passions and war—one would never suspect that it had any relation to the cold, dead hand of money that the renowned German sociologist Georg Simmel sees. To modern man all things appear in a uniformly flat and gray tone, with no one of them deserving preference to another. This frame of mind is the true subjective reflection of the thorough permeation of a money economy, in that money takes the place of all the diversity of things and expresses all qualitative distinctions between them through the distinction of "how much." In so far as money with its colorlessness and impersonality appears as the common denominator of all values, it becomes a most dreadful leveler. In an irreparable manner it hollows out the core of things, their individuality, their particular worth, their uniqueness. They all float with the same specific gravity in the continually moving stream of money; they all lie on the same level, distinguishable solely through their quantities.[2]

Many others have documented the impersonalism of the modern scene with specialized studies of the rooming-house dweller, the hotel guest, or the marginal man. More or less, they have kept without the bounds of bias. For this reason one must turn to another source—the modern worker himself—to find protest against the competitive directive, protest unembellished with symbolism and unrestrained by fear of making moral judgments. Thus, competition:

They [the owners, the managers] begin by asking you to cut the other guy's throat, but what happens is that everybody's throat is cut—including your own.

Thus, impersonalism:

I don't know what the plants could do to make working conditions better. They're so big, you know that there isn't much friendliness in them. One plant has the kids of the workers in once a year for ice cream and a social affair in general. That's a nice thing. At least the kids enjoy it, and the workingman appreciates it.

Thus, rationalism:

They classify you as type 1 or as type 2, and they can put you wherever they want to, and when they want to. If they want to shove someone else ahead of you, they can do it, don't worry. The company's got you where the hair is short. They don't care about their men.

Enough, for that cardinal triad. Protests against activism can be just as amply documented:

Hell, supposing I do get a better job. It will be a nickel an hour more, that's all. . . . That's right. There's no sense in being pushed around by foremen if you don't have to. Mine is a Simon Legree. He jumped a guy the other day for taking too long off to go out to the can. My God! It's drive, drive, drive all day long. No visiting at the bench. No nothing.

The son of a bitch across the street is one good reason why a lot of men are leaving that plant. Him and a lot like him. He is a foreman. He started a friend of mine running two milling machines instead of one. Jesus! Naturally Jack says no, so the foreman calls for the superintendent. The superintendent says what's the matter with you G.I.'s—are you afraid to work? Jack tells him no, I'm not afraid to work, but that's just too much; you know what you can do with your job. The bosses are just laying it on too thick. They expect too much. There are a couple of bad foremen at the plant where I work. Just a couple of days ago a G.I. went out to the can, and my foreman tells him he stayed too long. He said the war's over now. Can you imagine that? In another department. a G.I. made a mistake, or didn't get his work done fast enough, or something, and the foreman says—where have you been? So the guy cracks back, "In Italy, taking care of you." That story did my heart good.

Sure, I think most of us would admit that we could double our take-home if we wanted to shoot the works, but where's the percentage? A guy has to get something out of life. Now my little lady would rather have me in a good humor than have the extra money. The way it works out none of us are going to be Van-Asterbilts so why not get a little pleasure out of living together and working together?[3]

It is evident that complaints against the competitive and activist directives have been registered. Still, these statements by workers are only protests. By themselves they merely locate the source of trouble. Has anomie as described in the Introduction to Part I been seen? It will be remembered that one of its salient features was a feeling of pointlessness or that no certain goals exist. If you were to ask the psychologist Carl Gustave Jung what was the most frequent question put to him by an international clientele in his quarter-century of clinical experience, he would answer:

The most ordinary and frequent of questions [is]: What is the meaning of my life, or of life in general? Men today believe that they know only too well what the clergymen will say—or, rather, must say—to this. They smile at the very thought of the philosopher's answer, and in general do not expect much of the physician. But from the psychotherapist who analyses the unconscious— from him one might doubtless learn something. He has perhaps dug up from the depths of his mind, among other things, a meaning for life which could be bought for a fee! It must be a relief to every serious-minded person to hear that the psychotherapist also does not know what to say.[4]

Franz Alexander, a psychoanalyst, sees a similar lack of purposefulness:

> After long hours of daily work, spent listening to the suffering victims of these unsettled times and trying to extract sense from the kaleidoscopic variety of sincere self-revelations, a hypnagogic vision appears before the eyes of the pondering psychoanalyst. The analyst sees his patients—physicians, lawyers, engineers, bankers, advertising men, teachers and laboratory research men of universities, students, and clerks—engaged in a Marathon race, their eager faces distorted by strain, their eyes focused not upon their goal, but upon each other with a mixture of hate, envy and admiration. Panting and perspiring, they run and never arrive. They would all like to stop but dare not as long as the others are running. What makes them run so frantically, as though they were driven by the threatening swish of an invisible whip wielded by an invisible slave driver? The driver and the whip they carry in their own minds. If one of them finally stops and begins leisurely to whistle a tune or watch a passing cloud or picks up a stone and with childish curiosity turns it around in his hand, they all look upon him at first with astonishment, and then with contempt and disgust. They call him names, a dreamer or a parasite, a theoretician or a schizophrenic, and above all, an effeminate. They not only do not understand him—they not only despise him but "they hate him as their own sin." All of them would like to stop—ask each other questions, sit down to chat about futilities—they all would like to belong to each other because they all feel desperately alone—chasing on in a never-ending chase. They do not dare to stop until the rest stop lest they lose all their self-respect, because they know only one value—that of running—running for its own sake.[5]

And Erich Fromm, too, notes the uncertainty of goals:

> [Today one sees] the destruction of any kind of structuralized picture of the world. . . . The adult does not see the meaning of the "whole," the pieces of which come into his hands. He is bewildered and afraid and just goes on gazing at his little meaningless pieces.

Modern man seems, if anything, to have too many wishes and his only problem seems to be that, although he knows what he wants, he cannot have it. All our energy is spent for the purpose of getting what we want, and most people never question the premise of this activity: that they know their true wants. They do not stop to think whether the aims they are pursuing are something they themselves want. In school they want to have good marks, as adults they want to be more and more successful, to make more money, to have more prestige, to buy a better car, to go places, and so on. Yet when they do stop to think in the midst of all this frantic activity, this question may come to their minds: "If I do get this new job, if I get this better car, if I can take this trip—what then? What is the use of it all? Is it really I who want all this? Am I not running after some goal which is supposed to make me happy and which eludes me as soon as I have reached it?" These questions, when they arise, are frightening, for they question the very basis on which man's whole activity is built, his knowledge of what he wants. People tend, therefore, to get rid as soon as possible of these disturbing thoughts. They feel that they have been bothered by these questions because they were tired or depressed—and they go on in the pursuit of the aims which they believe are their own.

Fromm's analysis, moreover, begins to shade off into another aspect of anomie, the vague fear and uneasiness resulting from the lack of consistent directives:

> However, this feeling of individual isolation and powerlessness . . . is nothing the average normal person is aware of. It is too frightening for that. It is covered over by the daily routine of his activities, by the assurance and approval he finds in his private or social relations, by success in business, by any number of distractions, by "having fun," "making contacts," "going places." But whistling in the dark does not bring light. Aloneness, fear, and bewilderment remain; people cannot stand it forever.

His analysis of an important segment of the American cinema is worthy of quotation:

> The extent to which the average person in America is filled with the same sense of fear and insignificance seems to find a telling expression in the fact of the popularity of the Mickey Mouse pictures. There the one theme—in so many variations—is always this: something little is persecuted and endangered by something overwhelmingly strong, which threatens to kill or swallow the little thing. The little thing runs away and eventually succeeds in escaping or even harming the enemy. People would not be ready to look continually at the many variations of this one theme unless it touched upon something very close to their own emotional life. Apparently the little thing threatened by a powerful, hostile enemy is the spectator himself; that is how *he* feels and that is the situation with which he can identify himself. But of course, unless there were a happy ending there would be no continuous attraction. As it is, the spectator lives through all his own fears and feelings of smallness and at the end gets the comforting feeling that, in spite of all, he will be saved and will even conquer the strong one. However—and this is the significant and sad part of this "happy end"—his salvation lies mostly in his ability to run away and in the unforeseen accidents which make it impossible for the monster to catch him.[6]

Indeed, the entire thesis of Fromm's book *Escape from Freedom*, hinges on the conclusion that man's present freedom is fraught with inordinate fear.

The third characteristic of simple anomie, the feeling of separation or isolation from the group, not only has been observed but its causal antecedents have been pointed out in a well-packed paragraph by no less a sociological authority than Robert E. Park:

> Everywhere in The Great Society the relations of men, which were intimate and personal, have been more or less completely superseded by relations that are impersonal and formal. The result is that in the modern world, in contrast with earlier and simpler societies, every aspect of life seems to be mechanized and rationalized. This is particularly true in our modern cities which are in consequence so largely inhabited today by lonely men and women.[7]

No one has been more explicit in linking this loneliness and isolation to the competitive directive than the psychiatrist Karen Horney:

> All these factors together—competitiveness and its potential hostilities between fellow-beings, fears, diminished self-esteem—result psychologically in the individual feeling that he is isolated. Even when he has many contacts with others, even when he is happily married, he is emotionally isolated. Emotional isolation is hard for anyone to endure.

Thus the paradox appears that although he lives in crowded cities, areas where the population density is the world's highest, where morning and night he pushes, bumps, and jostles people, the person feels himself to be alone, isolated, uncared for. Horney does not stop with noting the individual's feeling of isolation but proceeds to set down the solution he seeks:

> It is this situation which provokes, in the normal individual of our time, an intensified need for affection as a remedy. Obtaining affection makes him feel less isolated, less threatened by hostility and less uncertain of himself. . . . Hence the individual—and I still mean the normal individual—is in the dilemma of needing a great deal of affection but finding difficulty in obtaining it.[8]

She has not been the only one to notice this need for affection. James Plant goes even farther in identifying its nature. In his work on *Personality and the Cultural Pattern* he observes that persons today exhibit a "need for belongingness" which everyday life does not satisfy. The inclusive affection with which a family binds its members together is the missing element. Thus Plant clearly realizes that the difficulty at bottom is a difference from a previous kind of communal relationship.

Perhaps the most convincing demonstration is provided by the academic studies of industrial morale that have been made in recent years. With few exceptions, these studies have been unsuccessful in getting frank protests from workers of the type previously quoted. But by roundabout methods[9] they have uncovered a fact which persons would find difficult to admit openly: The modern worker needs affection. No matter which schemes or devices were tried to increase production, they seemed to be successful only on one condition. An instructive example is that of a workroom in one plant where the experimenters found that when the walls were painted green as part of the usual redecorating, production stepped up. Then they tested the obvious possibility that the new color improved the vision of the workers and in this physical fashion had increased efficiency. The difficulty with that hypothesis, however, was that after a while production dropped back again. Moreover, no matter what color they used to decorate the walls, an upswing in output was the consequence. After much interviewing, they learned the simple fact that painting the walls was felt to be personal attention from the management; for the time, at least, the workers got the impression that their employers cared for them.

The entire series of the now famous experiments at the Hawthorne Works in Chicago presented the same facts. Originally set up to test physiological factors in production, these studies measured the effects on output of humidity and temperature, of fatigue and rest, of illumination, of menstrual cycles, and many other factors. No significant relationships were found. Then, on the basis of certain clues earlier uncovered by Elton Mayo, psychological factors were tested. Almost invariably, it was discovered, output per man increased whenever the workers felt that they were being given considerate attention.[10] Studies in other places reached the same generalization. Sometimes the factor was referred to as "special attention," at other times as "recognition of the individual," "taking an interest in the worker," "taking cognizance of the human needs of the worker," "sympathetic understanding of his problems," or "more intimate contact." Because of the varying terminology it has not yet been duly appreciated that at *all* times the factor referred to was the individual's need for affection, a need arising from conflicts in directives and an affection sought especially from the *rulers* on whom he is dependent, an affection assuring him that he is doing right and will be provided for. The full significance of the intensified need for affection in simple anomie has been as yet imperfectly realized.[11]

This chapter has shown that simple anomie exists in America. Documented by sociologists and psychotherapists, this form of anomie—less severe but more persistent, a constant distraction—has been found expressed in the world of literature and art, in the clients of clinical psychologists, and in factory workers, the army of modern industry. The next step is to determine whether acute anomie, too, can be seen.

CHAPTER SEVEN

OBSERVATIONS OF ACUTE ANOMIE

THE starting-point in a search for acute anomie nicely fits the proverb: Strike the shepherd and the sheep shall be scattered (Zech. 13:7). The *ruler*'s power of reassurance over the political community is one of immeasurable importance. Ordinarily it can scarcely be discerned in people. Yet let an extraordinary event occur, though but the mere presence of supreme authority, and emotions stand out more clearly, like a flat map put in relief. With unsurpassed descriptive skill, Virginia Woolf once captured the feeling of just such an event:

The violent explosion which made Mrs. Dalloway jump and Miss Pym go to the window and apologise came from a motor car which had drawn to the side of the pavement precisely opposite Mulberry's shop window. Passers-by who, of course, stopped and stared, had just time to see a face of the very greatest importance against the dove-grey upholstery, before a male hand drew the blind and there was nothing to be seen except a square of dove grey.

Yet rumours were at once in circulation from the middle of Bond Street to Oxford Street on one side, to Atkinson's scent shop on the other, passing invisibly, inaudibly, like a cloud, swift, veil-like upon hills, falling indeed with something of a cloud's sudden sobriety and stillness upon faces which a second before had been utterly disorderly. But now mystery had brushed them with her wing; they had heard the voice of authority; the spirit of religion was abroad with her eyes bandaged tight and her lips gaping wide. But nobody knew whose face had been seen. Was it the Prince of Wales's, the Queen's, the Prime Minister's? Whose face was it? Nobody knew. . . .

Everything had come to a standstill. The throb of the motor engines sounded like a pulse irregularly drumming through an entire body. The sun became extraordinarily hot because the motor car had stopped outside Mulberry's shop window; old ladies on the tops of omnibuses spread their black parasols; here a green, here a red parasol opened with a little pop. Mrs. Dalloway, coming to the window with her arms full of sweet peas, looked out with her little pink face pursed in enquiry. Every one looked at the motor car. Septimus looked. Boys on bicycles sprang off. Traffic accumulated. . . . Lucrezia herself could not help looking at the motor car and the tree pattern on the blinds. Was it the Queen in there—the Queen going shopping?

The chauffeur, who had been opening something, turning something, shutting something, got on to the box. . . . The motor car with its blinds drawn and an air of inscrutable reserve proceeded towards Piccadilly, still gazed at, still ruffling the faces on both sides of the street with the same dark breath of veneration whether for Queen, Prince, or Prime Minister nobody knew. The face itself had been seen only once by three people for a few seconds. Even the sex was now in dispute. But there could be no doubt that greatness was seated within; greatness was passing, hidden, down Bond Street, removed only by a hand's-breadth from ordinary people who might now, for the first and last time, be within speaking distance of the majesty of England. . . .

It is probably the Queen, thought Mrs. Dalloway, coming out of Mulberry's with her flowers; the Queen. And for a second she wore a look of extreme dignity standing by the flower shop in the sunlight while the car passed at a foot's pace, with its blinds drawn. The Queen going to some hospital; the Queen opening some bazaar, thought Clarissa.

The crush was terrific for the time of day. Lords, Ascot, Hurlingham, what was it? she wondered, for the street was blocked. The British middle classes sitting sideways on the tops of omnibuses with parcels and umbrellas, yes, even furs on a day like this, were, she thought, more ridiculous, more unlike anything there has ever been than one could conceive; and the Queen herself held up; the Queen herself unable to pass. Clarissa was suspended on one side of Brook Street; Sir John Buckhurst, the old Judge on the other, with the car between them (Sir John had laid down the law for years and liked a well-dressed woman) when the chauffeur, leaning ever so slightly, said or showed something to the policeman, who saluted and raised his arm and jerked his head and moved the omnibus to the side and the car passed through. Slowly and very silently it took its way.

Clarissa guessed; Clarissa knew of course; she had seen something white, magical, circular, in the footman's hand, a disc inscribed with a name—the Queen's, the Prince of Wales's, the Prime Minister's?—which, by force of its own lustre, burnt its way through (Clarissa saw the car diminishing, disappearing), to blaze among candelabras, glittering stars, breasts stiff with oakleaves, Hugh Whitbread and all his colleagues, the gentlemen of England, that night in Buckingham Palace. . . .

The car had gone, but it had left a slight ripple which flowed through glove shops and hat shops and tailors' shops on both sides of Bond Street. For thirty seconds all heads were inclined the same way—to the window. Choosing a pair of gloves—should they be to the elbow or above it, lemon or pale grey?—ladies stopped; when the sentence was finished something had happened. Something so trifling in single instances that no mathematical instrument, though capable of transmitting shocks in China, could register the vibration; yet in its fullness rather formidable and in its common appeal emotional; for in all the hat shops and tailors' shops strangers looked at each other and thought of the dead; of the flag; of Empire. In a public house in a back street a Colonial insulted the House of Windsor which led to words, broken beer glasses, and a general shindy, which echoed strangely across the way in the ears of girls buying white underlinen threaded with pure white ribbon for their weddings. For the surface agitation of the passing car as it sunk grazed something very profound.

Gliding across Piccadilly, the car turned down St. James's Street. Tall men, men of robust physique, well-dressed men with their tail-coats and their white slips and their hair raked back who, for reasons difficult to discriminate, were standing in the bow window of Brooks's with their hands behind the tails of their coats, looking out, perceived instinctively that greatness was passing, and the pale light of the immortal presence fell upon them as it had fallen upon Clarissa Dalloway. At once they stood even straighter, and removed their hands, and seemed ready to attend their Sovereign, if need be, to the cannon's mouth, as their ancestors had done before them. . . .

A small crowd meanwhile had gathered at the gates of Buckingham Palace. Listlessly, yet confidently, poor people all of them, they waited; looked at the Palace itself with the flag flying; at Victoria, billowing on her mound, admired her shelves of running water, her geraniums, singled out from the motor cars in the Mall first this one, then that; bestowed emotion, vainly, upon commoners out for a drive; recalled their tribute to keep it unspent while this car passed and that; and all the time let rumour accumulate in their veins and thrill the nerves in their thighs at the thought of Royalty looking at them.[1]

On the Death of the Ruler

Of course this is not a setting for acute anomie but the reverse, the feeling of solidarity. Theoretically, however, to make the transition from solidarity to acute anomie it is only necessary to concentrate on events which appear to affect the *ruler*'s ability to carry out his primary obligations to the political community. What happens, for example, when the *ruler* dies? Few studies on the subject exist. But if only the hypothetical question is asked of moderns, "What difference would it make in your daily life if you became convinced that there is no loving God caring for you?" it becomes possible to see the dark clouds of acute anomie gathering in their minds:

Life would just go black.

I couldn't keep on at all if I didn't believe God cares for me! It's so wrong to lose faith; it isn't God's fault that there's trouble in the world—it's men's sin.

There has been some kind of staying power during these hard times. I have faith in it, as I've always had faith in it. . . . What is true is that *there is something controlling things for good*.

How on earth would we get along without the thought of God? I could never have stood the last election without the thought of God helping the right side.

It would take all the courage out of me.

Life wouldn't hold out no hope for me or all my children. I just trust Him and know He won't disappoint me.[2]

In their heartfelt sincerity, these are rather persuasive expressions. Consider the problem from the *political* side. What is known about it? No one has undertaken to ask the question, "What difference would it make in your daily life if your country ceased to exist as a nation?" That is the very issue that sends men to war. One of the most famous photographs early in World War II showed a picture of a group of Parisians watching the conquering Germans march down the Champs Élysées. The anguish of one Frenchman in particular, evident in pained grimace and bitter tears, seemed to represent the whole group's feeling over the dreaded loss of national identity. The psychological effects of the *ruler*'s demise were more visible, however, in the days of the *ancien régime*, when the *ruler* was a mortal being. Lord Acton said that men, Englishmen and Frenchmen, respectively, died of shock on hearing of the execution of Charles I and Louis XVI.

There is ampler information on the death of more recent *rulers*. When Edward VII of England died, a broadsheet sold on the street at his funeral contained this verse:

> Greatest sorrow England ever had
> When death took away our dear Dad;
> A king was he from head to sole
> Loved by the people one and all.

Apparently the spontaneous appearance of broadsheets in London is a good indication that popular emotions are deeply stirred. Upon the death of George V on January 20, 1936, a correspondent gave the following account of popular behavior:

When George V died, however, no one who talked to his neighbour on the bus, to the charwoman washing the steps, or to the sightseers standing on the street corner could doubt the almost universal feeling of loss. Nor could any perceptive observer fail to notice the peculiarly personal character of this emotion. People who had never even seen the King and who had only heard his voice over the radio talked about him with tears in their eyes as if he were a personal friend or near relative cut off in his prime. . . . I think the clue is to be found, perhaps, in a remark that one heard very frequently at the death of George V. People constantly reiterated that King George "was a father to us all."[3]

During the grave period of George V's illness a psychoanalyst closely observed the reactions of three British patients. All showed aggravated mental and physical symptoms. On the evening following the king's death, one dreamed that he had shot a man resembling his father, one was depressively reminded of his own father's death, and the third dreamed that her own father was dead.[4] An event psychologically similar to the death of a king was the abdication of Edward VIII in December of 1936. In one critical week, while the king held the decision to abdicate in the balance, the public gave signs of extraordinary turmoil. An increase in absenteeism and a spectacular fall in trade were apparent. People seemed to have left off buying, going to theaters, or attending meetings.

The end of World War II provided a unique opportunity to study the psychological role of *rulers*. In Italy, Il Duce, Mussolini, was shot and hanged by his heels; in Germany, Der Führer, Hitler, committed suicide; in Japan, the Sun God, Emperor Hirohito, turned mortal. What happened to the public mind at these crucial times may remain forever a matter of inference. This is particularly regrettable since each of the heads that fell had once occupied the position of *ruler*.

In the studies of royal mortality reviewed above, the picture of acute anomie is not complete. There can be no doubt, however, of (1) the existence of great mental shock, (2) the realization that the *ruler* stood in a paternal relationship to his subjects, and (3) the occurrence of unusual popular behavior.

The one thing lacking is the all-important change in the subjective image of the environment which appeared so clearly in the hypothetical death of the religious *ruler:* "Life would just go black." The most detailed analysis of the psychological effects of the mortality of political *rulers* was made after the death of the President of the United States on April 12, 1945. The reactions of thirty psychoanalytic patients were closely watched for one month. Some of the results are pertinent enough to be given verbatim:

All persons expressed great initial incredulity that the event had actually occurred and some related the unusual measures they had taken to verify the
news. Once belief was definite, all persons felt for a time that "the world" had
changed. Absence of direction in the environment was a dominant fear. "What
will we do?" Another remark was, "What is there to live for now?" Or, "Now
we're all alone." The environment was pictured as potentially hostile. "Who
will save us now?" Or, "Who's going to save the world? Everything's stopped."[5]

The physical symptoms of anxiety were also prominent:

All persons showed a grieving or mourning type of reaction. Many wept at
the news, including one who never before lost emotional control under the anxious rigors of analysis. All persons seemed tense and more strained than usual.

All persons reported abdominally-located sensations and most of them had
gastric disturbances. At the news, they said, their stomach knotted or tensed, or
their stomach seemed to drop, or they had a sinking feeling. The gastric disturbances were mainly of a diarrhoeic character.

It should be clear from the evidence presented in this section
that acute anomie has been observed in adults on the death of the
ruler. Can an event be found that demonstrates what happens
when people believe that their *rulers* are indifferent or uninterested in them, feel no obligation toward them, prefer others to
them, cannot, in short, be counted on to protect them?

On a Political Estrangement

In chapter v a hypothesis concerning acute anomie and the
alienation of *ruler* from community was given, and the case of the
unexpected and vicious revolts of Polish peasants against their
lords was presented in illustration. It may well be that an analogous event never occurred in the United States; still there is one
period in American history which bears a striking resemblance
and should be briefly discussed in this light even though the evidence falls short of proof.

It is almost a banality to repeat that in the United States the
rise of the labor movement has not been colored by the presence
of intense class consciousness or class hatred. But the last quarter
of the nineteenth century was a time when this proposition did
not hold. A series of labor explosions—1877, 1886 (there were
eighteen hundred labor conflicts in this year alone), and 1894—
shattered the peace of the period. Haymarket, Homestead, and
Pullman are names of three of the bloodiest riots in America's

chronicles. Public indignation heightened the blasts of trust-busters and muckrakers. Three now famous critics of capitalism levied their attack—Bellamy, Veblen, Henry George. Memberships swelled in radical organizations; new causes—Populists, Grangers, Socialists, Knights of Labor, Nationalist clubs, bands of the type led by "General" Coxey—sprang up like weeds; armies of unarmed men from all parts of the country marched on Washington. If ever there was class consciousness, it descended on the United States in these years.[6] Whereas before, mass movements of various kinds could have been called radical, these agitations were often revolutionary in the full sense of the word. Inflammatory utterances like that of Governor Waite of Colorado, "It is better that blood should flow to the horses' bridles," filled the air. Propertied persons shivered in apprehension of imminent rebellion. Terrified by strikes, riots, and bombings, they demanded the building of armories in cities. Backed by government cooperation, they crushed with a thoroughness born of fear every stir of radicalism, employing for the purpose police, militia, injunctions, and Pinkertons. On the other side, the muckrakers: Tarbell, Steffens, Baker, Samuel Hopkins Adams, Myer, Russell, Lindsey; the novelists: Howells, Norris, Sinclair, Garland; the scholars: Ross, Croly, Smith, and Lloyd; all testified to the sin and iniquity of the rich. How did this happen in a country so indisposed to class hatred?

The only serious theory given for the frenzied and violent hatred of this period is an economic one. The writers and the historians have more or less taken for granted that the vituperative upheaval naturally followed the sporadic declines in these years of the incomes of farmers and workers. But it is risky to assume that if a wage cut of, say, 10 per cent is announced by a firm, a strike or revolt will ensue. The thesis that class hatred and revolts are provoked by intolerable poverty or hardship in the lower strata of the population does not stand up under scrutiny. Revolutions have occurred in good times and bad with almost equal frequency, and, conversely, they have been absent in times both of severe economic contraction and of general well-being. Indeed if even semistarvation is widespread, rebellion becomes physically impossible. Will disappears with energy. If the flesh is weak, the spirit is unwilling.[7]

One of the few quantitative studies in existence relating economic conditions to social disorders applies in part to this particular case. The economist A. H. Hansen analyzed the number of strikes and strikers in the United States and Canada for the period from 1881 to 1897, a decade and a half of falling prices. The coefficient of correlation between wholesale prices and the number of strikers was −0.388, in the author's own words, a "not entirely convincing relationship."[8] Moreover, the most careful economic analysis of this period makes it difficult to say that the *real earnings* of the workers, agrarian and industrial, actually declined greatly.[9] In fine, the unsupplemented economic theory falls short of real persuasiveness.

The necessary supplementary fact may be that the leaders of business, absorbed in the rich industrial aftermath of the Civil War, enthusiastically overstepped the bounds in their haste to adopt what they thought to be the appropriate way of life of an élite:

The last two decades of the nineteenth century offered a spectacle of parvenudom without a peer. Ostentatious display was given the utmost press publicity, for a man like "Silver Dollar" Tabor was only too anxious to have the world know that even the door-knobs in his palace were of silver. No more abashed in their magnificence than royalty of the European baroque, were the American business men, who had, like kings, made a nation; but the splendor of kings had seemed, not personal, but an integral aspect of their office. . . . It was this difference which caused the naïve whims of the new-rich to exercise so fatal an effect on the public mind of America. . . . In Waldorf's "Peacock Alley" and in San Francisco's "Poodle Dog," millionaires paraded in their newest finery. . . . The very streets of the cities became filled with visions of elegance: ladies "like butterflies . . . with their brilliant and vari-colored dresses, their glittering jewels, their air of sprightly and reckless extravagance." Beside them stalked imposingly solid men: "glossy-headed old nabobs with rubicund noses, bald foreheads, heavy side whiskers, portly bodies and great watch seals, types of prosperous sons of commerce; there are dapper little dandies and ponderous big dandies."[10]

Their wholesale adoption of supposed English customs and clothes, Renaissance paintings and sculpture, Roman orgies and extravaganzas, and extended sojourns on the Continent was well publicized in the press of the day. Nor was the public completely unaware that titled foreigners were being handed five hundred American daughters and two hundred and twenty million American dollars. In these crucial years the society page made its real debut.

Anyone living in the Gilded Age could have recounted numerous tales of the great, their rivalrous expenditure and waste galore. Now ordinarily in well-knit political communities people like to believe the *ruler* lives richly and gives generously—so long as he remains one of them, so long as he is *their ruler*. Even if they are themselves living on a bare subsistence level, they will see that he gets the lion's share.[11] But in this period the captains of industry unwittingly separated themselves from the community at a time when they should have been reaffirming mutual ties. The introduction of Savile Row trouser cuffs was greeted on the streets with the taunt, "It must be raining in London." Some of the "swells" of the time tried what Mencken abbreviates as PSP—British public school pronunciation. Many individuals experimented with "been," "jolly well," "dontcherknow," "right you are," and "frightfully"; while at the same time "high tea became a fashionable rite, and pink coats came into favor among huntsmen." A song of the late eighties went to the heart of the matter:

> O, the things that we say and the queer things we do
> Are "English, you know! Quite English, you know!"[12]

By importing alien cultivation, accents, clothes, and manners, they repudiated their leadership of a community which had believed in them and banked on their support. In a figurative sense they deserted their family in an hour of need. And in a literal sense, too, for the cult of the freshly discovered family tree dates from this period's race for genealogies, coats-of-arms, and sundry other proofs of European roots. Another event of the day which may have held a like meaning for the populace was the vast immigration from Europe. The "taking of jobs from Americans" and the giving of them to foreigners, although a logical result of the internationalism of capitalism, must surely have added to the feelings of neglect. In the political system of beliefs, preference should be shown the citizen. Even had the times been good, such action would have created great resentment and disunity. The mass embracing of third-party movements, of panaceas like the single tax, and of utopias like the Nationalist clubs (which, inspired by Edward Bellamy, numbered one hundred and sixty-three in the year 1891) indicated that people felt leaderless and protectionless, without a system of beliefs to guide them in their troubles. In a word—anomic.[13] And hatred fanned by the seeming hypocrisy of their rulers fiercely burned:

> Wall Street owns the country. It is no longer a government of the people, by the people, and for the people, but a government of Wall Street, by Wall Street, and for Wall Street. . . . Our laws are the output of a system that clothes rascals in riches and honesty in rags. The parties lie to us, and the political speakers mislead us. . . . the people are at bay, and the bloodhounds of money who have dogged us thus far beware![14]

The turbulence generated in spots of real economic distress, a turbulence which otherwise might not have grown, swiftly spread out of its local origins. The immediate situation was exploited by propagandists who—and this is what makes the gulf between *ruler* and ruled the crucial factor—by propagandists who, without a plan, were co-operating with fellow-propagandists in other areas by attacking a common symbolic enemy—the "Capitalist," the bloated monopolist, with checkered suit, white vest, top hat, heavy in paunch and jowl, and bedecked with a miscellaneous array of diamonds. The era gave birth to the greatest period of cartooning in American history. If, as one student of the subject says, the cartoonist "starves in times of brotherly love,"[15] in the three decades after 1875 he grew fat. A flood of cartoons and caricatures arose mocking the *ton* and the aping of English customs. The century culminated in the Bradley Martin ball of 1897 at the Waldorf, costing a third of a million dollars, while the next century began with the James Hazen Hyde ball at Sherry's to the somewhat thinner tune of $200,000. Was it any wonder that the public uproar drove both hosts into European exile?

The activities of the parvenu in this period bear an amazing resemblance to the phenomena described by Mosca. In the Bradley Martin ball, for example, not one "restored feather on a pheasant served *à la mode*" escaped popular notice. Even the fact that for days a *quadrille d'honneur* had been rehearsing at Mrs. Astor's under the tutelage of Professor Karl Marwig was brought to public attention by a scare headline in the *Times*. As for the Hyde affair:

A gilded youth, James Hazen Hyde, eight years after the Bradley-Martin Ball at the Waldorf, gave one more brilliant at Sherry's which was transformed into the Palace of Versailles. But where Mrs. Martin had chosen the period of Louis XIV, Hyde selected one with yet more unfortunate associations, and greeted his guests in the robes of the ill-fated Louis XVI. Promptly the people intimated that they knew history too, and were prepared to play their part, if drama was desired. Amid the general roar of rage, a sweeping investigation was started which uncovered startling frauds in the Equitable Life Insurance Company, a concern bequeathed to Hyde by his father. Hastily abdicating, the "last of the Capetians" fled to France. But the popular storm, gathering volume, swept on to the muckraking and trust-busting explosion that carried Theodore Roosevelt to triumph.[16]

It might be wondered, since many of the participants in these prodigalities were not far removed from "the generation of shirtsleeves," how they could be so far removed from the pulse of the public. Mrs. Bradley Martin's statements and actions, for example, disclosed a yawning chasm between the upper and lower strata: "One morning at breakfast during the winter of 1896-7 Mrs. Bradley Martin, reading of depressed conditions and the sufferings of the poor, suddenly decided to have a ball 'to give an impetus to trade.' As she pursued this ideal it grew grander and grander, until she ended by stimulating trade to the extent of $369,200."[17] An explanation for the lack of simple foresight may be found in the growth of trusts and absentee ownership in this period, a period generally described as in transition from industrial to finance capitalism and one which more and more separated the owner from his workers, interposing a wall of paper. Somewhat later Theodore Roosevelt recognized the trend with the following words:

The old familiar, intimate relations between employer and employee were passing. A few generations before, the boss had known every man in his shop; he had called his men Bill, Tom, Dick, John; he inquired after their wives and babies; he swapped jokes and stories and perhaps a bit of tobacco with them. In the small establishment there had been a friendly human relationship between employer and employee.

There was no such relation between the great railway magnates, who controlled the anthracite industry, and the one hundred and fifty thousand men who worked in their mines, or the half million women and children who were dependent upon these miners for their daily bread. Very few of these mine workers had ever seen, for instance, the president of the Reading Railroad. . . . The workman saw . . . that the labor problem was not only an economic, but also a moral, a human problem.[18]

In 1867 stock tickers were installed on Wall Street. The following year the exchange dealt in securities to the value of three billion dollars, marking a good beginning for high finance.

Perhaps it is to be wondered instead, then, that someone did have enough presence of mind to summon Pinkerton detectives, even though they marred the illusion of a hall in Versailles, for rumors were afloat that persons had been caught planting bombs under the Bradley Martin home and that others planned to hurl them through the Waldorf's windows.

In seeking causes for the end of the embryonic revolution in this part of American history, one must not neglect the clear fact of *force majeure* in the hands of the authorities. This lone fact, however, cannot account for the quick collapse of the struggle, for the subsequent legality of mass movements, for the "business unionism" and "class collaboration" in succeeding years. Nor does it help much to cite the progressive legislation of 1896 to 1912 which greatly benefited neither labor nor "little business." But one thing is certain. All sources agree that after the popular storms of the era the difference in appearance between the big businessman and the rest of the population dwindled:

This tendency was more marked after the popular storms of the "trust-busting" era; then business men put away flashy waistcoats and embroidered braces and, from the heights to the depths, from the tremendous hog-slaughterers to the simplest salmon-canners, went into quiet suits and quiet manners, with mildly twinkling eyes. They assured biographers that, though "public-spirited," they were averse to public posts, that their hobbies were far from eccentric and their characters, simple and genial, were not distinguished in any particular. At the same time, they surrendered the passion for horse-flesh which has ever been associated with the social climbing of business men into a "horsy" feudal aristocracy; some went so far in their renunciation that they took up cow-fancying instead, as did the banker, James Stillman, who explained: "The more you see of horses the faster you get, but the more you see of cows, the more refined you get."[19]

In 1911 the brother of Bradley Martin published a book entitled *The Passing of the Idle Rich*. Many persons have cited this work for the tales it contains of the lives of the profuse rich, but few have realized that it marks the beginning of a new philosophy of rulership.[20] From the 1880's on there had been Catos warning the dominant group in the Republic to mend its ways, but Martin's book entombed a dying "age of arrogance." The public demanded that the gods reflect its own image. "Idleness," proclaimed Martin, "is doomed as a vocation." The queen bees, like the drones, began to ask one another what each did for a living. Businessmen penned volumes protesting the intensity of their labors and the simplicity of their tastes. By 1910 the American Baroque was over. As Miriam Beard concluded in her *History of the Business Man*, "If fond of displaying themselves in the robes of Bourbons, it must be said that the American rich were not so blind. They swiftly wrapped tissue paper about their crowns and put away their royal robes in moth-balls. . . . The American at least knew when to take off his Louis-Quatorze ruffles and hide away his wig and sword." In more ways than one, this was the end of a century.

On the Failure of Ruling Obligations

The third and final angle from which observations of acute anomie will be sighted reverses the proverb in this fashion: If the sheep are scattered, the shepherd must lie smitten. In a country where an essential part of the *ruler*'s obligations is military victory the rout of his armies in the field frequently leads to his overthrow at home. The populace has firsthand evidence that in this matter so vital for them the *ruler* is impotent. Chiefly for this reason defeats in war are often followed by revolutions. In capitalist countries prosperity is the primary obligation of the businessman. Prosperity means the provision of jobs to all who follow the directives of the economic ideology. Possession of a job insures the holder of his status in the community; he has the income and respect which fend off separation-anxiety. Periods of deep unemployment, therefore, ought to contribute much to the existing stock of observations, for if the jobholder loses the job, he should be gripped by acute anomie.

All students of the psychological effects of unemployment seem to agree that a definite sequence appears in persons who have lost their jobs: First, there is shock or great fear, followed (after an attempt to calm down) by an intensive hunt for work. If all efforts fail, the person becomes anxious, suffering active distress. This, say the writers, is the most critical stage, with attacks of fear and thoughts or attempts at suicide. And, third, the individual becomes fatalistic or resigned, his behavior marked by sober acquiescence or dumb apathy.[21] Both the first shock and the anxiety of the second period are attacks of acute anomie. The unemployed frequently resemble patients suffering from anxiety neurosis. As one study observed, "Fear seems to be taken into account far too little when considering the experiences of the unemployed. However, it seems that fear of the cruel tomorrow, the feeling of being hunted to earth, of being hemmed in, and absolute helplessness, are very typical."[22]

This is a lucid statement of the image of a hostile environment which characterizes the anxiety of acute anomie. The "hemmed in" and "trapped" feeling has etymological connections with the Latin *angustiae*, the French *angoisse*, and the German *Angst*, which all stem from a root meaning "pressure," "constriction," or "narrowness." Variations in the image will appear, for in each case different individual factors will have contributed to the person's conception of the environment. But in almost every instance the feeling of a hostile world is present. One author states that the unemployed feel that "life has forgotten them." The members of one family feel "as if the end of the world had come and they almost lost their desire to live." Others say that there are many times when "we feel the water closing over our heads." While yet another person asserts that "for a time, awakening in the morning is unbearable. The world becomes ever gloomier and viler. One sees in it neither pity nor friendship."[23] These statements should not be accepted as mere figures of speech. To regard them as such is to follow the example of the man who said, "I don't believe in ghosts, but I've been afraid of them all my life." People actually feel themselves in the fell clutch of sinister circumstance. At the moment the blow falls—"Your services are no longer required"—the world turns darker and chillier. Later, in a period prolonged by anxiety, it has grown cold, bleak, and hostile.

Biographical and autobiographical accounts are perhaps best for depicting the anxiety and subjective change of the environment in acute anomie. The following narrative is told by the wife of an unemployed man:

Then—crash! . . . "Sorry, Mark, but your job is no good any more."

I remember the sense of bewilderment and the all-gone feeling I had at the pit of my stomach at that time. It was as though the floor had suddenly floated out from under me.

I nursed [my husband] through a short physical illness that the shock and anger caused by such treatment had brought on.

As autumn wore on and so many bright prospects faded into thin air, while our precious bank account was painfully shrinking toward its last hundred, our mutual anxiety was sharpened into agony. We would find each other lying awake at night, tense with worry. . . . My own nerves were threadbare, and very often I gave way to fits of weeping when alone.

I knew, with every nerve quivering, that the "wolf at the door" proverb was a real, actual horror, beside which a real wolf from a Russian forest would have been as little to be feared as a large tabby cat. For the first time I have come to realize what is back of the commonplace paragraph I have so often encountered in the newspapers: "Man Out of Work Commits Suicide." And I have trembled if the step at the door was late, lest such a thought might have occurred to my own breadwinner.

Mark no longer tried to hide his despondency. His nervous state was such that each night, if he were a little late for supper and had not 'phoned, I became anxious. One night six o'clock came, then seven, then eight, but no husband. I telephoned to all the places where he might have been likely to be. At ten I found him on a neighboring park bench, sobbing like a child. . . .

We still bear the scars of those "five months out of work." In the back of our minds is always the fear that through illness or unforeseen circumstances, the experience may be repeated. . . .

Always, we have the dim sense of living close to a precipice—the common fate, I suppose, of the average skilled or unskilled worker who sells his services for a weekly wage in this great era of prosperity.[24]

Soon, other human beings begin to be eyed with suspicion and fear. For one reason or another, the unemployed man goes through a period when he feels more and more alone.[25] Not only men, but man-made machines take on a threatening, animistic mien. The operation of man and machine is not the cool, superficial relationship that the term "tool" conveys. Even in days of

full employment, the machine possesses for the worker an uncanny significance.[26]

But why talk about men? There's a new machine being developed in my
plant right now. I've seen it. It's almost human. When they get that ready, it
will knock ten or twelve men out of work. That's the problem.

Did you ever hear of the Shoemaker's Union? No, of course you didn't. There
ain't none. It's the Shoe *Operatives* Union. . . . Damn the machines, anyway.

It's a race between the machine and labour, and the machine is winning.

When, to a man who is minding a machine, that machine appears uncanny
because of its great strength or because of the complicated nature of the task it
can perform, it assumes a threatening, sinister, and hostile aspect, producing an
impression like that aroused in a man who for the first time has to deal with a
horse or with an element.[27]

It should not be surprising that the unemployed view the machine as a demonic force, a *daemon ex machina*. The constant bring-
ing-in of new machines gives them the impression of an uncontrollable, merciless swarming. E. Wight Bakke's observations of
The Unemployed Man are pertinent: "Machinery is the most prominent feature of his world. It is most quickly blamed for the
uncertainties of employment. It is almost a personal diabolical
force to him. Each man has at his tongue's end a number of concrete instances of the victory of machine over man."
The impact of the environment's depriving nature comes from
its utter disorderliness, its unpredictability, its rulelessness. There
seem to be no directives for securing assurance against anxiety.
The key the person holds in his hand no longer opens the gate.
Yet it is the same key that smoothly tumbled the lock before. The
confusion of jobless men in a depression is that they can see no responsibility of their own, no evil action on their part, with which
to rationalize their loss of status. "If I only knew," cries the man
out of work, "if I only knew what handsprings these chaps want
me to turn for them, I'd turn them; but I just can't find out."[28]
Despite the hopelessness of continued attempts, the unemployed
often will go back again and again to their last place of work.
The sense of futility of all efforts is a regular finding in unemployment researches:

Somehow the plans don't come like they used to. I reckon I've tried them all. And it's up at five-thirty or six in the morning to start out again. But you don't wake up feeling like going again. For you don't know which way to go. But you do. . . . *It isn't the hard work of tramping about so much, although that is bad enough. It's the hopelessness of every step you take when you go in search of a job you know isn't there.*

Bakke further observes that the root of the person's demoralization is buried in his aimlessness:

The usual state of mind [of the unemployed] in the morning is "What way shall I turn?" . . . The sense of bewilderment, of having exhausted the possibilities, of not knowing which way to turn . . . are factors which are made only partly less severe by the granting of unemployment benefit. Pack these conditions into a man's mind and heart and you will realize that each step he takes on the long trek in search of a job which he knows is not there, jolts the very foundations of his faith.[29]

Sooner or later, the splintering frame punctures the portrait of the *ruler*. The highest figure in the economic ideology, like the painting of Dorian Gray, begins to change in the eyes of the jobless, eyes which grow more jaundiced as the workless period lengthens.[30] If there are no effective directives, where are the *rulers?* The businessman, whose eminence is due to his imputed ability to provide jobs, retains his uppermost status position so long as unemployment is not lasting and widespread. Once more the perspicacity of Bakke has a special relevance:

An exceedingly important factor in moulding the attitudes of the working-class man is the impression that his destinies are controlled by beings outside his ken. Those who tell him what he may do, how much he may have for his work, and whether he may work at all; those who make the rules which govern his daily routine, the paying of his rent, the buying of his food, and the education of his children; these live in another world. He vaguely refers to them as "they." . . . He reads of their doings in the newspapers. He learns something of their activities from the cinema. He sees them sometimes from a distance, he may have occasional encounters with them and, if he is particularly fortunate and socially acceptable, he may "edge his way" into some organization or society to which members of the master class belong. But for the most part, "they" are remote, impersonal and unknown to him.

The fact that certain people habitually control has, in the minds of numerous workmen, created the feeling that special qualifications are required for that function. . . . As long as his job runs smoothly and the organization of his daily life is carried on with a fair degree of comfort, the faith that those who make the decisions must be especially qualified for that task and that on the whole those best qualified are members of the "master" class is not seriously shaken. . . .

These workers respect their employers and their rulers. They are proud of them when they are worthy according to the worker's standard of worthiness. . . . The individual worker realizes that in decisions, he is not at home. He knows that some men are at home in that world and he admires them for it.

Thus, with the following words, a youthful speaker met the taunts of a revolutionary party. "These agitators, they say, 'Away with the bosses,' but what will they put in their place? We need bosses, don't we? Otherwise we are like sheep without a sheep dog. If the sheep have a good sheep dog they keep together and all is well. If not, they scatter and get into bad places."[31]

Now this section of the chapter began with the twisting of a proverb about the scattering of sheep. As the rejoinder of the young speaker implied, if the sheep are in a bad way, the average person deduces that they lack a good sheep dog. And in this vein, Bakke continues:

Luck is assumed to be much more directly and completely in the hands of this "master class" than in supernatural hands. The unknown is there. It is undetermined by the workers' will. But its operation, though not understood by him, is assumed to be understood by the Olympian rulers of his destiny. . . . In case an uncomfortable state of affairs occurs, the worker blames indiscriminately any man or group of men belonging to this world . . . not because the worker knows for a fact that they are to blame; but because they belong to the "boss class" and therefore must be to blame.

In a nation where an economic *ruler* is not completely committed to prosperity, the political ideology may be questioned: "Now where is the Fatherland which the poets sing about, which should be a mother for a citizen who loves his country? . . . Should happiness and welfare be the lot of only a few lucky gamblers? Should the Fatherland be like this?"[32] In America there can be no doubt but that the businessman has been held responsible for jobs.[33] The beginnings of a dubious wonder appear in the following account of a man without a job:

The suffering, spiritual and mental and physical, entailed in an epidemic of unemployment must be greater than that of an epidemic of mere physical illness. If our business executives . . . could but see the unemployment problem in that light, instead of as a sort of Act of God, as the smallpox we no longer have was viewed years ago; if they could but understand—as I now do—what agony it brings to its victims, would they not be able to do away with it? Or must we be forced to believe that, as the radicals tell us, American business will never learn to think in human terms?[34]

But the individual's specific attitude toward the *ruler* who has been derelict in his obligations has several potential variations. In this book it was necessary to select mass unemployment as a situation in which to observe acute anomie because intensive psychological work had been done with the victims of economic contractions. Nevertheless, much depends on whether a man sees himself alone out of work or sees a queue of others like himself outside an employment office. Generally it determines the measures he will take to free himself from anomic tension. This problem, therefore, must await the next chapters. Here it remains to be said that in either event the individual feels that the ministrations of the *ruler* do not include him and that he is once again alone in an unmanageable, hostile environment; in either event, the anxiety of separation sweeps over him. The possibility of being able to live out his complex and, within broad limits, culturally inflexible pattern of satisfactions seems washed out, a total loss.

PART IV

THE THEORY OF ANOMIE
II. CONSEQUENCES

INTRODUCTION

MANY and diverse are the ways in which the person can react to anomic conditions. To predict the manner of the individual's adjustment is impossible without an intensive analysis of his prior reactions to separation-anxiety, combined with detailed knowledge of his immediate situation. In speaking of a collection of individuals, however, one can distinguish a factor that greatly affects the modes of adjustment. It is an important element in determining whether the response will be individual —an attempt to reach a solution within one's own mind and body; or collective—an attempt at a solution involving numbers of other persons. This factor is the amount of popular approval or disapproval attached to particular individual versus particular collective adjustments. In the United States, for example, a person's conversion to communism, an attempt at collective adjustment, would arouse more popular disfavor than another person's chronic alcoholism, an individual effort. And acting upon this factor itself are two other influences: (1) the possible effect of the mode of adjustment on the prevailing systems of beliefs (thus communism, in the above example, invites mass violation of the competitive directive, whereas alcoholism is merely a lone and indirect impairment of the work directive) and (2) the incidence of anomie, simple or acute, in the community.

A comprehensive chart here might help to visualize not only the relation of earlier chapters but also the last-mentioned possibility of different incidences of anomie. The graph on the next page portrays fluctuating levels of separation-anxiety and anomie through the life-span of one generation in several fictional communities.[1]

The curves $A-B$, $C-D$, and $E-F$ represent the different levels of simple anomie in separate communities, each reflecting a degree of conflict between belief-systems: $A-B$ the highest, $C-D$ a midway position, and $E-F$ with little or no simple anomie. The point now is that in communities with levels $A-B$ and $C-D$ there will be a greater propensity for collective adjustments to

HYPOTHETICAL LEVELS OF SEPARATION-ANXIETY AND ANOMIE IN COMMUNITIES

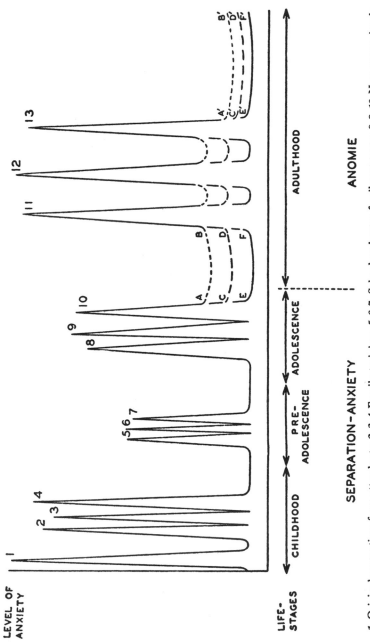

1, Original separations from attendants; *2, 3, 4*, Family training; *5, 6, 7*, School and extra-family contacts; *8, 9, 10*, New-status rituals; *11, 12, 13*, Unemployment, loss of *ruler*, mass-movement temper.

anomie than in a community with level E–F.[2] Similarly, in all communities at times of prevailing acute anomie, represented by curves *11*, *12*, and *13*, there will be a greater propensity for collective adjustment than in communities even with so high a level of simple anomie as A–B, for the fact that persons suffering from anomie do not call it that nor recognize it as a diagnosable condition does not mean that they cannot perceive and sympathize with the feeling in other persons. Once the perception that many others are in the same miserable state occurs, a greater inclination appears toward attempting adjustments in concert. From the political standpoint, the collective reactions to anomie are the more important. Therefore, although in a systematic discussion of possible consequences the individual solutions cannot be ignored, more attention will be paid the former category, that is, the collective attempts to reduce anomic tension.

CHAPTER EIGHT

ADAPTATIONS TO SIMPLE ANOMIE

IT IS not difficult to show logically what the reactions to anomie must be. The case of simple anomie has already been described by theory and by observation as showing an unusually strong need for affection. Simple anomie is the persistent low-level tension which, practically speaking, can be relieved only by affection.[1] No quantitative measures exist, however, for the measurement of a high or low need of affection. Perforce, then, in the pages that follow, comparative standards will be used.

The only way of judging whether the need for affection is great is to employ contrasting data, data comparing the adaptive behavior of groups of anomic persons or communities to that of less anomic groups.

Affection in Work Life

Outside a life of reverie[2] the sole manner in which individuals can satisfy a need of affection is by human intercourse. In the work activities of modern man, where the competitive and activist directives apply in fullest force, opportunities for personal relationships are circumscribed.[3] There is no even balance, however, but a variation among jobs. Some are popularly supposed to be less competitive, less impersonal, less rationalistic, and less activistic; others, more. A review of the usual occupational groups listed by the United States Census or similar classifications shows employments catalogued as farming, fishing, mining, clerical, manufacturing, trade and transportation, domestic and personal service, professional service, and so on. It is not contended that all persons accurately know of the working conditions of every one of these categories or have the freedom to move in whatever bracket they choose. But each person does have notions of the characteristics of some occupations or classes of occupations within his ken—lawyers, doctors, bricklayers, machinists, laborers—and these notions, in so far as they fit his preferences, influence his movement inside the range, however small, of his choice. Some jobs are "friendlier," they "deal with people," "you don't punch a time clock," "you can come or go when you please." Possibly the professions, as a class, with teachers, musicians, lawyers, artists, doctors, authors, actors, and so forth, would be rated the lowest in competitive and activist directives by the public. And despite the introduction of civil service systems, governmental employment also has a low rating. The commercial, mechanical, and agricultural pursuits probably receive the highest rankings. By no means, however, can finer classifications be avoided. Thus, in the field of transportation, it is one thing to be a clerk or a dispatcher at a desk, and quite another to be a truck driver in the open air with a host of different associations. Finding himself planted in a commercial field, the person who feels conflict over the competitive or activist directives will lean toward the less competitive or less activist areas of business. Consider the case of this former foreman whose wife tells the story:

> The men are treated just like a number. The men themselves don't matter, it's just the work. I may be prejudiced. . . . Another thing my husband didn't like about working at that company, he was supposed to push the men too hard. He didn't like to drive them as hard as he was supposed to. . . . The company expected to get too much work from its people. Ed never did blame his workers for not putting out as much as was expected of them. . . . The company was always jumping them for everything. My brother-in-law was a nervous wreck there, like my husband, but he's a changed man now. He got out of the shop because he hated it. Many is the time that the four of us have sat right here in this room, and talked about nothing but the shops. . . . Luckily, the both of them are now out of that. My husband used to ask to be put back on the line. He didn't make enough more with a better job to make up for all the grief he had. The company wants very much to get Ed back. The foreman came around to the garage where he works and everything, but Ed says he never will go back, and I hope he never has to.[4]

Now Catholics, more than Protestants, should endeavor to give a wide berth to those occupations which they believe to be saturated with the competitive and activist directives, for was it not shown in the previous analysis of the differences between Catholics and Protestants in impersonalism, rationalism, and activism that the clash of the family and religious belief-systems with the business ideology is greater among Catholics? To the extent that statistics on the subject can be found they bear out the thesis of a Catholic disinclination for the business directives. Max Weber summed up the researches:

> A glance at the occupation statistics of any country of mixed religious composition brings to light with remarkable frequency . . . the fact that business leaders and owners of capital, as well as the higher grades of skilled labour, and even more the higher technically and commercially trained personnel of modern enterprises, are overwhelmingly Protestant.[5]

A better indication of the Catholic demurral is the extent to which students of that religious affiliation go into humanist or professional schooling rather than into the technical studies of commercial and industrial occupations. Statistics for Baden, Bavaria, Prussia, Württemberg, Alsace-Lorraine, and Hungary demonstrate that among the Catholics graduating from higher educational institutions, a considerably lower proportion (as compared to Protestant graduates) had chosen academic training for a business vocation.[6] Although there is a total lack of quantitative studies of this type for the United States, writers have shown the different relationships of Protestantism and Catholicism to capitalism in numerous ways: by describing the important support for early capitalism given by the Protestant churches;[7] by following the many special connections of Calvinism and Puritanism with business;[8] by ascertaining the lack of Catholics among the great American magnates or the richer class in general;[9] by relating the practical dealings between Protestant churches and businessmen;[10] by scrutinizing the "Gospel of Wealth," wherein the deity is implicated by Protestant businessmen in a manner exemplified by the phrase, "God gave us our money";[11] by observing the increased business efficiency of workers who have acquired an invigorated Protestant sectarianism;[12] by tracing the development of business ethics among Protestant sects, like the Quakers and the Baptists;[13] and, finally, by describing the difficulties with the business ethic that afflicted not only the Catholic immigrants but also the emigrated followers of early Lutheranism, which least among the Reformation religions (it will be recalled) bore the impress of the competitive directive.[14]

A student of the occupational differences between Catholics and Protestants once said, "The Catholic is quieter, having less of the acquisitive impulse. . . . The proverb says jokingly 'either eat well or sleep well.' In the present case, the Protestant prefers to eat well, the Catholic to sleep undisturbed." To this well-put statement one can only add that the Catholic fights shy of commercial life not only because he feels a somewhat greater conflict in it than the Protestant but also because, to him, labor has no reinforcing motives. The Catholic feels no mission to change the face of the earth by his work. That "continuous labor of an unexciting kind" which J. S. Mill believed essential for real civilization seems naught but a striving after wind.

Affection in Life outside Work

It may be reasonably expected that, given a period of the day which consistently engenders conflicts in directives, persons in the remainder of their day will try somehow, through their relationships with other people, to restore their peace of mind. One simple way of classifying relationships is by the number of people involved in them. In this fashion man's daily nonwork life can be viewed as composed typically of intercourse with one other person, such as in courtship and friendship; with several persons, as in the fruitful marriage or the family; and with numerous persons, as in voluntary associations. These are the affiliations that should reveal, even more than the working relationships considered above, the expression of the need for affection in modern democracies. Each of them, as they are respectively discussed, should appear exaggerated in contrast.to other cultures.[15]

In *Othello* the dark-skinned hero is made by the poet to say:

> Excellent wretch! Perdition catch my soul
> But I do love thee! And when I love thee not,
> Chaos is come again.

This extreme need of affection from a unique member of the opposite sex is not characteristic of Shakespeare's time.[16] In the English renaissance that was the Elizabethan age, the more appropriate spirit was "Men have died from time to time and worms have eaten them, but not for love." The sentiment of the Moor of Venice better fits the age of the Industrial Revolution and, more particularly, the United States, now the irradiating center of a cultural trait known as "romantic love."

The characteristics of modern courtship practices and marriage ideals—"An engrossing emotional attachment between a man and a woman, exclusive and individualized, transcending at need all sorts of obstacles, involving some kind of idealization, and enveloping the sex relationship in an aura of tender sentiment"[17]— have not been typical of the time-hallowed affiliations of male and female. In truth it is difficult to find in any other culture the same phenomena comparably combined and called "love." According to the anthropologist Ralph Linton:

> Most societies are less keen on romance than on congeniality. They train their young people to believe that any well-bred boy and girl, once married, will be able to live together contentedly and will in time develop a real fondness for each other. In most cases this seems to be correct. The percentage of happy arranged marriages is probably as high as that of happy romantic marriages, and they are likely to be much more satisfactory to the families involved.

In the days of knight-errantry marriage was considered the death knell of romantic love. For the Greeks marriage was distinct from sexual relations or love. They too thought the sentiment of love a thing apart from juridical marriage. To find in Greek life or literature a free-born Greek woman who married for love is well-nigh impossible. The Greeks preferred a division of labor among women. "We have hetaerae for our delight," said Demosthenes, "concubines for the daily needs of our bodies, wives in order that we may beget legitimate children and have faithful housekeepers." Though the ideals of Greek love varied greatly from period to period and even from city to city, they never sought to unite men's affection for hetaera, for concubine, and for wife into an apotheosis of love for one woman.

The ancients, it is true, recognized something akin to romantic love, but they thought it an affliction, a temporary insanity, and vigorously warned the young against it. The counsel of Lucretius, the Latin poet and philosopher of the Golden Age, makes an ideal example:

> For the most part men act blinded by passion, and assign to women excellencies which are not truly theirs. . . . And one man laughs at another, and urges him to appease Venus, since he is wallowing in a base passion, yet often, poor wretch, he cannot see his own ills, far greater than the rest. A black love is

called "honey-dark," the foul and filthy "unadorned," the green-eyed "Athena's image," the wiry and wooden "a gazelle," the squat and dwarfish "one of the graces," "all-pure delight," the lumpy and ungainly "a wonder," and "full of majesty." She stammers and cannot speak, "she has a lisp"; the dumb is "modest"; the fiery, spiteful gossip is "a burning torch." One becomes a "slender darling," when she can scarce live from decline; another half dead with cough is "frail." Then the fat and full-bosomed is "Ceres' self with Bacchus at breast"; the snub-nosed is "sister to Silenus, or a Satyr"; the thick-lipped is "a living kiss." More of this sort it were tedious for me to try to tell. . . . Surely there are others too: surely we have lived without her before, surely she does just the same in all things, and we know it, as the ugly, and of herself, poor wretch, reeks of noisome smells, and her maids flee far from her and giggle in secret.

Be on the watch beforehand, even as I have taught you, and . . . beware that you be not entrapped.[18]

Among primitives, the

sentiments of romantic love play no part in the motives that lead to the association of the sexes in primitive society. [Yet] that conclusion does not by any means imply that primitive man is incapable of affection or of attachment. The reverse is, on the contrary, the truth. Other things being equal, there is probably a greater disposition to whole-hearted, if perhaps less deep and constant, affection in primitive than in civilised man. The whole structure of primitive human society rests upon such sentiments. "Affection, with the savage," justly remarks Miss Kingsley, "is not so deeply linked with sex; but the love between mother and child, man and man, brother and sister, woman and woman, is deep, pure and true." . . . Primitive man is prone as civilised man to sensual desire; he is equally capable of tender affection; what is unknown to him is the intimate combination of the two.[19]

But to return to modern times in the United States:

All societies recognize that there are occasional violent emotional attachments between persons of opposite sex, but our present American culture is practically the only one which has attempted to capitalize these and make them the basis for marriage. Most groups regard them as unfortunate and point out the victims of such attachments as horrible examples. Their rarity in most societies suggests that they are psychological abnormalities to which our own culture has attached an extraordinary value just as other cultures have attached extreme values to other abnormalities. The hero of the modern American movies is always a romantic lover just as the hero of the old Arab epic is always an epileptic.[20]

One might append to this: not only "the hero of the modern American movie" but of the popular song, novel, and radio drama and then agree that the forms of love are today peculiarly fused into the vision of a singular person of the opposite sex, at once sacred and profane, of this world and the next, desired supremely for a permanent attachment called marriage. Such a love offers nothing so much as an island of hope where two, at least, in a world raked by rivalry and dark with indifference, can ever be true to each other.

Friendship, perhaps more than romantic love, is a subject of delicate intricacy. Even Plato, the author of *Lysis, or Friendship*, Plato, whose name is attached to several varieties of it, confessed his perplexity:

> I can only, like the wise men who argue in courts, sum up the arguments. If neither the beloved, nor the lover, nor the like nor the unlike, nor the good, nor the congenial, nor any other of whom we spoke—for there were such a number of them that I cannot remember all—if, I say, none of these are friends, I know not what remains to be said. . . . Here is a jest: you two boys, and I, an old boy, who would fain be one of you, imagine ourselves to be friends, and we have not as yet been able to discover what is a friend.

It would be easy to sidestep the problem by simply reporting that the amount of scholarly writing on the subject is negligible. Indeed, to do so is almost imperative! Nevertheless, a few speculative remarks ought to be tried.

In *Civilization and Its Discontents*, Sigmund Freud inadvertently approached the subject by describing some of the modern restrictions on love:

> Present-day civilization gives us plainly to understand that sexual relations are permitted only on the basis of a final, indissoluble bond between a man and woman; that sexuality as a source of enjoyment for its own sake is unacceptable to it; and that its intention is to tolerate it only as the hitherto irreplaceable means of multiplying the human race. This, of course, represents an extreme.

If it be assumed that the lack of data on friendship is itself significant, is itself a datum, then the words of the Viennese physician are pertinent. In the United States deviation from heterosexual relations is a harsh transgression of morality. Legendary stories of friends—Patroclus and Achilles, Orestes and Pylades, Damon and Pythias, Theseus and Pirithous—do not appear in such a culture, for an exclusive association of two members of the same sex is suspect. The important philosophical works on friendships are to be found in communities that permitted greater freedom in this respect, for instance, the classical Greek and Indian

cultures. Think of the idea of friendship in Montaigne's *Essays*—
"each man doth so wholly give himself unto his friend, that he
hath nothing left him to divide elsewhere"—a completely exclusive view; "this amity which possesseth the soul . . . it is impossible it should be double." Turn to the *Essays* of Emerson:

> Let him be to me a spirit. A message, a thought, a sincerity, a glance from
> him, I want, but not news, nor pottage. . . . Should not the society of my friend
> be to me poetic, pure, universal and great, as nature itself? . . . Love is only the
> reflection of a man's own worthiness from other men. Men have sometimes ex-
> changed names with their friends, as if they would signify that in their friend
> each loved his own soul.

In the twentieth century these quotations sound like expressions
of romantic love. To speak or act in such manner would occasion,
first, general suspicion, then, unmistakable disapproval.

Perhaps for this reason an inverse relationship may exist between romantic love and *l'amitié à deux*. Where one is much in
evidence, the other is likely to be neither seen nor heard. The excellent researches of Lauren J. Mills in *One Soul in Bodies Twain*
enabled him to summarize the seesaw pattern in six formulas:

1. A and B are friends; B loves C; consequently A loves C, since A and B are
   alike in interests and equal in most ways—"One soul in two bodies." B resigns C to A. Friendship surpasses love.
2. A and B are friends; B loves C; A voluntarily or by request woos C for B.
   C loves A instead of B. B, learning of the situation, resigns C to A.
3. A and B are friends; B loves C; A woos C for B; C loves A (as in 2). B accuses
   A of unfair tactics. A duel ensues, followed by reconcilation or fatal results.
4. A and B are friends; B loves C but for some reason ceases to love her and resigns her to A. C refuses to accept A unless he kills B. A reconciliation or
   tragic results follow.
5. A and B are friends; B loves C and invites A to accompany him a-wooing.
   A refuses, lest he fall in love with C. C's curiosity is aroused and she visits A.
   Tragic results.
6. A and B are friends; both love C. But because of their friendship neither will
   take advantage of the other. A woos C for B; C loves A. Likewise B woos C
   for A; C loves B. Consequently, as C falls in love with both A and B, the
   solution of the *impasse* is still to seek.

On the other hand, in communities where the co-operative outlook on life predominates, friendship as such is also little considered. Persons are either brothers by kin or community, or
strangers. Thus it was in the Middle Ages.[21] And the absence of

a positive relationship today between the need for affection and friendship should be explained by the existence of the heavier counterweight of romantic love, itself part and product of simple anomie.[22]

The third type of affiliation, family or home life, may best be appraised by the store men set upon it for the affection they miss in other areas of their lives. As contended earlier, the human being's need for shelter leads almost unavoidably to the sentimentalization of a place known as home. Nevertheless, great variations are possible in the depth of this feeling. The home today is enhaloed and, in the ideals of modern men and women, made the repository of romantic love.[23] Although one cannot deny that sociological literature abounds in books and periodicals lamenting obliquely the "disorganization of the family," the fact has no contradictory bearing on the point. The authors, in truth, usually start with an ideal type of family and then designate divergences as family disorganization or disintegration. Yet, to find a pattern which differs from the type, one has but to flip back the pages of history to pre-Victorian England:

The pre-Victorian Englishman was not conspicuously a home-bird. There was indeed a vigorous and devoted home-life, more absorbing and creative than ours, but it was lived by women. Her house was a domestic workshop and nursery. . . . She produced the bread, the beer, the puddings, the cakes, the strong waters, the salves and most of the medicines; she manufactured the stockings, the collars, the shirts; it was her business to distil, carve, pickle, wash, mend, embroider, feed the poultry, distribute alms, keep accounts, and understand surgery, education and genealogies. Above all, she had to tend the ailing, squalling children. . . . There were fewer adults than now, but no lack of young ones, and the women had the task of tending their ailments and supplying their wants. Her life's work was decided for her.

Under these circumstances the men were better out of the way. They had their own public duties and avocations, and from the Civil War onwards they had acquired the habit of enjoying each other's company at the coffee-houses. . . . By the beginning of the eighteenth century, they had become the hearth and home of London life. Men went there to smoke, dine, write their letters, discuss pamphlets, recite their own poetic effusions, and get drunk. . . . Coffee-houses went out of fashion during the Napoleonic era. . . . But men did not abandon their gregarious habits. . . . The typical Londoner became a club-man, and his chosen resort continued to be a "home from home."[24]

Admittedly, knowledge on this subject, as on that of friendship, is short. One must expect this at intervals; a new theory will not fail to segregate new factors of significance for study. It happens, therefore, that researches on the family amid all their signs of family decay have missed for the most part the rise in the nineteenth century of the aura of ideals about the sanctity of home. Cowper's lines are heavy-laden with a sentiment inimical to coffee-house days:

> Now stir the fire, and close the shutters fast,
> Let fall the curtains, wheel the sofa round.
> . . . .
> So let us welcome peaceful evening in.

Thenceforth the husband began to spend more time at home. The furniture of Heppelwhite, Sheraton, and the Adams brothers met a huge demand. Household architecture and interior decoration followed the pace set by the lathes that were busy spinning out comfortable Victorian furniture. "Paternity had become an absorbing interest," says the literary historian, H. V. Routh, only to be laid aside at death. On the whole the prospect must have seemed exhilarating. One imagines that the average householder did not, indeed, wish to give up his club-life, and his man's talk in the smoking room, nor did most of them expect to find intellectual or spiritual companions in their wives and sons. But this was the age of hope. The men had now to give more thought to their home; they consoled themselves by thinking how well they could influence their children.

In return for his time, money, and elderly wisdom, the father pictured his declining years brightened by their affection and companionship:

The home was expected to be more than a haven of rest, and domestic sociability. . . . It suggested a "sacred spot identified with his life, in which his heart in the bustle and tumult of existence could take refuge." . . . He was trying to escape from the atmosphere of *the economic man*. There was much in his business life which seemed ignoble or accurst, but when he thought of his growing family, he could quiet his conscience by reflecting that he did it all for them. Even if he was helping to deface the countryside, to ruin his competitors, to defraud his customers and clients, to hasten his own death, others were to reap the benefit. All that was best in him could find expression in this unselfish selfishness.[25]

The home was run, furnished, and arranged to nurture the comfort, piety, and affection which he hoped to find within its walls.

Today, the Englishman's home is still his castle.[26] It is backed by legal precedents reflecting the declaration of the famous British jurist, Sir Edward Coke. *Et domus sua est unicuique tutissimum refugium.* In the United States, the private residence is a sanctuary whose inviolate nature is engraved on a bill of rights in one of the Constitution's most specific passages:

> The right of the people to be secure in their persons, houses, papers, and effects, against unreasonable searches and seizures, shall not be violated, and no Warrants shall issue, but upon probable cause, supported by Oath or affirmation, and particularly describing the place to be searched, and the persons or things to be seized.

The average young American, if asked of his aim in life, may reply—granting that anything at all comes to mind—that he wants something resembling the stereotyped ivy-covered cottage, with a pretty and ever loving wife, two "kids," and a car. He can bring up no grander purpose in life than this. In Middletown, people know that "the family is a sacred institution, the fundamental institution of our society," and "the final divinely ordained form." One is forced, then, to distinguish the ubiquitous sociological reports on the divorce and desertion rate from the dream of home life. Perhaps the inability of people to rise to the dream's requirement should be included in the sociologist's tabulation of causes of family disorganization. "In theory Middletown . . . talks about marriage as a 'sacred institution,' while daily in the courtrooms its businessmen lawyers work in the matter-of-fact spirit of their world of personal contractual relations." It is the persistence of this "theory" or idealization which the existence of simple anomie helps explain. The quest for idyllic intimacy in the circle 'round the hearth, like the search for the romantic lover or the friend, pursues associates who will treat the person "for what he is," not for what he achieves or possesses; not rationally nor competitively, but forever affectionately.[27]

There remains the important topic of the effect of simple anomie on associations of a voluntary nature. In this area the evidence substantially improves. Again one cannot escape the imputations of American uniqueness. America is "a nation of joiners," unequivocally state the observers. After the clear voices of Tocqueville and Bryce comes the twentieth-century echo of the

Beards in their history of *America in Midpassage*. The tendency of Americans to join organizations

> became a general mania as the means of communication and the routine of economic activity grew to be national in scope. . . . In addition to organizations primarily for mutual advantage, new types of fraternal societies were created, distinct from the established orders like the Masons, Odd Fellows, and Knights of Pythias. Business and professional men now flocked to Rotary Clubs, Kiwanis Clubs, Lions' Clubs, and a score of other associations. . . . Enthusiasm for organization also produced a bewildering number of clubs, orders, and societies—political, social, benevolent, religious, and reform. The directory of charitable enterprises in New York City alone in 1925 embraced more than 345 pages of fine print. It was a rare American who was not a member of four or five societies.

The last sentence of the quotation is undoubtedly an exaggeration, but only if one takes as the measure of voluntary affiliation the highly formalized association with rules and officers, records and government taxes. By this definition the cheap and informal associations of the poorer parts of the population are excluded. Yet these people, without the knowledge of the collector of data, may rent a dark basement somewhere or the backroom of a store and thereby establish a card-playing or "Jolly-Boys" club, certainly a voluntary association in the meaning here intended.[28] The clarifying criteria which need to be noted in a broader usage of the term are, first, the absence of an exclusive and avowed profit motive for association; second, regular or determinable meeting times; third, ascertainable rules of behavior; fourth, participation predominantly by adults and nonrelatives; and, last, a formal freedom to begin or discontinue membership at will.

In attempting to link the towering statistics on participation in voluntary associations[29] with the need for affection in modern life, two examples will be presented, one depicting with literary lucidity the motives for affiliation in the formal mode of free association and the other describing the behavior of the less formally organized type:

> The International Organization of Boosters' Clubs has become a world-force for optimism, manly pleasantry, and good business. Chapters are to be found now in thirty countries. Nine hundred and twenty of the thousand chapters, however, are in the United States.
>
> None of these is more ardent than the Zenith Boosters' Club.
>
> The second March lunch of the Zenith Boosters was the most important of

the year, as it was to be followed by the annual election of officers. There was agitation abroad. The lunch was held in the ballroom of the O'Hearn House. As each of the four hundred Boosters entered he took from a wall-board a huge celluloid button announcing his name, his nickname, and his business. There was a fine of ten cents for calling a Fellow Booster by anything but his nickname at a lunch, and as Babbitt . . . checked his hat the air was radiant with shouts of "Hello, Chet!" and "How're you, Shorty!" and "Top o' the mornin', Mac!" . . .

President Willis Ijams began that Boosters' Club luncheon by standing quiet and staring at them so unhappily that they feared he was about to announce the death of a Brother Booster. He spoke slowly then, and gravely:

"Boys, I have something shocking to reveal to you; something terrible about one of our own members."

Several Boosters, including Babbitt, looked disconcerted.

"A knight of the grip, a trusted friend of mine, recently made a trip up-state, and in a certain town, where a certain Booster spent his boyhood, he found out something which can no longer be concealed. In fact, he discovered the inward nature of a man whom we have accepted as a Real Guy and as one of us. Gentlemen, I cannot trust my voice to say it, so I have written it down."

He uncovered a large blackboard and on it, in huge capitals, was the legend:
George Follansbee Babbitt—oh you Folly!

The Boosters cheered, they laughed, they wept, they threw rolls at Babbitt, they cried, "Speech, speech! Oh you Folly!"

President Ijams continued:

"That, gentlemen, is the awful thing Georgie Babbitt has been concealing all these years, when we thought he was just plain George F. Now I want you to tell us, taking it in turn, what you've always supposed the F. stood for."

Flivver, they suggested, and Frog-face, and Flathead and Farinaceous and Freezone and Flapdoodle and Foghorn. By the joviality of their insults Babbitt knew that he had been taken back to their hearts, and happily he rose.

"Boys, I've got to admit it. I've never worn a wristwatch, or parted my name in the middle, but I will confess to 'Follansbee.' My only justification is that my old dad—though otherwise he was perfectly sane, and packed an awful wallop when it came to trimming the City Fellers at checkers—named me after the family doc, old Dr. Ambrose Follansbee. I apologize, boys. In my next what-d'you-call-it I'll see to it that I get named something really practical—something that sounds swell and yet is good and virile—something, in fact, like that grand old name so familiar to every household—that bold and almost over-powering name, Willis Jimjams Ijams!"

He knew by the cheer that he was secure again and popular; he knew that he would no more endanger his security and popularity by straying from the Clan of Good Fellows.[30]

The next example is imported from England. It records the behavior of the people living around a working-class shopping street in London called Lambeth Walk. The location is just off Lambeth Road and Kennington Road by the smaller streets of Lollard, Jaxon, and Old Paradise Street. In America it might be called a slum. Much of the housing is condemned, there is an open street market and a chapel which serves also as a cinema; and as the Walk runs into Tyers Street, it is flanked on both sides by huge blocks of working-class flats. Most of the people living in the tenements have moved there from other parts of London. The authors themselves, from this point on, can better carry the narrative:

Observers talked to many other Lambethians and attended some of the private parties where the dancing takes place. They confirmed the information given in this report. A spontaneous talent for dancing and song is a Lambeth tradition, having its connection with music-hall tradition but also having a life of its own. It has many features in common with primitive dancing. Men dress up as women or pretend to be animals. Beer plays its part, but observation showed that those who take part may be *half* drunk, but are certainly not whole drunk. It certainly is true of Lambethians having a bit of fun that:

> "Everything's free and easy,
> Do as you darn well pleasey. . . ."

On August Bank Holiday night, an observer was asked along to one of the parties. It was the end of the holiday, most of them had "been to Hampstead and got all boozed up. . . ." Most would have to be starting work at 6 or 7 next morning. After closing time the whole party proceeded from the ———— ———— to a house nearby, carrying crates of beer, each holding four quart-bottles. Already at the ———— ———— they had started swaying into the dance, and on the pavement outside two of the women were dancing with linked arms.

The party was held in an upstairs sitting-room, about 14 by 12 feet, with a piano, two settees and chairs round the wall, and an elegant blue-tiled fireplace —the tiles came unstuck later in the evening. Men and women were there in equal numbers, and including one or two who came in and went out, there were 24 all told—and 28 quart bottles of beer. The party lasted from 11.30 to 1.30 A.M. Four performers took turns at the piano; they all played by ear, and they all played very well. Three others took turns with the accordion. Dances alternated with songs—there were solos by a woman, a young man, and an old man of 83. He was the best singer and his age didn't in the least prevent him from having a good time with the rest. His songs included "Up Goes the Price of Meat, Ta Ra Ra" and "My Bradshaw Guide." All joined in the choruses of these and others, such as "Lily of Laguna," "The Lambeth Walk," and "What Does It Feel Like To Be Poor?" . . .

The first time the observer's glass was filled he emptied it. Then he noticed that the others after taking a swig from theirs, handed it on. Perhaps on the same analogy, when one man's nice-looking wife came in half way through, another man, friend of the first, gave her a good kiss. It was all free and easy and went with a terrific swing, but order was kept and there were certain rules like keeping silence during the solos. Mostly the women asked the men to dance. Everyone danced, old, middle-aged and young.

The striking feature of the dancing was the rolling tempo. . . . This tempo the pianists and dancers managed to introduce into waltzes and fox-trots, but it was most obvious when they danced their "own" dances, with improvised steps. The dancers faced each other, by two and two, or by three and three, with linked arms. They did jigging steps with their feet, plus some high kicking, then the two lines crossed over, turned and re-formed. As they crossed, they walked in the half-lilting, half-swaggering way that Lupino Lane used in his Lambeth Walk. For the men it is a swagger, arms out from the sides, like a boxer playing for position; for the women it is more of a lilt, with hips swaying. The two get mixed, though, when the men dress as women and behave like them—which is part of the tradition. Also, men dance with men and women with women free-ly. . . . Finally, the party broke up in the best of good temper, singing:

> "We play the Lambeth way,
> Not like you but a bit more gay,
> And when we have a bit of fun
> Oh, Boy ———."

This quotation speaks for itself. But the fate of the "Lambeth Walk" is interesting for another reason:

> "Any time you're Lambeth way
> Any evening, any day
> You'll find us all doin' the Lambeth Walk."

This is the song that half the world started singing in 1938. To the song a dance was added, a dance that was half a walk, and it caught on as no new dance has done for years. You could, and can, find them doing the Lambeth Walk in Mayfair ball-rooms, suburban dance-halls, cockney parties and village hops. Scotland and the industrial north took it up as keenly as the south. From all sorts of out-of-the-way places came news of its penetration. An observer who visited the far-away isle of Arran reported that the "natives" were doing it there. It spread to New York and thence right across America.

Its diffusion illustrates a contemporary characteristic of democratic countries—a blotter-like receptivity to "crazes," fads, societies, cults, groupings of all sorts that bring their joiners temporarily into personal intimate contact. After the song and dance had spread far and wide, the observers asked questions of devotees who were not Lambethians. Here are some of their remarks:

A good dance to "break the ice," for after shouting "Oi!" to a stranger, in some strange way he ceases to be one.

The dance gives a sense of complete unity to the whole body of dancers and not just individual pairs.

I thought it was a jolly dance, and a lot more friendly than most of the dances danced nowadays, more like the old style of dancing. The part that seems to amuse is the slapping of knees, turning the thumbs up and shouting "Oi!"

The authors add a concluding remark to these comments: "The Lambeth Walk succeeded in a big way, because it made everyone do the same thing at the same time, and express their togetherness with smack and shout."[31]

The tune found its way into the British Labour party which sheared it of its lyrics and clothed it in new ones designed to "swell the Labour vote." But this is a negligible illustration of the political effect of the intensified need for affection. The popular propensity for affiliation extends to political groupings. The proliferation in the nineteenth and twentieth centuries of socialists, guild-socialists and syndicalists, communists, fabians, anarchists, land-taxers, revisionists, organicists, fascists, monarchists, nazis, anarchico-syndicalists, technocrats, pietists, fundamentalists, "moral re-armers," and so on reveals not only a spread of ideas about political communities but also a vast assortment of live political associations. Lewis Mumford once said in his *Story of Utopias* that "in this new world of falling water, burning coal, and whirring machinery, utopia was born again. . . . About two-thirds of our utopias have been written in the nineteenth century." And whether or not the utopians have been able to hie themselves to isolated communities, their ideas are embodied in societies, or associations.

Edmund Burke's famous definition of a political party called for "a body of men united" and sought "friendship's holy ties" for its support. Let former Senator George Washington Plunkitt of New York's Tammany machine portray such a body of men at a political get-together:

You ought to attend one of these meetin's. They're a liberal education in patriotism. The great hall upstairs is filled with five thousand people, suffocatin' from heat and smoke. Every man Jack of these five thousand knows that down in the basement there's a hundred cases of champagne and two hundred kegs of beer ready to flow when the signal is given.[32]

Or listen to him describe the fixed duties of Tammany district leaders to give outings, dinners, and dances:

> As to the balls, they are the events of the winter in the extreme East Side and West Side society. Mamie and Maggie and Jennie prepare for them months in advance, and their young men save up for the occasion just as they save for the summer trips to Coney Island.
> The district leader is in his glory at the opening of the ball. He leads the cotillion with the prettiest woman present—his wife, if he has one, permitting—and spends almost the whole night shaking hands with his constituents. The ball costs him a pretty penny, but he has found that the investment pays.
> By these means the Tammany district leader reaches out into the homes of his district, keeps watch not only on the men, but also on the women and children; knows their needs, their likes and dislikes, their troubles and their hopes, and places himself in a position to use his knowledge for the benefit of his organization and himself. Is it any wonder that scandals do not permanently disable Tammany and that it speedily recovers from what seems to be crushing defeat?

Or, to call on a more modern representative, listen to the words of one of the greatest political experts in America's party history—James Farley:

> It doesn't hurt my feelings when some sophisticated gentleman of the writing craft describes me as the kind of fellow who likes to go back to the old home town and salute the neighbors by their first names while they greet me in return with a hearty "Hello, Jim." The radio is a wonderful thing . . . but, to my way of thinking, there is no substitute for the personal touch and there never will be, unless the Lord starts to make human beings different from the way he makes them now.[33]

Not only in Babbitt's Booster Club or in the inexpensive nuclei of the working-class neighborhoods but in the political arena, too, one finds this constant attempt to break down impersonality, to call the Honorable Philip La Follette, "Phil," to hold parties and dances, give boat rides and bus rides, sponsor card parties and teas, and have dinners and picnics:

> The range of entertainment offered at political club socials surpasses belief. Every type of dance program is arranged from *surprise* dances to *patriotic* dances, *sport* dances, *balloon* and *confetti* balls, *barn* dances, *novelty* dances, *masquerade* and *civic* balls, *shirt-waist* dances, *pajama* dances, *pirate* dances and *cake-walks*. . . .
> The writer has been invited to attend a *dance and pretzel party* in the Bronx, a *spaghetti dance* in Queens, a *turkey dance* in Union City and a *chop suey dance* in Westchester.

The investigator of these phenomena justifiably concludes that "the most popular and, one is inclined to believe, effective activity of the political clubs is that which is ordinarily known as 'social.' "[34]

Once the hunger for fellowship is assuaged by means of a particular association, the individual ethicizes that association. The ostensible purpose for the group's existence may be minor, as, for example, in a bowling or luncheon club, yet the person clings to it. It seems that he exaggerates its importance. Charles Ferguson, in describing the activities of *Fifty Million Brothers*, wonders at this:

> American secret and non-liturgical societies are in many respects singular. Whatever may be true of the rest of the world or of past history, we present an array of orders altogether baffling not so much in their starlike multiplicity as in their vitality and endurance. The impact of the whole array upon the eye keeps one incessantly curious to know for what earthly reason we have gone at organizing with such abandoned enthusiasm—an enthusiasm which shows no sign of abating.

But when it is remembered that these organizations serve the function of relieving simple anomie, the mystery grows less dense. The voluntary association's importance to the individual seems no longer exaggerated. The need for fraternal fellowship is the one reason he seldom gives. It nonetheless exists. It is especially apparent in the constant use of the word "belong," a term which when frequently employed should call to attention the possibility of an intensified need for affection. What does it mean to say, "I *belong* to the Democratic Party"? Ostrogorski was close to the answer:

> [The factor] which impelled the American to herd with his fellows in the party fold, is one of the primordial facts of American social existence—the isolation of the individual. True, nowhere is man more unfettered in his movements; nowhere can the individual launch forth more freely; nowhere are political and, to all appearances, social barriers brought so low as in the United States; and yet nowhere else is man reduced to that atomic condition, so to speak, in which he finds himself on the western side of the Atlantic. . . . The American lives morally in the vagueness of space; he is, as it were, suspended in the air, he has no fixed groove. . . . He creates mechanical [grooves, therefore,] in the form of associations, as numerous and varied as they are superficial, but all revealing the uneasiness of the American mind assailed by a sort of fear of solitude. . . . Party filled a portion of the moral void: it met an emotional need; it offered a groove exclusive enough to permit of the growth of genuine or con-

ventional feelings of hatred and devotion, and comprehensive enough to unite in these feelings men with no other bond between them, and even dispersed in space. . . . The American finds in his nomadic existence everywhere, from the Atlantic to the Pacific, from Maine to Florida, a Republican organization or a Democratic organization, which recalls him to himself, gives him a countenance, and makes him repeat with pride the cry . . . "I am a Democrat," or "I am a Republican."

The person who has never come face-to-face with electoral statistics is astounded to learn that three out of every four American voters never alter their party allegiance; three out of every four are "hereditary voters." Come what may—bad candidates, bad platforms, or good—once a Republican, always a Republican; once a Democrat, always a Democrat. Unquestionably, the staunch allegiance of 75 per cent of the voting population is the most important element in the study of political attitudes; yet political scientists have done little more than call it the traditional vote and ascribe it to the "power of tradition."[35] The loyal party voter is voting for the victory of his team, the association in which his fellow-members know him and greet him, help him and are in turn helped. Graham Wallas claimed that the voter seeks in his party "something which can be loved." True enough, but the cart precedes the horse. He loves his party because it loves him; it provides him with the personal attention, friendliness, and affection he needs and does not receive in the competitive, rational, and impersonal world of business. Thus to vote for the other party is to vote against his own psychic welfare. The fact that he cannot verbalize this feeling explains why the traditional voter—in deference to the folkway of "independent thinking"—will sometimes say before the election that he may vote this way or that, that he has not yet decided. But when election day rolls around, he casts his ballot for the party that garnered his votes on all previous polling days[36] and, in all probability, his father's before him, too.[37] Only a period as peculiar as the 1890's could produce a queer-sounding stanza like this:

> I was a party man one time,
> The party wouldn't mind me,
> So now I'm working for myself,
> The Party's left behind me.

The customary finding is a tenacious party allegiance, a second-class patriotism.[38]

When a favorite stanza on Middletown club programs is

> So many gods, so many creeds,
> So many paths that wind and wind
> While just the art of being kind,
> Is all the sad world needs;

and when, as Ostrogorski says, "the mere fact of having a trade or an occupation or even an external peculiarity in common is taken as a pretext for pleasure parties [like] the barbers' picnics, the tailors' excursions, the dinners of men weighing more than fourteen stone"; when men defend their voluntary associations against all intrusions; it is small wonder that there has sprung up a modern political doctrine called pluralism. A respectable number of political theorists have asserted that the political grouping of the state or nation has no greater claim to the allegiance of the person than many of the present-day associations of trade-unions, of local communities, of employers, professions, and recreational groups. As the most prolific writer of the school, Harold J. Laski, said, "I have termed this view the pluralist theory of the state because it is rooted in a denial that any association of men in the Community is inherently entitled to primacy over any other association." In fact, the theorists say, other groups often elicit *deeper* loyalties than the state which, after all, is "only one among many forms of human association."[39]

Thus the intensified need for friendly contacts, symptomatic of simple anomie, has impelled men into legions of voluntary associations and into high estimations of their value; the high evaluations, in turn, partially account for the rise of modern pluralist doctrines. A serious criticism of pluralist theory emerges in light of these facts. Whenever the philosophers of pluralism imply that the present-day intense craving for association is part of human nature, as, for example, in the remark that "man is a creature of competing loyalties," they are in error. It was just seen that the extreme need today for the affectionate contacts of associations is circumstantial. Furthermore, as the early chapters of this book showed, conscience cannot develop without a series of unconflicting directives. Man is a creature who must avoid competing loyalties.[40]

Mental Effects of a Divided Life

All along man's course in history, the student can find him making distinctions between work and play. Michelangelo could not complete his work on the sculpture of the exquisite slave without stopping to carve on its back a grotesque gargoyle. The good times of old times even in so young a country as the United States were seldom wholly divorced from work: cornhuskings, barn-raisings, church-raisings, sugar boildowns, spelling bees, quilting parties. Even taffy pulls were related to food preparation. Today, however, the difference between work and nonwork is uncompromising. Essentially, it is the general inability to secure affectionate relations in work that opens up the modern chasm between labor and leisure.

The previous sections of this chapter endeavored to show how people in their off-work hours try to obtain a comradeship which is doubly vital for its mitigating effect on simple anomie. The salutary effect, however, is limited. A system of beliefs does not hesitate to cross even the threshold beyond which good fellows get together. The rationalistic component of the competitive directive is particularly persuasive. Men in their relationships with one another suspect ulterior motives, which usually mean pecuniary or instrumental motives. They wonder whether or not they are being "used."[41] Accordingly, they persistently search for affectionate relationships and consistently find that the ideal is not the spotted actuality. They surround themselves with associations, and for the small measure of relief they eke out they defend their pluralistic membership with all the intensity at their command, for the measure of relief is great when compared to the asymptotical amount they obtain in work life.[42]

Though associative behavior were more healing than it seems, the problem yet would be unsolved. The human conscience cannot rest on contradictory morals. "Religion is one thing; business is another." "Business and sentiment don't mix." To compart areas of living and assign a different directive to each brings only a superficial solution. The earliest entrepreneurs learned that lesson late in life. Their moral conflict and anxiety were well presented by Henri Pirenne, the medieval scholar. One can still read the numerous wills of bankers and speculators directing that the poor, whom they said they had defrauded, should be repaid and repentantly bequeathing to the clergy the ill-got portion of their property.[43] Today clinical records bulge with cases described as having "isolation" tendencies. No moral problem seems to be troubling the patient. In discussing matters that should cause him great anxiety he remains calm; he maintains *la belle indifférence*. Patients of this type do things without any guilty feeling. Then suddenly they develop great emotion, guilt, or anxiety over an event whose importance seems incomprehensible. To their associates they appear to have no conscience—until the crack-up. In actuality they had isolated their feelings of guilt, but not without ultimate repercussions. Not everyone can pulverize competitive and co-operative directives so as to blend them. Most men wind up with sausage.

CHAPTER NINE

WAR AND SIMPLE ANOMIE

AS HE gazed at the myriad associations in the United States, Ostrogorski felt that "in the morbid need of friendly contact that they reveal they have something pathetic about them. In America everything is done in a crowd, by troops."[1] He could just as well have said, "they have something dangerous about them," especially since he used the word "troops." Everyone who dislikes war should take interest in the possibility that underneath the many factors which have already been weighed by students of the subject simple anomie may be uncovered. Should it exist, it would probably hasten the resort to war.

The reciprocal influence of anomie and war begins when the threat of war is at the focus of popular attention. It may have been brought there by any means—the ominous reporting by the press or radio, for example, of movements or increases in strength of another nation's military personnel or matériel; the method by which the menace reached the public mind is not important here. But once in the forefront of attention, the prospect of war throws into relief the changes in the ways of life it may bring. The likelihood of war then makes persons consider what bad or good effects it will have for them and for those dear to them. The task of examining all the prognoses of things to come "if we get into war" cannot be attempted here. Admittedly, the thought which flashes first through the minds of most democrats is uncontained horror. They unhesitatingly subscribe to General Sherman's dictum. War is hell! But to accept this feeling without further examination leaves a curious contradiction. It is said that a modern war must be supported by public opinion.[2] The paradox summons up the analogy of a man driving a car and saying to himself, "I don't want to run into that wall; I'd better not run into that wall," and the next instant smashing straight into it. The fact therefore should not be allowed to hide itself: there may be certain aspects of war which suggest beneficial results, though the individual may be loath to confess such thoughts even to himself. With some excuse one can turn Von Moltke's epigram around slightly and say that war is a dream and not entirely a bad dream. The strains of peace, as the distinguished English psychologist, Edward Glover, called them, exist. That cannot be denied. And anomie is high on the list. Thus there is a proposition to be examined here, namely, that people generally expect war's changes to reduce the mental tension of simple anomie.

Above all, people anticipate that war will give the political system of beliefs precedence over the capitalist ideology. Their intuition proves true. Mounting nationalism with its affirmations of unity, brotherhood, and common defense accompanies the march toward war. By subordinating business directives to the political, the principle conflict of belief-systems in democratic nations is liquidated. The idea of competition with its logical extension, internationalism, vanishes.[3] There is no question now: Co-operation and the commonweal are to the fore. H. G. Wells once wrote that "when the contemporary man steps . . . into the barrack-yard, he steps to a higher social plane, into an atmosphere of service and cooperation and of infinitely more honourable emulations." One need not agree with Wells's judgment of the nobility of war to accept the facts of the statement. A member of the Royal Air Force in a visit home during World War II told his parents:

I shall never go back to the old business life—that life of what I call the survival of the slickest; I now know a better way. Our lads in the R.A.F. would, and do, willingly give their lives for each other; the whole outlook of the force is one of "give," not one of "get." If tomorrow the war ended and I returned to business, I would need to sneak, cheat, and pry in order to get hold of orders which otherwise would have gone to one of my R.A.F. friends if one of them returned to commercial life with a competing firm. Instead of co-operating, as we do in war, we would each use all the craft we possessed with which to confound each other. I would never do it.[4]

In the same war, numbers of women who joined the American Women's Auxiliary Corps said: "Until now, I did this for a private firm; now I want to do it for my country."[5] Companionship or association or co-operation is no problem. Cities become like villages.

Women leap to the breach. In 1941, for example, under the headline, "80,000 Women Eager To Help if U.S. Needs Them," a newspaper article's lead paragraph began: "Eighty thousand Illinois clubwomen who only recently were most concerned over the latest cake and salad recipes today are ready and eager to leap to the breach in any emergency confronting the country." Such items for the United States and England could be multiplied indefinitely. One remembers, too, how quickly the suffragettes at the approach of the first World War put the suffrage ship in dry dock. And in World War II women burst out of their shells into a warm companionable world—not the cold cruel world of pre-war years: "It was not difficult to mobilize women for work. Women of every age and of all classes went to work. Working in factories and on the farms, even in offices, became glamorous." Truly, for many women the war was a solution for a lonely existence.[6]

Of the men, those regarded as too old or too essential in civilian activities have all the advantages of a reduction in the competitive directive with none of the dangerous apprehensions of the soldier. But even the soldier finds more of the good life in the army than he may have foreseen. As the threat of war appears and develops, the nation's status system changes; to the community, military activities now become the most necessary and therefore the most honored. And in the army there is no conflict of directives: to military leaders is due obedience and faith or, as usually phrased, discipline and loyalty; to comrades-in-arms brotherly affection is due.[7] If men never met with co-operation in the world outside their family, they meet with it in the camaraderie of army life. With all the mud, blood, and excrement of such an existence, this one gift appears like a pearl in muck. In the previous war the writings of Erich Maria Remarque and Siegfried Sassoon bore unimpeachable testimony.[8] Said Sassoon's alter ego George Sherston, "watching the men as they plodded patiently on under their packs, I felt as if my own identity was becoming merged in the Battalion"; and, later, while perplexed over his great desire to return to the troops after a leave in England, he decided that he believed in nothing more than the "Battalion spirit": "The Battalion spirit meant living oneself into comfortable companionship with the officers and the N.C.O.'s around one; it meant winning the respect, or even the affection, of platoon and company."[9] In the more recent world war the observations of two psychiatrists, Grinker and Spiegel, working with both ground force soldiers and air force personnel, are incomparably useful for the purpose at hand:

> We have already described the intensity of [soldiers'] feeling for each other as resembling the closeness of relationship between members of the same family. In truth, they are brothers-in-arms in more than a figurative sense. They actually feel toward each other as if they were brothers. It is a very common thing to hear a flier say of his buddy, "He reminds me of my brother" or "I felt closer to him than to my own brother." The men in the combat teams are brothers by virtue of their constant enforced association, their dependence upon each other, their common ideals and goals, and their relation to their leaders. In the family circle of the combat group, the leader is in the position of the father. Again it is extremely common to hear a combat flier describe his commanding officer as reminding him of his father. As with the fraternal feelings of the men toward each other, this seems to have less to do with the physical appearance of the leader or his actual personality than with his relation toward the men in combat. From a psychological point of view, the combat leader is a father and the men are his children.[10]

War is thus the Great Association. To revert to the chart above (p. 132), in countries at war the curves $A–B$ and $C–D$ will drop, one may assume, to the levels $A'–B'$ and $C'–D'$. The importance of this readjustment of beliefs (and hence conduct) in prewar and wartimes cannot be overstressed. It is a powerful factor encouraging an acquiescence in, acceptance of, and hastening into war conditions.[11] And, viewed from this vantage, it puts men in the peculiar position of fighting to preserve a nonanomic way of life that was ushered in by the fraternal atmosphere of imminent war.[12]

By and large, war's early remedial influence on simple anomie more than fulfils expectations. For the men-in-arms, if they meet with battle, disenchantment comes soon. Yet even they, once returned to civilian life, look back with longing to the fellowship of the barracks. It is too soon yet to get much expression of this sort from the veterans of World War II, but the recollections of the first war's veterans can still be heard. One of them, in 1933, wrote a letter to the *New Republic:*

A lot of people like myself enjoyed the war. I don't think there was anything monstrous about me for liking it. The things I loved about it were all things denied us in peacetime . . . : i.e., close association with large numbers of one's fellow-men in a common purpose, the chance to put forth intensive and disinterested effort in a cause greater than one's own personal concerns, economic equality, freedom from economic worries, adventure.

This frank statement can be supplemented by the more philosophical sensitiveness of the hero of *All Quiet on the Western Front:*

The days, the weeks, the years out here shall come back again, and our dead comrades shall then stand up again and march with us, our heads shall be clear, we shall have a purpose, and so we shall march, our dead comrades beside us, the years at the Front behind us:—against whom, against whom?

In the words of the song of the troops, "old soldiers never die." Scarcely can it be said that "they simply pass away."[13]

Disillusionment comes later to the noncombatants. They are more reluctant to part with war conditions. Even the partial carrying of the war to the hinterland, removing as it does some of the differences between civilian and fighting groups, accomplishes surprisingly little to offset civilian tenacity:

Terrible too was the dismay of the men in the trenches who failed to get any response to pleadings with friends, when they realized the depth of moral apathy at home. In the *Nation*, December 27, 1919, a letter is published from "A Soldier in the War," who describes how terrible this dismay of the men in the trenches had been, of the men who, having told cheerful lies about the conditions they were living in, having endured the unendurable, had at last, some of them, written home and told the truth and asked that everything might be done to stop the war. The only answer they received was "to stick it."[14]

British psychiatrists in the last war were almost puzzled at the willingness of the civilian population to continue the war ad infinitum even in heavily bombed areas like English cities. Parents bore their deprivations so well that even the children suffered no grave psychological evil. Psychiatrists expected many psychoneuroses but found only a few.[15] They were less at a loss, however, when the war came to an end. Suddenly, things began to happen. Persons who had lived in close harmony during the long war years grew irritable with each other. The fights in taverns and the arrests grew at an alarming rate. Everywhere people began to fall sick. Not only were the psychiatric clinics pushed beyond their greatest wartime limit, but the other clinics and physicians who handled only the apparently organic illnesses found themselves unexpectedly swamped with cases.[16] The war was over.

Let it be clear what these few paragraphs on war offer. They are not meant to be more than suggestions. The evidence for the propositions is scanty, but theoretically the consequences are clear. If simple anomie is present, the prospect of a war will augur for its relief. Immersed in the imbroglio of actual war, people will find their salutary anticipations confirmed. This is especially true of noncombatants. The progression of the war not only validates many of their presuppositions but reveals welcome possibilities not bargained for. In these senses, then, simple anomie may be both a factor in the resort to war and one prolonging its duration.[17] Perhaps there is within grasp here at least a fragment of the reason that Fascist leaders, having repeatedly convinced themselves of the softness of the decadent plutocracies, stood agape at the militancy of the democracies.[18]

CHAPTER TEN

ADAPTATIONS TO ACUTE ANOMIE

A LADY in the distress of a heated philosophical argument once had the mishap of saying, "I accept the universe." On learning of this, the cantankerous Carlyle remarked, "Gad, she'd better." Some time later, another learned person heard the story and improved it by rejoining, "Gad, she'd better not." The humor in this cosmological exchange is not without its relation to acute anomie. It serves as a reminder that all attempts at a solution—no matter how variform—aim at controlling a hostile world. Since acute anomie is an anxiety, attempts to remove it, both individual and joint attempts, will be more drastic and radical than in the case of the lesser type discussed in chapter viii. The dangerous lawlessness of the environment must be banished and an orderly world restored.

Mental Disorder and Suicide

Mental disorder and suicide are examples of the extremities to which individual adaptation may proceed. It may seem unusual to use a term with voluntarist connotations, such as "adaptation," to analyze mental disease, but this meaning is intended. The symptoms by which a person resolves his anxiety are part of the behavior of people about him. A very small part, to be sure; so small that the behavior should not be given the name of cultural traits. But, nevertheless, the individual who is considered psychotic is unconsciously imitating action which he has previously seen or, in most instances, heard described. Thus one finds that each section of the modern city has a favorite type of mental disorder: in rooming-house areas, paranoid schizophrenia; in areas inhabited largely by immigrants or Negroes, catatonic schizophrenia; in rooming-house and immigrant areas, alcoholic psychoses; in high rental areas, manic-depressive psychoses, and so on. Among the poorer and less educated groups the signs of mental disease often appear in bodily infirmities, such as paralysis or hysteria; while among the richer and more educated, symptomology leans toward the symbolic infirmities, such as obsessive psychoneuroses. Persons have even predicted in their dreams the type of mental derangement they later acquired. And it seems that the classes that once got the gout now favor manic-depressive psychoses. In like manner, not only the resort to suicide but the method of suicide is suggested by the milieu. T. F. Powys expressed this vividly in his novel *Mr. Weston's Good Wine*. When the girl, Ada, asks a kind neighbor what ways there are "to put an end to a poor maid," she learns "that Dodderdown were the village for hanging, Madder the place to cut a wold throat, and that the folk of Folly Down do like drowning best." Ada consummated the deed by throwing herself in a deep stream. Were she in America, her choice, being a feminine choice, might have been poison or asphyxiation. Had she been a man in the United States, she probably would have employed firearms or the noose. On the other hand, if she had been a Yahgan of the Tierra del Fuego in South America, she would never have heard of suicide.

Mental disorder as a way out occurs only in the case of acute anomie. Yet the boundary line setting off the consequences of each type of anomie is thick and blurred. For example, among the leaders of voluntary associations are found persons with a high "neurotic score" which has intense loneliness as its most prominent feature.[1] Also, as was pointed out, cases involving an extreme division of everyday life into moral and unmoral spheres developed into the "isolated" psychoneuroses and sometimes into full-blown schizophrenia. Furthermore, falling ill to gain affectionate attention is a trick so commonly played that it is not discussed, yet it borders on the whole newly expanding field of psychosomatic medicine. The late Otto Fenichel, who had one of the most logical minds among psychoanalysts, drove this point home with an amusing anecdote:

It is often stressed that the main . . . gain consists in getting attention by being sick. But what type of person is especially in need of "getting attention"? Attention is needed either as . . . a substitute for love or, more frequently, as reassurance and a promise of help and protection. . . . Very often this is no either-or; the most intense struggles for "compensation" are fought by patients who are much less in need of money than in need of a sign of parental affection and of

assurance against abandonment. No illustrative anecdote must be told to ana-
lytic patients as frequently as the story about the inmate of an asylum who implied, when special privileges of his were denied: "Then what am I nuts for?"

Nevertheless, for the most part, the differences between the effects
of simple and acute anomie are gross enough to be separated.[2] It
is not the demarcation of these two that makes an assessment of
the relation of acute anomie and mental disorder difficult. It is
the variety of ways in which acute anomie alone may be dispelled
that creates the problem. Any subjective reconstruction of belief-
systems will effect a cure. As will be seen, several forms of psychosis answer the bill; so do suicide and certain types of ideological mass movements. The first task is to examine briefly the
belief-systems of the two forms of mental derangement which
from their frequency alone are the most important—mania in
manic-depression and schizophrenia.[3]

The manic's distinction lies in the fact that he believes himself
powerful enough to control the environment. In this respect he is
acting as he did as a child, when he frequently fancied that he
was as powerful as his attendants and that therefore he need fear
no separation from them. The triumphant air that the manic has
"is a derivative of the pleasure the child feels whenever his growing ego achieves the feeling 'I no longer need to be afraid because
I can master something which until now I looked upon as dangerous; now I am as powerful as omnipotent grownups are.' "[4]
The emotion experienced in this fantastic scheme is sheer relief
at the riddance of separation-anxiety. Whereas in the depressive
phase of his illness the patient feels, "I have lost everything; now
the world is empty," in the manic stage the world is not hostile
but subject to his desires. "Life is rich." In an almost literal sense
this type of patient wills himself to power. He frequently believes
himself to be the king or the president or God. In short, in the
manic's system of beliefs, *he* is the *ruler*.

In schizophrenia two sets of similar fantasies are discernible—
world destruction and world reconstruction. In Otto Fenichel's
experience, as set down in his *Psychoanalytic Theory of the Neuroses*,

the fantasy frequently met with in the early stages of schizophrenia [is] that
the world is coming to an end. The patients who experience such a feeling are
correct, in a sense; so far as they are concerned, the objective world has actually

broken down. . . . The world is felt as vital and significant as long as it is invested with libido. When a schizophrenic complains that the world seems "empty," "meaningless," "monotonous," and that he feels as if something has changed, as if people were mere fleeting images, when he states that he feels perplexed and abandoned in this new world, he reflects in all this the withdrawal of his libido from the objects.

In the later stages of schizophrenia various fantasies of reconstruction often occur. These states of mind show greater passivity than the manic's passion for control. There is often the feeling that a salvation or rebirth is anticipated:

> The world does not seem to be empty and meaningless any longer but instead particularly rich and full of new and indescribably grand meanings. Everything perceived has another meaning, sometimes a hidden, sometimes a clear one, but nearly always a prophetic and symbolic one.

In other schizophrenic cases the patient's attitude is more active. He himself has the task of saving the world or perhaps has been chosen by God to restore order to a cruel, empty world.

It is evident that in some of the most important forms of mental disorders the patient's difficulties lie in his system of beliefs. The world may be perceived to be so hostile and himself so helpless that the person may (as in hebephrenic schizophrenia) "let the world go," make himself invulnerable to its slings and arrows, incase himself in mental armor so that all stimuli from the environment leave him unmoved. He gives the appearance of just vegetating. On the other hand, the patient may believe himself able to subdue the animate, inimical world through his own strength. Like Archimedes he thinks that he can move the world; unlike Archimedes he does not ask for a place on which to stand before he tries the task. Both solutions, the passive and the active, are successful in that they remove the preying anxiety.

The centrality of anxiety in mental disorder is now well established. It is less known that it is also prominent in suicide. Of necessity little is recorded of the emotions experienced by suicides just before they kill themselves. Once dead, their thoughts and feelings, though cold for but a few moments, are lost to science. Most data come from the attempted suicides which by circumstance or design miscarried. From these cases and from hospital records of patients who later became successful suicides, it is clear that the self-destroying individual is desperately trying to free himself from anxiety. But the specific features of the terror are enveloped in a haze of unclear data. In the cases of attempted suicide, moreover, the seriousness with which the person tries to dispatch himself can often be disputed. Often, he merely wants to convince others that he is serious about the project. Prospective suicides often leave open an opportunity for recovery should they find their effort more painful than anticipated. Some persons are known to have attempted suicide only to be forced by the chill of the cold water to swim to safety. Recent statistics from the Seine area of France, for example, show that in 1927 over one-quarter of all attempted suicides ended in failure; in 1931 the number of failures increased and continued to rise rapidly until 1937, when the proportion reached nearly one-half; the following year it decreased and by 1943 had gradually dropped back to around one-quarter.[5] In light of these facts one cannot be sure that the person whose attempt at suicide was foiled was really in earnest.

A fictional document exists, however, which describes the suicidal thought and deed of a man named Septimus Smith. Again, one pays homage to the art of Virginia Woolf:

He stared so . . . and made everything terrible; sky and tree, children playing, dragging carts, blowing whistles, falling down; all were terrible. . . .

Men must not cut down trees. There is a God. (He noted such revelations on the backs of envelopes.) Change the world. No one kills from hatred. Make it known (he wrote it down). . . .

Look the unseen bade him, the voice which now communicated with him who was . . . the scapegoat, the eternal sufferer, but he did not want it, he moaned, putting from him with a wave of his hand that eternal suffering, that eternal loneliness. . . .

Once you stumble, Septimus wrote on the back of a postcard, human nature is on you. . . . So he was deserted. . . . This last relic straying on the edge of the world, this outcast, who gazed back at the inhabited regions, who lay, like a drowned sailor, on the shore of the world. . . . How does one set about it, with a table knife, uglily, with floods of blood,—by sucking a gaspipe? . . .

Now for his writings; how the dead sing behind rhododendron bushes; odes to Time; conversations with Shakespeare; Evans, Evans, Evans—his messages from the dead; do not cut down trees; tell the Prime Minister. Universal love: the meaning of the world. Burn them! he cried. . . .

Human nature, in short, was on him—the repulsive brute, with the blood-red nostrils. The whole world was clamouring: Kill yourself, kill yourself. . . . Getting up rather unsteadily, hopping indeed from foot to foot, he considered

Mrs. Filmer's nice clean bread knife with "Bread" carved on the handle. Ah, but one mustn't spoil that. The gas fire? But it was too late now. . . . Razors he might have got but Rezia . . . had packed them. There remained only the window, the large Bloomsbury-lodging house window. . . . "I'll give it you!" he cried, and flung himself vigorously, violently down on to Mrs. Filmer's area railings.[6]

The author of this psychological study gave the subject of suicide serious thought. In the last week of March in 1941 she walked into the sea to her death.

In the above paragraphs on mental disease and suicide the intention is to demonstrate that (1) in the emotions and thoughts of major types of the mentally ill and the suicidal the typical syndrome of acute anomie appears—anxiety accompanied by the image of a menacing world—and (2) the solutions adopted by such persons are radical attempts to banish this terror and to procure an indulgent, orderly environment. A part of the purpose behind this presentation is to show that Durkheim's hypothesis, given in the Introduction to Part I, about the connection of suicide and anomie, a hypothesis which he largely derived from statistical data, could be supported by psychological evidence. The clinical evidence here on mental illness, however, and the evidence to be given below on mass movements point out also that Durkheim in trying to use suicide as an index to anomie erred on the side of oversimplification. The error is understandable, for intricate psychological theories of the possibilities of displacement or substitution in mental conflict have only recently been given scholarly standing. But the fact remains: suicide is only one of a number of possible reactions to the anxiety of acute anomie.

Recognition of this complication leads to another consideration—the present inadequacy of statistics for an appraisal of the extent of anomie. In the first place, the traditional classifications of mental disease, such as the Kraepelin, are not sharp enough to permit confidence in the frequencies of the various categories as presented in statistical tables. Second, the statistics on frequencies represent only the mentally ill who are committed to institutions and, for the most part, only those who are committed to public hospitals. All the factors which operate to keep certain categories of the mentally deranged out of institutions must be ascertained, not to mention that they must also be weighed. For example, certain ethnic groups feel that "the old folks," even though demented, should be taken care of at home; a prejudice seems to exist against committing women, even though men with the same degree of derangement would be speedily packed off; the more conspicuous hysterics must be put away, yet the quieter obsessional types can be kept around without too much embarrassment. Even the totals of suicides cannot be fully trusted. Care is not taken properly to tag every cadaver that comes into the municipal morgue, especially if the body happens to be part of the floating unidentified population of the big city.

Finally, and most important, the traditional classifications are based either on the symptomology or (as in the case of some psychoanalytic categories) on the genesis of the symptomology. A patient may be first classified as a schizophrenic because he exhibits bizarre relationships of emotions and ideas. Then, if he gets more and more withdrawn, passive, and uncommunicative, his behavior may be labeled "schizophrenic surrender" and his case may be further classified as hebephrenic schizophrenia. Such classifications are presumably made to give information useful for therapy, but they tell next to nothing of the events which touched off the disorderly behavior. An actual case can illustrate the point. One day "a young pretty woman of the working class" came to the psychiatric clinic with two boys and an infant. She was unable to talk. She wrote on a piece of paper that a few weeks previously she had lost her job and shortly thereafter she had lost her speech. The psychoanalyst's description and disposition of the case follow:

> Analysis was out of the question; so I attempted to eliminate the speech disturbance by suggestion. After a few hypnotic sessions, she began to talk in a low, hoarse and apprehensive voice. . . . The father of the children had deserted her, and she and the children were on the verge of starvation. [After losing her job] she tried to make a living by sewing at home. Then she began to think of murder. She was about to push her children into the water when she was gripped by terrible anxiety. From then on she was tormented by the impulse to confess to the police, in order to protect the children from herself. This intention also aroused violent anxiety. She was afraid of being *hanged. The mere thought of it constricted her throat.* Being afraid of her own impulse, she protected

herself against its realization by way of her mutism. The mutism was really an *extreme spasm of her throat* (the vocal chords). It was not difficult to find out what infantile situation was expressed in it. In her early life an orphan, she had been brought up by strangers. They had lived six or more in one room. As a little girl, she . . . was tormented by the longing for a protective mother. In her phantasies she was a protected infant at the breast. *Her throat had always been the seat of her choking anxiety and of her longing.* Now she was a mother and saw her children in a situation similar to her own, and felt that they should not go on living. In addition she had transferred her hatred of her husband (for his desertion) to his children. In brief, an unbelievably complicated situation which nobody could understand.

From this case it can be seen that, if the symptoms alone of this patient were to be explained, the analyst could correctly say that they were based on unconscious fantasies of nursing at the mother's breast. On the other hand, if the woman had not been unemployed and in financial straits, she might have remained a useful and respected member of the community. But this fact would never have been reflected in the typical statistical table which probably would have used the patient's mutism as the basis for classification. The clinician sensibly concluded:

I helped her to the extent that she became able to master some of her difficulties. The boys were taken to a good institution. She managed to resume work. We collected money for her. But in reality the misery continued, only somewhat alleviated. . . . There I had before me not the lofty problems of etiology of the neuroses, but the question as to how a human organism could possibly tolerate such a life, year in, year out.[7]

The point at issue is that if some idea is to be obtained of the anomic factor in mental disease or suicide, a classification by precipitating factors rather than by therapeutic categories should be attempted.[8] There is much to be said for the French practice of tabulating suicides by the *motifs-présumés*. Although offering many difficulties, data thus organized would reduce the number of equally plausible explanations for statistical correlations of mental disorders with indices such as business conditions. The interpreter of the data would be brought logically closer to the operative psychological motives.

Existing statistics, of course, are not useless. If one sets aside all reservations and accepts only the higher correlations, one will find much supporting evidence for the theory presented here of the consequences of acute anomie. The statistics on suicide, however, are the only ones reliable enough to be entertained, for, while the border lines between normality, neurosis, and psychosis are often hard to draw, the distinction between a suicide and a nonsuicide is much clearer. Perhaps for this reason statistical correlations clearly show that suicides increase during a depression,[9] while mental disorders do not. Mental disorders, in fact, show few reliable fluctuations. But the parallelisms of the ups and downs of the suicide rate and business cycles support the proposition that the loss of employment during economic contractions leads to acute anomie and that part of the consequences appears in the higher suicide rate. Another pertinent and reliable relationship is that between suicide and type of religious beliefs. In every European locality where differential data were compiled, the Protestant suicide rate was much higher than the corresponding Catholic rate.[10] This discovery supports the finding made here and often referred to, that the Catholic's psychological investment in the business system of beliefs is less than the Protestant's. Loss of economic status for the Catholic—being not so closely entwined with his religious system of beliefs—may less often bring him to the brink of acute anomie. The higher suicide rate among Protestants and also a possibly higher mental disorder rate[11] provide the germ of truth in Rousseau's remark: "Protestantism forces a man to be free."

There is one more correlation which is high enough to be trustworthy, namely, the inverse relationship between the suicide rate and war. In all twentieth-century wars and in the nineteenth-century wars for which, like the American Civil War, there are reliable figures the suicide curve dips deeply.[12] The anomic explanation for this has already been fully treated in the previous chapter on war and simple anomie. At this point it is enough to recall that in war the major conflicts between directives of belief-systems and the major possibilities of the deterioration of belief-systems are eliminated for nearly all persons.

In conclusion one may say that if statistics on both mental disorder and suicide were to be compiled according to the precipitating factors and then treated together as interrelated consequences of acute anomie, knowledge of the extent of acute anomie would greatly increase in exactness. To these two possible consequences a third should be added in order to make the sum of potential re-actions, more complete. The mass replacement of a new system of beliefs for an old one that has disintegrated is the third possible adaptation. It is the collective solution to widespread acute anomie, and appears in the growth of ideological mass movements. The solution of the unemployed woman who resorted to mutism is not the only solution. Consider the following declaration of a miner's wife whose position, while not so grave, is nevertheless similar. "Sure," she said addressing a Sunday afternoon crowd in a western Pennsylvania coal town, "I'm a Bolshevist, and so's my man and my four kids. What of it? You'd be a Bolshevist, too, if you didn't have enough to eat."[13] This pale, bedraggled woman, a native American, had chosen the type of solution next in order of examination.

Mass Movements

When men find their present and future painful to behold, they search for new ideologies, and oftentimes, like the man with a toothache who believed the time when he had no toothache his happiest, they glance backward toward a golden age. Some writers delight in applying the psychological term "regression" to this tendency. This is an inexcusable usage, which seeks with mammoth subtlety to condemn the retrospection as infantile. Unless one is prepared to call "regressive" all learning which makes use of past knowledge or experience, one should simply state that these systems of belief are built around the history or traditions available to their adherents, for all mass movements contain archiaic elements.[14] Like Ortega's great bullfighter, they take a step backward to get forward momentum.

An ideological movement will not grow unless a thorough dis-ruption of existing belief-systems takes place. In the United States today many small sects exist.[15] Relative to the urban stand-ard of living they are extremely poor. They adopt devices to stir the emotions to high pitch. They are intolerant, allowing no de-viations from their way of life. All persons must think alike on sec-tarian matters, and departures even in minutiae cause lasting schisms. Nearly all hark back to the first century and believe it their holy duty to reconstruct the primitive Christian church. The larger number of them trace their ancestry back to Christ and the

Apostles. Toward modern scholarship, which they call "Modernism," they have nothing but hatred, a hatred balanced only by their worship of the remote past. The present world is evil and untrustworthy. Their one forward glance is toward the millennium.[16] Yet throughout the comparatively stable periods in America the small sects have not developed into mass movements.

In the Germany of the early twentieth century a political sect grew up around the ideas that Ferdinand Tönnies set forth in his book *Gemeinschaft und Gesellschaft*.

> The notion of *Gemeinschaft* has, since the beginning of the century, played an important and not always fortunate part in public debate and popular argument. From this time on, criticism of cultural and social traditions was rampant, especially among the younger intellectuals who rebelled against the "mechanization" and "atomization" of social life. There was also a radical reaction against the overestimation of the intellect and of positive research. . . . These trends found spontaneous expression in the middle-class youth movement. "Soul" and "blood" were invoked as against intellect and factual knowledge. . . . This neo-romantic rebellion against civilization prepared the soil for the literary success of Spengler. . . . The antithesis *Gemeinschaft-Gesellschaft* . . . was changed into the program: "Back to *Gemeinschaft*." . . . Thus *Gemeinschaft* was made the slogan of a cultural and social rebirth movement.[17]

In the belief-systems of these religious and political sects the negative elements are the protests against an inimical world, the absence of brotherly ties, and the lack of faith. Their positive features include the re-establishment of an old homeland and the banishing of a modern hostile world for one of a blood brotherhood with faith and love for a common ancestor who will actively intervene to effectuate all the necessary changes. By turning now to whole communities which have suffered a complete disruption of belief-systems, one will be able to see both the details and the diffusion of embryonic ideologies.

Let it be once more noted that belief-systems deteriorate when members are convinced of one or the other of two things—that their *ruler* is either unable or unwilling to provide for them in the manner prescribed in the ideology. To choose an example, the difficulties of the American Plains Indians affected the former conviction, the one concerning the power rather than the unwillingness of their *ruler*. The white man came in, killed off the buffalo, expropriated Indian lands, segregated the tribes on reservations—and then tried to force on them new systems of religious and political beliefs. But the new gods could not provide them with the patterns of satisfaction and nutrition that had been built about their buffalo-hunting life. Therefore the new gods were weak, not gods at all, tin gods. As it happens, twenty Indian messianic movements are recorded in the United States prior to 1890 alone.

Messianic movements are genuine mass movements: they include the whole community. Their doctrines assert that in the immediate future a hero will appear and lead the people to a terrestrial paradise.

Through the intervention of the Great Spirit or of his emissary, the earth will shortly be transformed into a paradise, enjoyed by both the living and the resurrected dead. In anticipation of the happy return to the golden age, believers must immediately return to the aboriginal mode of life. Traits and customs which are symbolic of foreign influence must be put aside. All members of the community—men, women, and children—must participate. . . . The exclusion of the whites from the golden age is not so much a reflection of hostility toward them as a symbolization of the fulfilment of the former way of life. The millennium is to be established through divine agency; believers need only watch and pray.[18]

Prophets in their visions depict the old regime. They see an old-fashioned buffalo hunt or they promise the restoration of original tribal lands or they describe a new order which, like the golden age, will give the unconflicting directives that make a warrior's life meaningful. Today, the anthropologist finds the Plains Indian without a messianic movement, spending his days in vivid fantasy. "Hunting and warfare, living in tepees, wearing the old Indian dress, and dancing the old dances are presented as things that, it is hoped, will come again. They are not recounted as past glories but as satisfactions that may return to make up for the hardships and fears of the present."[19]

Once the vast mass of people feel that the *ruler* cannot carry out his obligations, a belief-system that offers a new order, yet one in which the old will be revived, spreads like fire through dry brush. Such was the history of the Ghost Dance revival among the American Indians. Those tribes whose previous modes of life had been most disturbed participated with fervor; those whose life resembled the stage before the white occupation were little affected. Among the whites themselves, messianic and adventist movements surged up after the American Revolution, the Civil War, and World War I. During the Great Depression in the United States not only did the suicide rate shoot upward but so also did memberships in radical organizations like the Communist, Socialist, and Fascist-imitating parties.

To revert now to the small sects that carried the spark of *Gemeinschaft* in their bosoms, few persons thought that they would develop into a mass movement. "Before 1930," wrote a National Socialist party member, "most people looked upon us as immature hot heads, sacrificing their time and money for a chimerical cause."[20] Since 1930, many scholars have spent their time and money analyzing the conditions of the German people which gave rise to the N.S.D.A.P.—standard-bearer of the *Gemeinschaft*. It will not be necessary, therefore, to enlarge on the details; the recall of a few salient points will suffice. The Industrial Revolution came late to Germany; arriving tardily, it made up for lost time; between the years 1870 and 1930 the degree of urbanization increased nearly 100 per cent. (In the same period, Britain's urban growth was only 25 per cent.) Germany lost World War I. The inflation of 1919–23 wiped out all small savings. With the exception of Austria, Germany's suicide rate was the highest in Europe—25.9 per 100,000 persons per year from 1926 to 1930. The rate of crimes against private property between 1920 and 1930 was each year from two to four times as great as that of England. During the years from 1926 to 1931, in the process of rapid industrialization—scrapping, replacement, and improvement of machinery—two million persons were put on the streets, structurally unemployed. (In the same period production rose by 20 per cent.) The process of expansion of large-scale enterprise put many small proprietors out of business or into the factories. The differential in tariff walls, being high in the case of cereals produced by large landowners and low in the small farmer's province, for example, butter and cheese, brought in foreign agricultural produce which primarily competed with the livelihood of the small agrarian. The depression first hit the farming areas in 1928 and by the next year swiftly spread throughout the German economy. At the end of 1930 the number of unemployed was approximately four million, at the end of 1931 five million. By December of 1932 nearly six million were unemployed, plus an estimated two million more of the so-called "invisible unemployed"; 60 per cent of each new university graduating class was out of work, and over half of all Germans between the ages of sixteen and thirty were without jobs. On January 30 of 1933 Hitler and the National Socialist party reached power.

The cool recital of all these events tells nothing of their psychological effect on the German people. The impact can be condensed in one sentence: The belief-systems which had supported the German people collapsed like a house built of straws. Those without jobs or those with jobs in jeopardy, namely, the majority of the population, by that fact lost status. In the capitalist ideology the job-holder alone has status.[21] Whenever the closest conformity to ideological directives brings no reward—individuals work hard, competitively and rationally, and yet are discharged —they lose faith in their efficacy and in the *ruler* who rules only by grace of his ability to regulate the environment for his subjects' welfare. Ideological disintegration is complete. What should next occur, acute anomie, has often been described in these pages, but the following impressionistic account of the German and European psychological temper in the period before the rise of naziism deserves quoting for its almost empathic clarity:

> The despair of the masses is the key to the understanding of fascism. No "revolt of the mob," no "triumphs of unscrupulous propaganda," but stark despair caused by the break down of the old order and the absence of a new one. . . . Society ceases to be a community of individuals bound together by a common purpose, and becomes a chaotic hubbub of purposeless isolated monads. The great depression proved that irrational and incalculable forces rule peacetime society: the threats of sudden permanent unemployment, of being thrown on the industrial scrap heap in one's prime or even before one has started to work. Against these forces the individual finds himself as helpless, isolated, and atomized as against the forces of machine war. He cannot determine when unemployment is going to hit and why; he cannot even dodge it. Like the forces of war, the forces of depression reduce man's rational and mechanical concept of his own existence to absurdity, because they are the ultimate consequences of his rational and mechanical society. And like the forces of war, depression shows man as a senseless cog in a senselessly whirling machine which is beyond human understanding and which has ceased to serve any purpose but its own. . . .

The fact that the world has no order and follows no laws is all that is important to him . . . the individual is not concerned with historical "proofs," demonstrating that the world has not changed. All he need understand is that the attempt to comprise the universe in a mechanically rational order, in which life and death could be understood in terms of a calculable, logical sequence, has resulted in the *return of the demons* as the real masters of his destiny. . . . The demons of old were as natural as their manifestations in earthquakes or storms. The new demons, though no less inescapable, are unnatural. They can be released by man only; but once they have been turned loose, man has no control over them. . . . The average individual cannot bear the utter atomization, the unreality and senselessness, the destruction of all order, of all society, of all rational individual existence through blind, incalculable, senseless forces created as result of rationalization and mechanization. To banish these new demons has become the paramount objective of European society.[22]

This picture contains every element of acute anomie—the anxiety and animism, the hostile and uncontrollable environment.[23] And the last sentence poses the problem for any people which finds itself rulerless. Who or what can change the environment so that it provides good instead of doing harm? The American Indians sought a hero to straighten out the world for them. So did the Germans.

A social scientist in mid-1934 collected six hundred life-stories of Nazi party members. "The wish for a leader," he reported, "is frequently echoed in the autobiographies." Thus wrote a teacher:

Around 1923 I reached the conclusion that no party, but a single man alone could save Germany. This opinion was shared by others, for when the cornerstone of a monument was laid in my home town, the following lines were inscribed on it: "Descendants who read these words, know ye that we eagerly await the coming of the man whose strong hand may restore order."

And a businessman:

These were sad years. . . . As a cattle dealer, I had ample opportunity to observe the reactions of people. . . . The call for a second Bismarck resounded throughout East Prussia. The desire for a leader was evident in every political manifestation of East Prussians. . . . They could not understand why a great leader had not arisen to scatter Marxism to the four winds and give Germany a new lease on life.[24]

Before long the searchers found what they sought. Here are the testimonials of some party members:

I heard Hitler in Bonn, in 1926. . . . From that day on I could never violate my allegiance to Hitler. I saw his illimitable faith in his people and the desire to set them free. His conviction upheld us, whenever we weakened amidst our trials; we leaned upon him in our weariness.

His never-to-be-forgotten speech affected me as the words of a prophet.

I first saw Hitler at an *S.A.* Meeting at Gera in September, 1931. The experience was a revelation to us, and we should have rushed blindly anywhere Hitler commanded us to go. The sun shone all the time Hitler was there, in proverbial "Hitler weather." Before his arrival and after he left, it rained so hard we were drenched.

We, oldtime National Socialists, did not join the *S.A.* for reasons of self-interest. Our feelings led us to Hitler. There was a tremendous surge in our hearts, a something that said: "Hitler, you are our man."[25]

This overpowering desire to see in one being the capacity to regulate a hostile world and to repose in him physical and moral authority and full trust—this need has appeared in the ontogeny of the human organism whenever it has been afflicted with the separation-anxiety that follows each disintegration of belief-systems.[26]

It was not Hitler who made himself a demi-god; it was the masses who pushed him up on this pedestal. For only a demon, a superman and magician who can never err and who is always right can resolve the contradiction between the need for a miracle and the impossibility of producing one. Only unquestioning belief in the Führer can give the security of conviction which the masses crave in order to be spared from despair. . . . Hitler must be right because otherwise nothing is.[27]

It is this need to believe which most fully explains the vagueness of the theory of leadership succession in fascism. The same theory occurs in all messianic movements. The deity himself or his emissary will simply appear. And he does appear because the need for his presence is so great. The unspoken prayers of the mass of people are answered.[28]   This is no devious attempt to be mystical. Most of the population feels completely helpless and abandoned and anxiously seeks a *ruler*. As was learned in the preceding chapter, however, there usually exist a few persons whose reaction to acute anomie is the assumption of a great mission or (as psychiatrists or opponents of the mission might say) of paranoiac or megalomaniac delusions. The bulk of the population, vitally interested as it is in all missionary claims, gives them a larger measure of credence than it would under less anomic conditions. In this way do the special reactions of a few and the ordinary reactions of the many fit together. "We believe deeply and unswervingly that God has sent Adolf Hitler to us to save Germany."[29] The attributes of a messiah are the attributes of the Leader. No one has depicted the process of *Führer*-selection more accurately than the ill-starred American model, Huey Long, when he declared, "Just say I'm *sui generis*, and let it go at that."[30]

What was the program of the man who could win such a devoted following? Fascism had no philosophical past; in the embryonic stages of the movement both the Nazi and Fascist parties made platforms that they never realized; their doctrinal emphases shifted like an accordion, first to the left, then to the right.[31] They made many trials and errors to find the deepest groove. But once there, they did not stir except to make occasional hairsplittings (such as that between finance and industrial capitalism) for reasons of tactical politics. Hitler and the National Socialists did have a basic program. Without it they might never have come to power. It was simple. The complete opposite of the competitive directive with its rationalist and impersonal axioms. *Gemeinnutz vor Eigennutz! Blut und Boden! Gemeinschaft!* three phrases that overthrow the competitive ethic, three phrases that underline the family pattern in ideologies, three phrases that make up every new ideology and strengthen the defense of every old ideology. This emphasis on the commonweal, common ancestry, and brotherly cohesion was also seen in the small American sects and the messianic movements of the Plains Indians. There are scores of books on Nazi philosophy attempting to relate the ramifications of this creed. They write of the anti-rationalism or anti-intellectualism of the Nazis, their anti-individualism, anti-parliamentarianism, anti-Semitism, anti-capitalism, and anti-pluralism. Yet these doctrines could all be crammed into a vehement rejection of the competitive directive.[32] And from the positive viewpoint they outlined the cosmic adjustment which the German people desperately needed. The ideologies of the majority of Germans had disintegrated. What National Socialism did was to promise the German people what they no longer had—a system of political beliefs.

Hitler's first task, then, was the restoration of the political belief-system. Most writers on naziism have found its violence so reprehensible that they have not attempted to document its work in any other direction. But in so far as possible the National Socialists did carry out the job of ideological reformation. Certainly no one can say that their blood purification plan failed for want of execution or that economic profit and loss were supremely regarded either domestically or in foreign trade. Unemployment? Had not Hitler said, "economics is a secondary matter"? There was no unemployment. Perhaps less known are the efforts made by the Nazis to re-create the atmosphere of *Gemeinschaft*, that part of their work which looks to a homier past. In 1938 an English architectural expert toured Germany, and his remarks on building styles and art are interesting because they deal rather objectively with the relatively unfamiliar works of the Nazis. Having only an indirect political bearing, these deeds of theirs may smack less of duplicity:

Everything arty and crafty . . . is now staging a come-back in Germany. It is part of the flight from functionalism; and a hand-made tomb for the modern movement has been prepared. This arty-craft revival—which is part of the Nazi educational scheme that works through form and colour just as logically as it does through the printing-press and the radio set—is laying heavy hands upon the shape of all things. Furniture has lost any suggestion of lightness and gaiety; chairs, tables, sideboards and dressers are putting on flesh. The cabinet-maker seems to be trying to get back to the adze, and to derive his inspiration from the butcher's shop. . . .

"We don't want experiments in structure or materials," we were informed. The housing officials know exactly what accommodation a family needs; they prefer to use traditional materials and building methods; they want to create a comfortable setting for traditional family life. (No experiments are wanted in that direction either.) . . .

There can be no compromise between the experimental outlook of the modernist and the determination of National Socialism to establish the family with all its sacred traditional accompaniments in fecundity and perpetuity. . . .

German housing officials put first on the list: *the people hate a flat roof*. I was assured that people can't and won't think of a flat-roofed house as a home. I was too familiar with the echoes of this sentiment in our own country to dispute the assertion. Experiments have been made with various materials, but the most satisfactory structure has been produced by timber framing, with brick filling; similar to the half-timbered houses of the sixteenth and seventeenth centuries. These new farm-houses have a thatched roof; generous windows; walls thick enough to keep the house warm in the biting, raging winds that harry the plains; and an air of welcome and comfort. They are not copies of old houses—

they exemplify the use of a traditional method of building. They blend agreeably with existing buildings, and they are going to last and grow old gracefully.

The flight from concrete is interesting, for it is political in character; it is a flight from exciting and revolutionary shapes that might recall memories of modernism; it is an expression of reverence for tradition and abhorrence of any form of life that threatens the old, known and often inconvenient ways of mankind.

And everywhere—around Berlin, near big industrial cities, outside Munich, Nuremberg, Frankfort and Cologne—you see, as a reflection of these homely ideals, the little warm-roofed dwellings which are stopping the *landflucht*, spreading contentment and checking the growth of unconventional ideas.[33]

Hitler's role, as a discerning political scientist describes it, nicely fits this nostalgic preoccupation with the symbols of home life:

There is a profound sense in which Hitler himself plays a maternal role for certain classes in German society. His incessant moralizing is that of the anxious mother who is totally preoccupied with the physical, intellectual and ethical development of her children. He discourses in public, as he has written in his autobiography, on all manner of pedagogical problems, from the best form of history teaching to the ways of reducing the ravages of social disease. His constant preoccupation with "purity" is consistent with these interests; he alludes constantly to the "purity of the racial stock" and often to the code of personal abstinence or moderation. This master of modern Galahadism uses the language of Protestant puritanism and of Catholic reverence for the institution of family life. The conscience for which he stands is full of obsessional doubts, repetitive affirmations, resounding negations and stern compulsions. It is essentially the bundle of "don'ts" of the nurse-maid conscience.[34]

The place assigned to women in National Socialism, the traditional *Kinder*, *Küche*, *Kirche*, also dovetails with the goal of a healthy old-fashioned home life. The disparagement of female suffrage, the discrimination against bachelors, the heavier penalization of illegitimacy, and the increased difficulty of divorce in fruitful marriages all harmonize with the domestic symphony.

The tourist next turned his attention to the cinema:

But what of the films? . . . The only good films to be seen now are news films. For the rest, sentimental slush, only passably well photographed, and agonizingly long (they've forgotten everything about cutting), alternates with the dreariest and most prolonged documentary films dealing with nice established traditional things like the working of the solar system, the mating of tropical birds, and nature in all its safety-first aspects. Of course, a lot of health and joy pours off the screen—hulking wenches leap about, and somebody is always wringing melody from an accordion.[35]

Another favorite type of film was on the theme of *die gute alte Zeit* of old Vienna:

> As in the living theatre where Goebbels has encouraged the revival of Viennese operetta, as on the radio where Viennese waltzes have occupied a great deal of the broadcasting time, so in the cinema an increasing number of films has been produced on Viennese themes. An example of this type of film was *Operetta*, with Willy Forst the actor-producer. It was set in the classic age of Viennese operetta, the 1820's or '30's. Its atmosphere was the familiar one of spring, love, lilac, guitars, and Viennese wine, of whistling baker-boys and housemaids who sing and waltz as they flick dusters over gleaming doorknobs, of dashing guardsmen who flirt with pretty milliners. Out of this background emerged in the film *Operetta* the story of a young composer and his actress friend whose talent and love helped them to become famous and important forerunners of Johann Strauss. Many similar films have been made in German film studios during the last two years, among them *A Ball at the Opera* and a film version of Johann Strauss's operetta *Wiener Blut*.[36]

In music the modernists like Hindemith, Krenek, and Alban Berg were of course outlawed. In turn, the Ministry of Enlightenment encouraged the revival and rediscovery of nineteenth-century composers of both the light and the heavy variety, Lincke, Lehar, Ziehrer, Beethoven, and, assuredly, Wagner. The same effort was made in the fields of sculpture and painting. Back to *Gemeinschaft!*

This English visitor in Germany also went to a labor camp. Throughout his stay he endeavored to make correct discounts for the obvious attempts to present naziism's best side to the tourist:

> The Labour Service system gives every boy of every class the feeling that he has personally contributed something tangible to the improvement of the land, and also gives to future German citizens a practical appreciation of the farmers' life and problems. . . .
> "The spade is our machine," said the Commandant. They use nothing else. The mechanism which could cut drains and make embankments and roads has no place in this scheme. The rejection of machinery is as deliberate as the rejection of the modern movement in architecture. It is believed that only from muscular effort, from sweat, and from the skill acquired in handling the spade and the tools of the farm, can pride in work arise. There was a strong flavour of the teachings of John Ruskin and William Morris about all this.

A person may still doubt the sincerity and earnestness of even these less political projects. And on reading a eulogy of the *Kraft durch Freude* which runs in this vein, "It is much jollier and more cheerful in our company, because we are not a more or less casual gathering of 'individuals,' but a happy community in which social differences are obliterated and real good fellowship takes their place,"[37] he can jot it down as propaganda. But he should recall the German youth who in 1933 celebrated his acceptance in the fraternal order of the Brownshirts with a poem:

> Now I know well
> I am no more alone.[38]

Well would it be for him also to remember one of the Nazis' earliest slogans: "Rather a terrible end than an endless terror." It should be admitted, then, that Hitler and the National Socialists created a system of beliefs. They ended the endless terror. In doing that they freed themselves for the issuance of other directives—military conquests, world domination. And at these the German people could not balk, for they were still haunted by the panic of acute anomie. The most persuasive argument that could be made to keep them in line took the form of a question: "Would you rather go back to the chaotic days?"[39] The terrible end was chosen instead.

It is a recurring thing, this acute anomie. A few concluding words might be appended concerning its wider significance. In modern times its greater frequency is due to the widespread loss of status during economic contractions. On the basis of past experience, an authoritative statement declares, the American citizen may expect to spend one quarter of his life in periods of economic stagnation.[40] In a depression the American citizen too says, "I want belief, some ground to stand on. I do not want government to go on being a meaningless thing."[41] He is not immune to anomic anxiety. *Ergo, fas est ab hoste doceri.* It is one's duty to learn from the enemy, even though he is militarily vanquished or even though he may no longer be the enemy. The poet Yeats has properly placed the problem of the citizen in a rulerless world on a universal plane:

> Turning and turning in the widening gyre
> The falcon cannot hear the falconer;
> Things fall apart; the centre cannot hold;
> Mere anarchy is loosed upon the world
> .   .   .   .
> Surely some revelation is at hand;
> Surely the Second Coming is at hand.
> The Second Coming!

To sum up, if more than a majority of the adult population[42] in a political community loses primary secular status, faith in the ruling entity will dissolve and the entire political belief-system will disintegrate. In consequence the incidence of acute anomie will be high. Under pressure of anxiety people will attempt a solution which sets up the family pattern of political relationships. They will seek succor in one person who claims to be able to control the environment so that they will regain status, one person who directs them to love one another as brothers, one person who demands of them unquestioning faith and obedience. The identity of feeling among those with acute anomie will cluster them about such persons. This way of solving the problem is necessarily chosen; it involves the same attitudes and behavior patterns that the individual successfully maintained in earlier attempts to free himself from separation-anxiety. In time a mass movement starts, one person emerges clear, and the march toward a new ideology for the whole political community begins. The recency of popular anxiety colors the movement with a strong interrelatedness which invariably brings the blood brotherhood and the physical and moral authority of the *ruler* to the foreground. Conduct takes on the appearance of a strain to convert communal ties into the stereotypes of family bonds. The beliefs behind this action are extreme when compared to those that characterize the political and religious ideologies in periods without a disintegrating threat. The exaggeration can be likened to the growth of protective bony cells around the healing area of a fracture. Freshly recovered from panic, the mind takes extraordinary precautions to prevent a relapse. Had there been no breakdown of the system of beliefs, the political ideology would have performed its primary protective function in customary quietness. Once the psyche is long removed from the terror of acute anomie, it proves itself more adaptable than the soma. It sloughs off the extra growth.

C O D A

C O D A

THE theologian is right. Why not admit it? More than anything else, the world needs Love. These several hundred
pages have shown that unless a human being is welcomed to this
world with love, he might as well have been stillborn; that unless
his widening horizon continues to assure him of this love, he will
not grow; and unless the religious and political beliefs which secure this love are left unfouled, he will wander through life in a
maze. Love cannot follow its true course which is Justice unless
the competitive directive is removed from barring its path.
America, which was among the last to receive the competitive directive, may be the last to let it die. But die it must if man is ever
to cease to act the wolf of man. And this truth applies not only
to the community of the nation. The world's peoples will be
loath to accept America's leadership so long as they see it as the
promise of glittering objects in the clutch of competition. There
can be no single world-embracing political community until the
idea of competition as the guiding principle for the relation of
man to man is ruled out.

There is no other way. Theoretically the problem of eliminat-
ing conflict between the directives of belief-systems is that of
holding one directive constant while changing the other so that
the two harmonize. To a logician the possibility at once appears:
Why not then hold the competitive directive fast and vary the religious and political ideologies to fit it? The answer in plain words
is that the human being is not made that way. That is why one
of the first propositions in political science must always be Aristotle's dictum: Man is a political animal. In fact, this book could
be summarized by saying that it attempted to go beyond Aristotle's declaration, that it attempted to show why man is a political and religious animal and cannot be otherwise.

The co-operative ethic cannot be eradicated from the human
mind because from birth the individual needs the co-operative

help of a community or else he perishes. All persons receive this help, and therefore all persons organize their lives around belief-systems that assure them of it. No matter how diverse communities may be, they have this in common. They put their trust in supreme beings who are rulers not so much for their command over subjects as for their special ability to rule the environment. These supreme figures, the religious and political rulers, can thus provide for the community. But the secret of their success lies in their inviolable demand that brotherly co-operation be the spirit of communal relationships. Not all belief-systems present this directive. All of them, it is true, direct that love, faith, and obedience must be rendered the ruler. This is a constant, the one directive that appears in all ideologies. There are variable directives in ideologies, however, and the most important of these concerns the relationships among members of the group. Although a business ideology can ask for competitive relationships, the religious and political cannot. There lies the heart of the matter. There lies the reason that the political and religious systems of belief can never fundamentally conflict. Both of them are descended from the community of the family, an inescapable community bred in the very nature of the human species. Hence, if the community is to be regenerated, the competitive directive must be the one to go, for the co-operative directive can never be crushed out of men's lives. To search for compromise measures is futile. Halfway measures are what exist today, each half opposed to the other.

One should not fall into the belief, however, that a necessary connection exists between democracy and anomie. In *A Study of History*, Toynbee reports that most of the world's twenty-one civilizations were at some time affected with the "schism in the soul" that led to their disintegration. Yet none of them had the form of government that first struck root in the British Isles. Strangely enough, anomie is unrelated to any particular system of beliefs. So long as clear and consistent belief-systems prevail, anomie will spare the community, no matter what its brand of belief may be. Certain circumstantial factors, however, factors not of the essence of democratic philosophy, have led it toward a careless view of the problem of community. It is sometimes forgotten that democratic theory emerged out of four revolutions—two English, one American, and one French. A fifth could be added—the Industrial Revolution. The leading spirits in these struggles were bent on breaking, not forging, many of the physical and moral chains of existent regimes. But even the most seaworthy ship of state must have chains if for nothing but the anchor. Durkheim's merit is that he first openly declared that men without systems of belief are men without anchorage, floundering and tossing in mental turmoil. If there is one grand underlying cause for the continued existence of anomie, it is that the damage wrought by those revolutions has not yet been repaired. A sober realization of the psychological importance of the political belief-system poses a perplexing problem for the democracies. As was seen, they appear not to have the courage of their political convictions; they let the younger generation grow into adulthood without showing it the depth of their own faith. The wages of cynicism is death, death to the democratic community no less than to any other.

It is easy to see now how essential the ruler is for the political community. The wisdom of Confucius expresses it simply:

Tzu-chang asked about government. The Master said, "The requisites of government are that there be a sufficiency of food, sufficiency of military equipment, and the confidence of the people in their ruler." Tzu-chang said, "If it cannot be helped, and one of these must be dispensed with, which of the three should be foregone first?" "The military equipment," said the Master. Tzu-chang again asked, "If it cannot be helped, and one of the remaining two must be dispensed with, which of them should be foregone?' The Master answered, "Part with the food. From of old, death has been the lot of all men; but a people that has no faith in their rulers is lost indeed."

A political community exists among men who regard each other as brothers. But they will not think of themselves as a brotherhood until they have and avow filial love and faith for their ruler and for their God. If they have no faith in their rulers or if they allow opposing directives to sway them from the commandment of love for their fellow-men, they have no political community; they have anomie.

Once grasp this truth and the theoretical splitting of man into a creature of individual and social interests becomes an obvious distortion. In political science especially, the individual-collective dichotomy has been worked to barrenness. All political ideologies—monarchy, democracy, aristocracy—are protagonists of the common good. A political belief-system that claims to be for the benefit of an individual or a few is an impossibility. Man is the being who can attain his greatest happiness only in the political community. He will not be excluded from it.

Those political writers who would bring the political community down to the level of other associations invariably speak of a great "Society" or a great "Community" *within* which the state is merely one among many morally equal groups. When one asks on what is this "Community" based (for does not the word community imply living things with something in common?), the answer can only be labored and confused. Joseph de Maistre once said, "I have seen, in my time, Frenchmen, Italians, and Russians; I even know, thanks to Montesquieu, that one may be a Persian; but as for *Man*, I declare that I have never met him in my life; if he exists it is without my knowledge." Similarly, a person today can see the nationals observed by De Maistre, but he can say further, "I even know, thanks to Malinowski, that one may be a Trobriander; but as for a Societan!—I declare that I have never met him in my life." *Extra patria, nullum nomen*. Without the political community, a man is a nameless outcast. The state is the highest secular association because like its counterpart, the religious community, it exists to protect man from his greatest fear—isolation. If he lives in this fear, he can never rise to his fullest potentialities. It is rather ironic that in this age without a sense of community charges are often heard that the dignity of the individual is lost. Once the sense of community is regained, dignity again will envelop the individual.

How long the competitive directive will survive is unknown. In the perspective of centuries its history has been spotty and brief. Never being able to penetrate the family community as early as the political and religious directives, its foundation is comparatively shallow. Nonetheless, it has its greatest depth in the United States where, combined with the ethic of work, it has branched out into the creeds of science and progress. Its removal will not come without difficulties, but these difficulties should not be exaggerated. It must be remembered that a community without a competitive directive means no more than a community where rivalry among men for monetary acquisition is not given moral encouragement. Such a community does not require a new set of institutions for economic life but that a new, a less conflict-laden, a purer spirit should move men. It does not ask that people quit all competitive behavior. That they should is neither necessary nor desirable. There will always be striving for excellence in those activities which the community regards as honorable; is this not enough? The reward of higher respect from one's fellows, a reward present wherever men associate, suffices to maintain a competitive striving of this kind. And monetary incentives could be piled atop the reward; there could be no objection. But what need is there for indoctrinating men in the belief that other men are rivals for their basic position in the community, for their very status? As long as the doctrine of competition lasts, its uncomputed costs will include the misery and fear of pointlessness and isolation, eccentric lives that find nobility of purpose only in war.

The pervasive evil of anomie will certainly justify an honest effort to depict a community to which could be brought increased devotion. This is a further task in the theory of political organization. These last few pages obviously do not assume the task. They are literally a tailpiece, suggestive in intent, though broad in scope. The previous chapters have carried the brunt of evidence and generalization. They are the pages that should make easier now the task of assaying the character of a modern community without conflicting beliefs. Scholars had written before of the vital importance of beliefs to the political community. They were right-thinking men, but they pointed to the trouble from too far a distance. Unmodified, the word "beliefs" covered too long and wide a terrain. The area seems narrowed now. Henceforth any effort to describe the makeup of a community without anomie can focus immediately on the critical points in men's beliefs—the rulers and their directives. That task, however, requires a new volume to follow in the traditions of political science set by Plato and Campanella. In any event, it is not for one person to decide whether anomie is a greater evil than life without the competitive directive. The contribution of this book is toward making the causes of anomie and its debilitating effects on the political community known to many persons. The problem then rests in their hands. Only in finding the solution can they rightfully call themselves Citizens.

N O T E S

N O T E S

PART I

INTRODUCTION

1. The English word "anomy," which descends directly from the Greek *anomia*, meaning lawlessness, is obsolete, having been out of practical use since 1689. At that time it meant disregard of law and, in seventeenth-century theology, disregard of divine law. *Webster's New International Dictionary* (2d ed., unabridged; Springfield, Mass.: G. & C. Merriam Co., 1930) spells and accents the word, "an ' omy," placing more emphasis on a meaning of lawlessness or lack of uniformity in the physical order and quoting Karl Pearson in the following fashion: "Laplace has even enabled us to take account of possible 'miracles,' anomies, or breaches of routine."

The term "anomie" was first used by Durkheim in a descriptive fashion in *De la division du travail social* (Paris: Félix Alcan, 1893). In a later work, *Le Suicide* (Paris: Félix Alcan, 1897), the word was expanded into a concept and assigned a prominent position. And, finally, in the Preface to the second edition of the former work, "Quelques remarques sur les groupements professionnels," Durkheim made up for his previous neglect by treating the subject extensively.

This work will spell the word "anomie" without italics or quotation marks. The adjective of the noun, which in French is *anomique*, will be spelled "anomic," again without the use of italics or quotation marks.

CHAPTER I

1. For some of the biological peculiarities of man see Julian Huxley, *The Uniqueness of Man* (London: Chatto & Windus, 1941), pp. 3–33. The newborn infant does have a number of reflex and defensive responses—closing eyes to a bright light or restlessness under cold temperature—but unless it lives in a highly protective environment, which includes ministering adults, these responses alone cannot keep it alive. The defensive capacities of the infant are carefully examined in Mandel and Irene Sherman and Charles D. Flory, *Infant Behavior* ("Comparative Psychology Monographs," Vol. XII [1936]). See also William Stern, *The Psychology of Early Childhood up to the Sixth Year of Age*, trans. Anna Barwell (New York: Henry Holt & Co., 1924), pp. 70–79. Psychologists have reached fairly close agreement on the definition and enumeration of viscerogenic needs of the human organism. For technical classifications see E. C. Tolman, *Purposive Behavior in Men and Animals* (New York: Century Co., 1932); P. T. Young, *Motivation of Behavior* (New York: J. Wiley & Sons, Inc., 1936); Henry A. Murray and Associates, *Explorations in Personality* (New York: Oxford University Press, 1938).

2. See, especially, Sandor Ferenczi, "Stages in the Development of the Sense of Reality," in *Contributions to Psychoanalysis* (Boston: Richard G. Badger, 1916), pp. 171–251. Since the infant cannot speak, the evidence for the existence of the autarchic stage is in the nature of a logical inference from data on the physiological condition of the organism at this time. It has additional support in the more direct evidence of the development of self-consciousness (see n. 3, below) and in adult cases of drug usage or mental disorders of the manic variety which apparently reproduce the illusion of self-world unity.

3. See, e.g., J. M. Baldwin, *Mental Development in the Child and the Race* (New York: Macmillan Co., 1903); George Mead, *Mind, Self, and Society* (Chicago: University of Chicago Press, 1934); Stern, *Early Childhood*, pp. 112–23; Kurt Koffka, *Principles of Gestalt Psychology* (New York: Harcourt, Brace & Co., 1935); Gordon Allport, *Personality: A Psychological Interpretation* (New York: Henry Holt & Co., 1937), pp. 159–65, and Jean Piaget, *The Child's Conception of the World* (New York: Harcourt, Brace & Co., 1929), pp. 131 f., 389 f. For the development of self-awareness among children of simpler cultures see Dudley Kidd, *Savage Childhood* (London: A. & C. Black, 1906).

4. If adults in the culture, however, do not restrict consciousness to animals, in all probability neither will the children.

The literature on the animism of the child is voluminous. See, especially, Piaget, *The Child's Conception of the World*, pp. 171–251. An early theoretical formulation is contained in Ferenczi, "Sense of Reality."

The development of child animism as presented here allows of no exception for cultural differences. In support it should be noted that anthropologists almost unanimously agree that child animism is a universal phenomenon (see, e.g., Ruth Benedict, *Patterns of Culture* [New York: Pelican Books, Inc., 1946], p. 17). The one noteworthy exception is Margaret Mead, who maintains that animistic beliefs are not characteristic of children in all cultures (see her *Coming of Age in Samoa* [New York: Blue Ribbon Books, 1934]; *Growing Up in New Guinea* [New York: W. Morrow & Co., 1930]; and "An Investigation of the Thought of Primitive Children with Special Reference to Animism," *Journal of the Royal Anthropological Institute*, LXII [1932], 173 f.). Both her definitions and methods, however, have been severely criticized (see O. F. Raum, *Chaga Childhood: A Description of Indigenous Education in an East African Tribe* [New York: Oxford University Press, 1940], pp. 240–42).

5. See Jules Henry, "Some Cultural Determinants of Hostility in Pilaga Indian Children," *American Journal of Orthopsychiatry*, X (1940), 117–18.

6. Throughout this chapter the word "attendants" is used instead of "parents" to refer to those persons in a culture who traditionally minister to the infant or child. Malinowski has stressed the occurrence of child rearing by persons other than father and mother (Bronislaw Malinowski, *Sex and Repression in a Primitive Tribe* [New York: Harcourt, Brace & Co., 1927]). It often happens, too, that elder siblings rather than adults watch and care for the child, as among the Lepchas of Sikkim (see Geoffrey Gorer, *Himalayan Village* [London: Michael Joseph, Ltd., 1938], pp. 283–301).

7. Rainer Maria Rilke, *Duino Elegies*, ed. and trans. J. B. Leishman and Stephen Spender (London: Hogarth Press, 1939), p. 42. Rilke's writings on the child's toy also show a remarkable psychological insight. E.g., "Consider . . . whether everything—apart from it—was not in a position to hurt or wrong you, to frighten you with a pain or confuse you with an uncertainty. . . . If kindness was among your first experiences and confidence and not being alone—are you not indebted to it? . . . This small forgotten object, that was ready to signify everything, made you intimate with thousands through playing a thousand parts, being animal and tree and king and child,—and when it withdrew, they were all there" (p. 121).

8. Among some North American tribes, such as the Lummi and the Fox, the parents discussed religious affiliations with the child *before* it could speak, on the theory that even though speechless it understood all (see George A. Pettitt, *Primitive Education in North America* ["University of California Publications in American Archaeology and Ethnology," ed. A. L. Kroeber, R. H. Lowie, and R. L. Olson, Vol. XLIII, No. 1 (Los Angeles: University of California Press, 1946)], pp. 9–11).

9. Anxieties attributable to peculiarly familial or cultural factors will not be considered here. An example of familial and cultural factors promoting anxiety would be the situation of the Pilaga child on the arrival of a new sibling:

Although as the Pilaga child grows older he receives the breast less often, partly because he eats other things, partly because he is busy playing, and often because his mother is away working, he can still have access to her breast frequently. He is still very much the object of his mother's attention, and he spends many hours sitting on her thighs as she parts his hair looking for lice. Once a new sibling appears, however, this is radically changed.

Though the mother may nurse him even while she is in labor, when the new child is born the older sibling is absolutely denied the breast. Not only this, but the attention his mother and father once gave him is now directed to the new baby. Formerly when he wept he was given the breast and comforted by his mother. Now he is told to "Be quiet" and sent to play outdoors or to a relative, who may afford him some casual comfort in the form of a morsel of food.

This situation leaves the older sibling stunned. He wanders disconsolately about near the house and whimpers continually, apparently without cause. When he comes home, it is not infrequently to try out little schemes for doing away with the new baby, and his mother must be very watchful lest he injure the new sibling. Naturally this only intensifies the situation, for the mother's redoubled attention serves to isolate the older sibling even more [Henry, "Pilaga Indian Children," pp. 118–19].

This anxiety is familial in the sense that if the child had had no younger siblings or if the next sibling after him was born when he was ten or fifteen years of age, it would not have occurred; it is cultural in that the Pilaga make no attempt to give the child substitute attention, whereas in other communities, such as in Manus, Dobu, and among the modern Omaha, the father at this time may take over the care of the child, thereby lessening the psychological hardship. For variations in adult conduct upon the arrival of succeeding children see Margaret Mead, "The Primitive Child" in *A Handbook of Child Psychology*, ed. Carl Murchison (Worcester, Mass.: Clark University Press, 1933), p. 677.

10. As a matter of theory, anxiety is the core of the psychoneurosis (Sigmund Freud, *The Problem of Anxiety*, trans. Henry Alden Bunker [New York: Psychoanalytic Quarterly Press and W. W. Norton & Co., Inc., 1936]). Some psychiatrists define personal maladjustment simply by the extent to which anxiety of any kind is present. For the physical symptoms of anxiety see, especially, Henry Harris, "Anxiety, Its Nature and Treatment," *Journal of Mental Science*, LXXX (1934), 482–512, 705–15; H. L. Kozol, "Study of Anxiety Attacks," *Archives of Neurology and Psychiatry*, XLIII (1940), 102–10; and Kurt Goldstein, *The Organism* (New York: American Book Co., 1939), pp. 291–307.

11. See, e.g., Margaret A. Ribble, "Anxiety in Infants and Its Disorganizing Effects," in *Modern Trends in Child Psychiatry*, ed. Nolan D. C. Lewis and Bernard L. Pacella (New York: International Universities Press, 1945), pp. 11–26; Bert I. Beverly, "Anxieties of Children: Their Causes and Implications," *American Journal of Diseases of Children*, LXIV (1942), 585–93; W. Langford, "Anxiety Attacks in Children," *American Journal of Orthopsychiatry*, VII (1937), 210–18; Henry E. Utter, "Fears of Infancy and Early Childhood," *Rhode Island Medical Journal*, XXV (1942), 242–48. The pioneer venture in the investigation of children's anxiety is the "little Hans" case (Sigmund Freud, "The Analysis of a Phobia in a Five-Year-Old Boy," *Collected Papers*, trans. Alix and James Strachey [New York: International Psychoanalytic Press, 1924–25], Vol. III).

12. Psychiatrists and psychoanalysts of several opposing schools are now in accord on this anxiety. Each one, however, gives it a different name. Freud, whose writings on the subject are indispensable for the student, simply called it "anxiety" (or "primary anxiety") using adjectives before the term, such as "castration anxiety," to distinguish other types (S. Freud, *The Problem of Anxiety, passim*). Jones, who first called attention to its significance, used the Greek term *aphanisis* (Ernest Jones, "The Early Development of Female Sexuality," *International Journal of Psychoanalysis*, VIII [1927], 459–72). Horney used the name "basic anxiety" (Karen Horney, *The Neurotic Personality of Our Time* [New York: W. W. Norton & Co., Inc., 1937], pp. 79–90). Suttie gave it the name which was selected for use here—"separation-anxiety" (Ian Suttie, *The Origins of Love and Hate* [London: Kegan, Paul, Trench, Trubner & Co., Ltd., 1938], *passim*).

It may be reasonably objected that the child could not possibly describe the subjective aspect of this anxiety at the age in which it first occurs. This is correct. The frame of mind of the anxious child has been constructed from several sources: (1) logical inferences from what is known of the child's conception of the world at this time, (2) parental observations, (3) the direct statements and observed play of children at an age of clearer expression (two to six years of age) (see, e.g., Horney, *Neurotic Personality*, pp. 88–89; John Bowlby, "The Influence of Early Environment in the Development of Neurosis and Neurotic Character," *International Journal of Psychoanalysis*, XXI [1940], 154–78; Melanie

Klein, "Infantile Anxiety Situations Reflected in a Work of Art and in the Creative Impulse," *International Journal of Psychoanalysis*, X [1929], 436, and "Psychological Principles of Infant Analysis," *ibid.*, VIII [1927], 25–37; Dorothy Burlingham and Anna Freud, *Young Children in Wartime: A Year's Work in a Residential War Nursery* [London: G. Allen & Unwin, Ltd., 1942]), and (4) the expressions of adults under psychological observation whose anxiety revives such a picture. Thus an adult patient spontaneously drew a picture in which she was sitting in the midst of a scene as a tiny, helpless, deserted baby, encircled by all sorts of menacing monsters, human and animal, ready to pounce on her (Horney, *Neurotic Personality*, pp. 92–93).

13. The essays of Jean Jacques Rousseau and of Sigmund Freud on the inevitable conflicts arising out of the civilizing process were concerned with this fact (see Rousseau, "A Discourse on the Origin of Inequality" in *The Social Contract and Discourses*, trans. G. D. H. Cole [New York: E. P. Dutton & Co., Inc., 1913], and Freud, *Civilization and Its Discontents*, trans. Joan Rivière [London: Leonard and Virginia Woolf at the Hogarth Press and the Institute of Psychoanalysis, 1930]).

14. Ernest Jones was instrumental in pointing out that the anxiety aroused on such occasions was provoked not only by the fear of corporal punishment but also by the fear of loss of his parents' love, the much more drastic threat to the child, which results in *aphanisis* or separation-anxiety (Jones, "Female Sexuality"; see also Horney, *Neurotic Personality*, pp. 79–89).

15. See, especially, James S. Plant, *Personality and the Cultural Pattern* (New York: Commonwealth Fund, 1937), pp. 21–22, 95–97. The reassuring function of affectionate expression is well described in David M. Levy, "Primary Affect Hunger," *American Journal of Psychiatry*, XCIV (1937), 643–52.

16. See P. Bovet, *The Child's Religion* (London: Dent, 1928).

17. On the child's need at this time to know who has authority over such forces see the chapter "On the Relativity of Reality and the Genesis of the Need of Causality," in René Laforgue, *The Relativity of Reality*, trans. Anne Jouard (New York: Nervous and Mental Disease Monographs, 1940), pp. 37–59.

18. Plant makes this point in *Personality*, pp. 385–86. Murdock presents material about the agricultural Hopi Indians which bears on the subject (George Peter Murdock, *Our Primitive Contemporaries* [New York: Macmillan Co., 1934], pp. 347–48).

19. Raum, *Chaga Childhood*, pp. 339–40.

20. Rudolf Otto has stated that the feeling contained in the idea of the divine is appropriately expressed only in this term, *mysterium tremendum* (see *The Idea of the Holy*, trans. John W. Haney [New York: Oxford University Press, 1939], pp. 12–41).

21. Three excellent works supply abundant data for this proposition: A. M. Hocart, *Kingship* (London: Oxford University Press, 1927); Marc Bloch, *Les Rois thaumaturges* (Paris: Librairie Istra, 1924); and Sir James G. Frazer, *The Golden Bough* (one-volume abridged ed.; New York: Macmillan Co., 1941),

chaps. v–viii, xiii, xxiii–xxvi. On "Queens and Their Special Powers" see Robert Briffault, *The Mothers* (3 vols.; New York: Macmillan Co., 1927), III, 1–184.

22. Veblen's theory of the change in communities from sedentary agriculture to predatory warfare with corresponding change in status is related to this proposition. Also related are Marx's theory of economic determinism, which, however, includes more than political institutions in its applications, and John Dewey's concept of occupational psychosis, which calls attention to the extraordinary influence a community's productive methods will have on the other traits of the culture.

As the studies of Giuseppe Mazzarella, *Studi di etnologica giuridica* (Catania: E. Coco, 1903), and L. T. Hobhouse, G. C. Wheeler, and M. Ginsberg, *The Material Culture and Social Institutions of the Simpler Peoples* (London: Chapman & Hall, Ltd., 1915), have shown, the proposition seems to lose much of its value when applied to more complex societies, where the uneven life-spans of different institutional forms, such as religion, aesthetics, or marriage, complicate the picture of political leadership at any given interval. It should be noted in defense, however, that the important part of the hypothesis concerns those whom the members of a community *believe* to be the persons performing the activities most essential for the commonweal. Even in complex communities, as will be seen, persons have a rather simple idea that there is one homogeneous group of activities which is all important.

23. Hocart, *Kingship*, p. 46.

24. Malinowski, *Foundations of Faith and Morals* (London: Oxford University Press, 1936), p. 30. H. Richard Niebuhr has classified religions according to the aspects of the environment they are presumed to regulate (see his *Social Sources of Denominationalism* [New York: Henry Holt & Co., 1929]).

25. Malinowski, *Foundations of Faith*, pp. 25–27.

26. The term *ruler* also has the advantage of avoiding the selection of a word in an obsolete language (e.g., the Latin *gubernator*) which is likely to impart an ancient or unreal aura to the context. Furthermore, existing terms do not sufficiently resemble the meaning involved. Thus, "superhuman" was rejected because it was difficult to apply to mortals. "Superman" was impossible not only because of its Nietzschean and Nazi usage but also because of its comic-book popularity in this country. "Superbeing," a likely candidate in many ways, unfortunately had obvious "super" associations. The hardest to reject because of its affinity of meaning was Max Weber's "charismatic leader." Charismatic authority for Weber referred to a rule over men to which the governed submit because of their belief in the extraordinary quality of the specific *person*. As will be the case with the *ruler*, the charismatic leader could operate in the political, economic, or religious fields. Charismatic rule, however, contains many aspects irrelevant to, and inconsistent with, the concept of *ruler*, such as its irrational nature, its extraordinary conditions, its revolutionary ("Caesarist") denotations, and its predominant application to tangible persons (whereas *ruler* is to be applicable also to intangible entities). It is true that Weber spoke also of the "routinization of charisma," of *Erbcharisma* and *Gentilcharisma*, and here

approached more closely the definition of *ruler*, yet this usage was subordinated to the one of *ausseralltäglich* character.

27. Almost every book on adolescence treats of its *Sturm und Drang*. See, e.g., G. Stanley Hall, *Adolescence* (New York: D. Appleton & Co., 1904).

28. The concept of social mobility is given full and systematic treatment in Pitirim A. Sorokin, *Social Mobility* (New York: Harper & Bros., 1927). For the transitional procedures of puberty see especially A. Van Gennep, *Les Rites de passage* (Paris: Librairie Critique, 1909).

CHAPTER II

1. Joseph Kirk Folsom, *The Family* (New York: John Wiley & Sons, Inc., 1934), p. 20. It is altogether possible that the autarchic period of many modern infants is shorter than among primitives due to the scheduling habits and education of urban middle-class mothers. Primitive mothers apparently nursed their babies whenever they cried, whereas many new mothers of today believe that the baby almost from birth should feel hunger pangs only at regular intervals of three or four hours. Crying at intermittent hours is presumed to have some other significance (see especially A. I. Richards, *Hunger and Work in a Savage Tribe* [London: G. Routledge & Sons, Ltd., 1932], pp. 40–47; and for the effects of restricted nursing, see, e.g., Margaret A. Ribble, "Infantile Experience in Relation to Personality Development," in *Personality and the Behavior Disorders*, ed. J. McV. Hunt [2 vols.; New York: Ronald Press Co., 1944], II, 639–40).

For modern separations from the child see Folsom, *The Family;* John Dollard, *Frustration and Aggression* (New Haven: Yale University Press, 1939), pp. 64–65; and also the advice tendered by the Children's Bureau, United States Department of Labor, *Infant Care* (Washington: United States Government Printing Office, 1938), pp. 44–45. The growing proportion of mothers working outside the home and the expansion of the mother's horizon beyond homemaking in certain classes increase in some measure, of course, the extent of separation from the child. Freud, with typical insight, pointed out that the mother's familiar game of covering her face and then, to the child's joy, revealing it again promotes his learning that her disappearance is inevitably followed by her reappearance (S. Freud, *The Problem of Anxiety*, p. 155).

On modern disciplining of the child see Dollard, *Frustration and Aggression*, pp. 62–64, 65–68, 76–83; Robert S. and Helen Merrell Lynd, *Middletown* (New York: Harcourt Brace & Co., 1929), pp. 142–43; and "The Gallup Poll," *Chicago Daily News*, March 8, 1947. The last-mentioned source found that three out of every four American parents approve of the idea of spanking children, while eighty-four out of every hundred parents interviewed admitted that they had been spanked as children. No significant differences were found between the attitudes of mothers and fathers.

2. See Emanuel Klein, "The Reluctance To Go to School," in *The Psychoanalytic Study of the Child*, ed. Anna Freud, Heinz Hartmann, Ernst Kris (New York: International Universities Press, 1945), I, 263–79, which deals, for the

most part, however, with young children who have attended school for some time. In the same volume, two other articles are of interest for the problem of separation-anxiety in American life: Eleanor Parenstedt and Irene Anderson, "The Uncompromising Demand of a Three-Year-Old for Her Own Mother," pp. 211–31, and René A. Spitz, "Hospitalism," pp. 53–74. The latter article demonstrates that the high mortality rate in the orphanages of earlier times has today given way to an extremely high rate of psychiatric disturbances. The enforced separation of parents and children in England clearly showed that children feared bombings, death, and destruction less than the absence of their parents (see Anna Freud and Dorothy T. Burlingham, *Infants without Families* [New York: International Universities Press, 1944], and *War and Children* [New York: International Universities Press, 1943]).

3. It often happens that the father enjoys fostering the notions of parental invincibility and omniscience which the child automatically acquires (see Alice Bálint, "Identification," *International Journal of Psychoanalysis*, XXIV, 97–102). In this sense, the father may be transmitting a system of beliefs before the child learns speech—a religion of parents, as Bovet called it. But the child would acquire these beliefs in any case, and the father's influence here could only be to extend their duration.

4. Bálint, "Identification," p. 107. A recent study of two hundred published autobiographies showed that family guests are sometimes the first ones to present standards for the measurement of parental limitations (see James H. S. Bossard and Eleanor S. Boll, "The Role of the Guest: A Study in Child Development," *American Sociological Review*, XII [1947], 192–201).

5. See p. 14, above. See also Nina Searl, "Questions and Answers," in *On the Bringing Up of Children*, ed. John Rickman (London: Kegan Paul, Trench, Trubner & Co., Ltd., 1938), pp. 87–122, which, despite some emphasis on sexual questioning, conveys the intense insistence of the child; and Bálint, "Identification." For the religious questions of the child see Henry B. Robins, "The Religion of Childhood," *Biblical World*, LI (1918), 216–26. For political questioning see p. 36, above.

6. See, e.g., Stern, *Psychology of Childhood*, pp. 396–97.

7. Ernest W. Burgess, "The Family and the Person," *Publications of the American Sociological Society*, XXII (1928), 133; Susan Isaacs, *Social Development in Young Children* (New York: Harcourt, Brace & Co., 1933).

8. "The Story of the Mother Hen and Her Baby," *Little Visits with Jesus* ("Nursery Course," Lesson 47 [Philadelphia: Castle Press, n.d.]), p. 4. This lesson is one of a series of fifty-two.

9. Mary Alice Jones, *Tell Me about God* (New York: Rand McNally & Co., 1943).

10. See Angus Hector MacLean, *The Idea of God in Protestant Religious Education* (New York: Teachers College, Columbia University, 1930), pp. 5–49.

11. This story was told to J. C. Flugel by a well-known psychologist (see Flugel, *The Psychoanalytic Study of the Family* [London: Leonard and Virginia Woolf at the Hogarth Press and the Institute of Psychoanalysis, 1926], p. 84).

12. Other typical political questions are: "What is 'country'?" or "What does 'U.S.' mean?" For some examples of the role of policeman in the child's life see F. Henry Allport, *Institutional Behavior* (Chapel Hill: University of North Carolina Press, 1933), pp. 339–43; Theodore Reik, "Psychoanalysis of the Unconscious Sense of Guilt," *International Journal of Psychoanalysis*, V (1924), 448; and Otto Fenichel, *Psychoanalytic Theory of the Neurosis* (New York: W. W. Norton, Inc., 1945), p. 103. For some concrete descriptions of the informal political education of the child see Harold D. Lasswell, *Politics: Who Gets What, When, How* (New York: Whittlesey House, 1936), pp. 34–35, Frederick L. Schuman, *International Politics* (New York: McGraw-Hill Book Co., Inc., 1933), pp. 280–81, 285–89; and John Merriman Gaus, *Great Britain: A Study of Civic Loyalty* (Chicago: University of Chicago Press, 1929). For the more formal aspects of citizen training in this and other nations see the series of which C. E. Merriam, *The Making of Citizens* (Chicago: University of Chicago Press, 1931), is the summary volume.

13. The fact that policemen, soldiers, and firemen use guns, motor vehicles, fire-fighting paraphernalia, and so on, may suggest that the child's fascination lies in complex mechanical equipment. But motormen drive trolley cars, soda-fountain clerks operate elaborate mechanical devices, garbage collectors have enormous and complicated trucking machinery, and yet the child has not the same feeling of deference for them. The necessary element is the attitude of respect which the child soaks up from his attendants.

14. The most thorough research into the materials that make up the American child's patriotic education in public schools is Bessie Louise Pierce, *Civic Attitudes in American School Textbooks* (Chicago: University of Chicago Press, 1930). See also Helen Martin, "Nationalism in Children's Literature," *Library Quarterly*, VI (1936), 405–18, which concluded that the more nationalistic children's books were, the greater was their circulation within the country; and Arthur Walworth, *School Histories at War* (Cambridge: Harvard University Press, 1938). Harry Ordan in *Social Concepts and the Child Mind* (New York: King's Crown Press, 1945) made a worthy effort to trace children's understanding of a list of concepts through elementary school from the fifth grade upward. Although the study showed an early recognition of legal and governmental ideas, its choice of words to suggest concepts decreased the study's usefulness for the purposes at hand. Thus, while words like "patriot," "legal," "jury," "politician," "dictator," and "criminal" got an early and full understanding, others like "executive" and "electorate" were obviously too unusual for such children to admit the study's results to bear on the propositions here about "the President" or "the People." However, the words were not designed to exact those meanings from the children. Such a study, nevertheless, beginning with younger children and including political stereotypes, would be of much assistance.

15. The psychological function of law for the child is well analyzed in Jerome Frank, *Law and the Modern Mind* (New York: Brentano's, 1930), pp. 13–21. Frank deviates from the above analysis in that he concludes that the law is a substitute for the father, whereas it is maintained here that law becomes

not a symbolic person but the prohibitions of a symbolic person. As the child progresses through school grades, he becomes acquainted with the Constitution and its framers. Here, the part of the founding fathers is clear—they made the law. In their position as defenders of the Constitution, the Supreme Court justices have received analogous roles, roles made more complete by their age qualifications and their specific sphere of the highest law of the land (see chap. v above).

16. See MacLean, *The Idea of God*, pp. 87–117. The solutions of Chave and Fahs for what they consider unsatisfactory religious concepts in children advocate making use of this relatively quiet period in the child's life to elaborate his religious ideas (see S. L. Fahs, "The Beginnings of Religion in Baby Behavior," *Religious Education*, XXV [1930], 896–903; and Ernest J. Chave, *Personality Development in Children* [Chicago: University of Chicago Press, 1938], pp. 227–51). Unfortunately for this purpose, the child now is as uninterested in new beliefs as was Émile. He will seek new ones only in crisis.

17. Even for college students the proportion of those who express no occupational preference is significant. For a summary of the available studies on the subject see Edward K. Strong, *Occupational Interests of Men and Women* (Stanford University, Calif.: Stanford University Press, 1943), pp. 28–31.

18. Over a fourth (26 per cent) found no employment whatsoever in the period of a year. All the data cited are from Howard M. Bell, *Youth Tell Their Story* (Washington, D.C.: American Council on Education, 1938), pp. 101–51. An earlier study (1936) of San Jose, Calif., estimated an average of slightly over one-third of a year of idleness for all occupational levels (Percy E. Davidson and H. Dewey Anderson, *Occupational Mobility in an American Community* (Stanford University, Calif.: Stanford University Press, 1937). The Bell study is preferable, however, in terms of both numbers of respondents and the applicability of the results to national conditions. Neither work, unfortunately, made any effort to estimate the school-employment gap at other times. The Davidson and Anderson monograph clearly shows the number and duration of makeshift jobs and their effect on the career pattern of adolescents (*Occupational Mobility*, pp. 39–47, 70–83, 103–13). For similarly revealing data on an English industrial area see D. Caradog Jones (ed.), *The Social Survey of Merseyside* (3 vols.; London: University Press of Liverpool, 1934), II, 33–46, and III, 201–21.

19. Caroline B. Zachry, *Emotions and Conduct in Adolescence* (New York: D. Appleton–Century Co., Inc., 1940), p. 436. In a system of great occupational mobility a relative term is necessary to describe the aspirations of different groups for the jobs they consider worthy. A street cleaner's job is not a job for the son of a clerk, nor is the clerk's job a job for the son of a corporation's president. "Success" is the term in the business system of beliefs which has this variable meaning, the "bitch-goddess Success" of William James. "You'll never be a success" or "get ahead" or "amount to anything" or "get on in this world" "if you don't stick to a job and work hard." The "job" is the absolute term that comprises those activities deemed worth while on a nation-wide scale, rather than in, e.g., particular income groups.

Not only in this section but throughout the book, the belief-systems of women, which, incidentally, differ greatly from those of men, especially on the political side, were given much less attention. Similarly, the special problems of specific groups, e.g., businessmen, ethnic or racial minorities, and age groups, were not given separate consideration.

20. A useful measure of the extent to which a particular class of persons may have reached *ruler* proportions (in short time periods and among adults) is the percentage of popular biographies devoted to it. Unfortunately, the subject has been little studied. A promising start is Leo Lowenthal, "Biographies in Popular Magazines," in *Radio Research, 1942–43*, ed. P. F. Lazarsfeld and Frank Stanton (New York: Duell, Sloan & Pearce, Inc., 1944), 507–48. The categories chosen (especially the political and business biographies) are remarkably useful for the purposes here entertained. Regrettably, the work extends only over the last few decades.

21. Hocart, *Kingship*, p. 7.

22. In the prosecution of the aims of this study, the field of analysis, as was indicated in the Introduction, had to be arbitrarily restricted. Thus not all belief-systems are discussed (the possible individual varieties are legion) but only those considered to be widely and tenaciously held. For this reason, science, for example, was not separately treated here as a system of beliefs and also for the reason that its kinship to the economic ideology through its resemblances in rationalism, activism, and impersonalism should be clear without elaboration. "Individualism" as an ideology, to take another example, is here equivalent to the economic ideology. It could have another meaning—belief in self-sufficiency—but such a system of beliefs is held by only the minutest fraction of the world's population (see p. 226, n. 1). For a further limit to this study see chap. iii, n. 1.

PART II

INTRODUCTION

1. The practice of Christian pastors and educators in Japan is almost exemplary in respect to the problem of eight hundred ancestral deities in Japanese religious teachings (see D. C. Holtom, "Christianity in the Modern Japanese Environment," in *Environmental Factors in Christian History*, ed. J. T. McNeill, M. Spinka, and H. R. Willoughby [Chicago: University of Chicago Press, 1939], pp. 348–58).

2. See, especially, the works of the Viennese ethnologist, W. Schmidt, e.g., *High Gods in North America* (Oxford: Clarendon Press, 1933).

3. See Sebastian de Grazia, "Status as a Political and Religious Motive," *Journal of Liberal Religion*, VIII (1947), 91–101. The findings of clinical psychology support the fact that man can have many gods. They can trace in detail the number of persons, actual and ideal—older brothers, teachers, ministers, politicians, doctors, scientists, film stars—to which the individual temporarily paid homage of the type he once gave his attendants (see, e.g., J. C. Flugel, *Man, Morals and Society* [New York: International Universities Press, 1945], p. 176;

and chap. v, above). See also A. M. Hocart, *Kings and Councillors* (Cairo: Print-ing Office, Paul Barbey, 1936), pp. 101–25, for assignment of duties and the relevant departments of nature to assistant gods and officials in primitive and ancient ideologies.

CHAPTER III

1. A phrase which both in word and meaning approximates the term here used is "major cultural directives," an expression used, e.g., by Ernest Beagle-hole in "Character Structure." (*Psychiatry*, VII [May, 1944], 145–62). Since it is held here that the significance of directives lies in their psychological relation to *rulers*, the insertion of the word "cultural" involves an unnecessary ambiguity. For fuller treatment of this important point see above, pp. 85–86. Muzafer Sherif approximates the view held here of the influence of directives in his at-tempt to relate the autokinetic effect to the absence of social values (see his *The Psychology of Norms* [New York: Harper & Bros., 1936]). Although he fully ap-preciates the lasting effect of norms laid down and interiorized in childhood and calls it "value-fixation," he fails to distinguish between ethical norms and prac-tical folkways. The meaning of the word "directive" bears a relation also to Sumner's "mores." The mores as understood here are those directives which were transmitted in childhood and are associated (to some extent consciously, but mostly unconsciously) with the most immediate and terrible family or com-munity disapproval. Directives which are established later in life (such as those of the business system of beliefs) never have the same powerful (interiorized) motives for conformity. These directives better fit what Sumner called "success policy." The mores, then, are not synonymous with, but part of, the directives. All mores are directives, but not all directives are mores. (It might be reiterated at this point that the only directives considered in this work are conflicting di-rectives. There are more directives to the business system of beliefs than those of competition and activism discussed here. Lasswell has attempted to describe them for the lower middle class, e.g., in *World Politics and Personal Insecurity* [New York: Whittlesey House, 1935], pp. 257–65.)

2. For less bizarre examples of difficult directive adjustment see Matthew Spinka, "The Effect of the Crusades upon Early Christianity," in McNeill, *et al.*, *Environmental Factors*, pp. 252 f.; and Marvin Henry Harper, "Christianity and the Culture of India," in the same work. Among the ethnological studies showing varying degrees of adjustment are Edward Spicer, *Pascua: A Yaqui Village in Arizona* (Chicago: University of Chicago Press, 1940); Charles C. Rogler, *Comerío* (Lawrence, Kan.: University of Kansas, 1940); and Robert Redfield, *The Folk Culture of Yucatan* (Chicago: University of Chicago Press, 1941).

3. William H. Rivers, "The Effect on Native Races of Contact with Euro-pean Civilization," *Man*, Vol. XXVII (1927).

4. An excellent drawing-together of data on the religious and political sig-nificance of head-hunting and the depressing effects of its prohibition can be found in Ludwig Krzywicki, *Primitive Society and Its Vital Statistics* (London: Macmillan & Co., 1934), pp. 88–100, 108–14.

5. Knight in Frank H. Knight and Thornton W. Merriam, *The Economic Order and Religion* ([New York: Harper & Bros., 1945], pp. 32–50), has stressed that the directive "Love thy neighbor" is impossible of fulfilment because it asks for indiscriminate love. Freud in *Civilization and Its Discontents* voiced a similar objection. Three points, however, should be considered: (1) Outsiders are not given brotherly love nor are immoral persons (disbelievers). Thus, "the meanest believer is above the most glorious hypocrite." (2) Imposed in childhood, the directive exists in the mind as an ideal and deviation from it results in some degree of mental discomfort. (3) Belief in it as a possible mode of conduct affects prevailing theories of human nature (e.g., those of the nineteenth-century anarchists) which hold that man is "basically good." In other words, action based on the idea that the world is filled with friendly animals will differ significantly from action stemming from the conception that the world is a jungle of man-eaters.

6. This definition follows that of Werner Sombart in "Capitalism," *Encyclopedia of the Social Sciences*, Vol. III, (1930). Actually, the definition leaves unstated many familiar characteristics of the idea of economic competition; e.g., it is mutual (all parties compete with others), theoretically nonviolent (only the services that money can buy are used; it is not the war of all against all), and both personal and collective (individuals or groups can compete).

Definitions of *general* competition, not uncongenial to this one, are perhaps helpful in clarifying the concept. Mark A. May and Leonard W. Doob define it as "behavior directed toward the same social end by at least two individuals but toward an end which can be achieved in equal amounts by some but not by all the individuals seeking it" (see their *Competition and Cooperation* [Social Science Research Council Bull. 25 (New York: Social Science Research Council, 1937)], p. 6 and also pp. 3–5). In *Cooperation and Competition among Primitive Peoples*, ed. Margaret Mead (New York: McGraw-Hill Book Co., Inc., 1937), p. 17 and also pp. 8, 16–17, a definition of competition (credited to Folsom) is noteworthy: Competition is behavior oriented toward a goal in which the other competitors for that goal are secondary.

Economic competition in an exchange economy means buying and selling, letting and hiring, lending and borrowing *for money*. Countries where the end is acquisition in terms of money are likely to be characterized (in Balzac's phrase) by *l'omnipotence, l'omniscience, l'omniconvenance de l'argent*. In the United States, since the unit of exchange is the dollar, "in snatches of conversation caught on the streets, the restaurants, and the cars, the continual cry is always dollars, dollars, dollars!" "Hard cash," "money talks," "dollars and cents," and "cash value" are phrases familiar as the ring of the cash register.

The definition of perfect and imperfect competition now in vogue among economic theorists, which depends on the conditions of atomism (no firm in the economy being large enough so that its decisions can effect the market price) and freedom of entry and exit, is of no interest since it applies to relationships among firms. Those works are also of slight relevance which attempt to describe the actual state of competition among firms as nonexistent or monopolistic, in major or minor part. This study deals primarily with persons' ideologies; in this case, with persons' *beliefs* about competition as a way of acting which they ought to follow.

7. Francis A. Walker, *Political Economy* (New York: Henry Holt & Co., 1887), p. 92. For the necessity, under the competitive ideal, of cutting off affiliative relationships see May and Doob, *Competition and Cooperation*, pp. 17, 49–50, 82. Werner Sombart discusses the same point in the form of the antithesis ancient economists posited between love and business (see *The Quintessence of Capitalism*, trans. M. Epstein [New York: E. P. Dutton & Co., 1915], pp. 207–9). Theodore Abel in "The Significance of the Concept of Consciousness of Kind" (*Social Forces*, IX [1930], 1–10) makes a basic distinction between "sentiment" and "interest" relationships corresponding more or less to the conflicting directives here described. Paradoxically enough, the demand for freedom from sentiment in competition makes it almost impossible to extend credit without legal force. For this reason, in order to secure credit, early American businessmen often found it expedient to belong to religious sects which emphasized thrift and honesty and could thereby guarantee the credit standing of their members.

8. Frank H. Knight, *Risk, Uncertainty and Profit* (New York: Houghton Mifflin Co., 1921), pp. 76–79.

9. See Sombart, "Capitalism"; Max Weber, *The Protestant Ethic and the Spirit of Capitalism*, trans. Talcott Parsons (London: G. Allen & Unwin, Ltd., 1904–5), pp. 19–27, 75–78; and *General Economic History*, trans. Frank H. Knight (New York: Greenberg, 1927), pp. 352–68. A word of clarification should be given here. Actually, no ideology in full force suffers critical discussion of its *rulers*. In precapitalist times it is seditious to question the majesty of the king; in capitalist times it is subversive to question the worth of the businessman and "crazy" to take no thought for the morrow. In each case there exist pious or taboo areas which must not be rationally considered.

10. However, the promotion of the businessman as the key figure in the new business ideology had been foreshadowed by the economists, especially David Ricardo in his *Principles of Political Economy* with its discussions of "manufacturers" and their profits. Of course, the burden of promulgation was eventually taken up by businessmen themselves, like Andrew Carnegie (see, e.g., his *The Empire of Business* [New York: Doubleday, Page & Co., 1902] and Ralph Henry Gabriel, *The Course of American Democratic Thought* [New York: Ronald Press Co., 1940], pp. 143–60).

The discussion here of the development of the idea of competition ranges over two and one-half centuries of fluctuating ideas and changing conditions. The amount of space devoted to it would be considered too slight, except that the purpose at hand is merely to illustrate that from its origins the idea of competition was supposed to benefit the entire commonweal because of the natural identification of interests in the world's scheme. For an excellent volume which is set in the center of the related ideas of the eighteenth and early nineteenth centuries see Élie Halévy, *The Growth of Philosophic Radicalism*, trans. Mary Morris (London: Faber & Gwyer, Ltd., 1928). One of the clearest of modern expositions on the automatic and harmonious regulation of the economic process through competition is Frank H. Knight, *The Economic Organization* (Chicago: University of Chicago Press, 1933), pp. 31–68.

11. See, e.g., Edwin G. Nourse, "Competition as Method and as Goal" (Pamphlet 33, Brookings Institution [Washington, D.C.: Brookings Institution, 1942]), p. 1; Max Radin, *The Lawful Pursuit of Gain* (New York: Houghton Mifflin Co., 1931), pp. 81–90; May and Doob, *Competition and Cooperation*, p. 3; Sombart, *Quintessence*, pp. 151–52; Gardner Murphy, Lois Barclay Murphy, and T. N. Newcomb, *Experimental Social Psychology* (New York: Harper & Bros., 1937), pp. 754–59; and Miriam Beard, *A History of the Business Man* (New York: Macmillan Co., 1938).

12. Raymond T. Bye, *Principles of Economics* (4th ed.; New York: F. S. Crofts & Co., 1944), p. 51.

13. From an unpublished series of interviews (1946) of plant workers in a large industrial city. The materials, in the possession of the author, will henceforth be cited as "Plant Interviews." For the competitive sentiment among salaried workers see especially Carl Dreyfuss, "Occupation and Ideology of the Salaried Employee," trans. E. Abramovitch (2 vols.; New York: Columbia University, 1938) (mimeographed).

14. C. G. and B. Z. Seligman, *Pagan Tribes of the Nilotic Sudan* (London: G. Routledge & Sons, Ltd., 1932), p. 519. For an example of utopian noncompetition see Edward Bellamy, *Looking Backward 2000–1887* (New York: Houghton, Mifflin & Co., 1889); for a survey of co-operation and competition as actually tried in utopian communities see May and Doob, *Competition and Cooperation*, pp. 58–62. An excellent account of the absence of the feeling of economic competition among the classical Greeks can be found in Alfred Zimmern, *The Greek Commonwealth* (Oxford: Clarendon Press, 1911).

15. Briffault, *The Mothers*, I, 635.

16. See John Adam Moehler, *Symbolism: Doctrinal Differences between Catholics and Protestants*, trans. J. B. Robertson (2d ed., 2 vols.; London: Charles Dolman, 1847), I, 31–114; II, 1–135.

17. See the interesting work of Svend Ranulf, *Moral Indignation and Middle Class Psychology* (Copenhagen: Levin & Munksgaard, Ejnar Munksgaard, 1938), pp. 12–95. In consistency with set limits, this study offers no place for the interesting theory (partially emanating from this work) which could be formulated concerning the psychological origins, reinforcement, and projection of the aggressive tendencies in early Protestantism. Undoubtedly they are directly related to the greater restrictions on the flesh (a term which, some psychologists would contend, includes innate human drives) characteristic of the period. For the degree of sensual restrictions among Protestants see, e.g., Ranulf, *ibid.*, and V. F. Calverton, "Sex and the Social Struggle," in *Sex in Civilization*, ed. V. F. Calverton and S. D. Schmalhausen (New York: Garden City Pub. Co., 1929), pp. 249–84. A recent study of four thousand men in the American army indicated that the greater sexual restrictions demanded by the present-day Protestant system of beliefs carries directly over into the actual sexual conduct of

Protestant men. When compared to the Catholic group, the Protestant group in the study contained a significantly greater proportion of virgins (see Leslie B. Hohman and Bertram Schaffner, "The Sex Lives of Unmarried Men," *American Journal of Sociology*, LII [1947], 501-7). On the greater impersonalism of Protestantism see Weber, *Protestant Ethic*, pp. 108-9, 224-26. For the varying Catholic attitudes see J. Huizinga, *The Waning of the Middle Ages* (London: Edward Arnold & Co., 1937), pp. 176 f.; Henry Charles Lea, *Historical Sketch of Sacerdotal Celibacy in the Christian Church* (Boston: Houghton, Mifflin & Co., 1884), pp. 144-408; and G. G. Coulton, *Ten Medieval Studies* (Cambridge: Cambridge University Press, 1930), pp. 123-200.

It can be said on a high level of generality that the Reformation revived and pushed farther early Christianity's turning of men's attention from themselves and others toward the natural environment. This simply stated complex hypothesis requires lengthy and intricate researches but should be extremely valuable, for it explains many facets of modern technological civilization.

18. Perry Miller, *The New England Mind* (New York: Macmillan Co., 1939), p. 205.

19. Its influence might be evaluated indirectly in areas of highly concentrated Protestantism, such as Middletown, where even immediately after the depression the attitude still lingered that "if some plague were to come along . . . and wipe them all out [i.e., those who 'would not work if they had jobs'] that would not be a tragedy but a big relief" (see pp. 70-71, above, and n. 38, p. 214, below).

For the Protestant church's neglect of the poor in the United States see Aaron Ignatius Abell, *The Urban Impact on American Protestantism 1865-1900* (Cambridge: Harvard University Press, 1943), pp. 3-26; and William Clayton Bower, "Facing the Future," in *The Church at Work in the Modern World*, ed. W. C. Bower (Chicago: University of Chicago Press, 1935), pp. 275-77. For an unusual comparison of Protestant and Catholic treatment of the poor throughout the world see Alfred Young, *Catholic and Protestant Countries Compared* (New York: Catholic Book Exchange, 1895), pp. 388-430 and *passim*.

20. By eschewing this formulation, one avoids the toils of a fierce academic controversy over the effect of Protestantism on emerging capitalism, a battle that has lasted since the publication in 1904-5 of Weber's lengthy essay on *The Protestant Ethic and the Spirit of Capitalism*. See Ephraim Fischoff, "The Protestant Ethic and the Spirit of Capitalism, the History of a Controversy," *Social Research*, XI (1944), 52-88. Whether or not Protestantism fostered the development of the capitalist spirit is a question beyond present scope. This book, however, including the next section on the activist directive, which gives a more intensive psychological analysis of the ideological interrelationships, supports the thesis that whichever is first, the hen or the egg, the two—Protestantism and capitalism—when found together provide for greater acceptance of the capitalist directives than the combination of capitalism and Catholicism.

21. Margaret Mead has endeavored to present a convincing case for the existence of the competitive directive in the American family (see her *And Keep*

Your Powder Dry [New York: W. Morrow & Co., 1942]). She confuses, however, a system of rewards and punishment with competition. Thus, she speaks of the American mother's "conditional smile," which appears or vanishes depending on the child's performance. Naturally so. All educational smiles are conditional. In every culture attendants somehow show their approval or disapproval of a child's behavior. How else can he be fitted into communal life? And to say that the American mother does not love her child if its marks are not in the higher grade brackets is patently inaccurate. The mother of the lowly dunce loves her child as much as the mother of the puny pundit and bestows as much affection on him for attaining the mark of D as the other on her son for the grade of A. The exceptions to this rule are few. As a matter of fact, local government authorities frequently meet with great difficulty in attempting to place young idiots in sanitariums, often having literally to tear them from their mothers' arms. It was shown here that affiliative contacts (and the ordinary mother-son relationships are affiliative) prevent the making of competitive judgments. The observations of the specialist in the American family are more to be trusted in this case (see Plant, *Personality and the Cultural Pattern*). It is possible to emphasize monetary acquisition in the family (see Otto Fenichel, "The Drive To Amass Wealth," *Psychoanalytic Quarterly*, VII [1938], 69–95), e.g., by giving children penny banks for birthdays; but it is not easy to vitiate Paul's injunction that no man circumvent or overreach his brother in business (see n. 37, p. 213, below).

22. Again excluding the Church of England. The High Church wing of the Puritans in America, however, increasingly accepted the views of Arminius, and therefore no exception need be made for it as far as a work ethic goes.

23. It is convenient to start the discussion with the religious directive of labor because the body of religious beliefs in the Reformation has been given detailed, systematic treatment by careful scholars. Once again, it should be recalled that no attempt is being made to give prior influence to religious factors. It may be that the economic conditions of life of certain strata of the European population first required the sanctification of work, which thus led them to the acceptance and encouragement of a new religious work ethic (see for some attempts at an appraisal of the effects of economic conditions of life A. M. Robertson, *Aspects of the Rise of Economic Individualism* [Cambridge: Cambridge University Press, 1935]; F. J. Turner, *The Frontier in American History* [New York: Henry Holt & Co., 1920]; and Bernard Groethuysen, *Origines de l'esprit bourgeois en France* [Paris: Gallimard, 1927]).

24. See Adriano Tilgher, *Work, What It Has Meant to Man through the Ages*, trans. Dorothy Canfield Fisher (New York: Harcourt, Brace & Co., 1930), pp. 47–50.

25. Martin Luther, "An Open Letter to the Christian Nobility," 1520, *Works*, trans. C. M. Jacobs (6 vols.; Philadelphia: A. J. Holman Co., 1916), II, 69.

26. It is possible to be brief and yet so certain about the Protestant doctrines of Luther and other Reformers only because of the extensive writings of Troeltsch, Max Weber, Tawney, and others. Since there is no space for a more detailed presentation of Protestant and Catholic religious ideas and practice,

discussion here will be limited only to those directives relevant for this study. More full-bodied descriptions can be found in the works of the scholars above.

27. Although the Puritans relied heavily on Luther, Beza, Melanchthon, and other reformers, Calvin had for them a special prominence, and in America his *Institutes* was the chief religious and political textbook of the New England Puritans. It was noted earlier that the term "salvation" in its historic Christian usage corresponds in the psychological sense employed in this work to the assurance of protection by *rulers* obtained through proper following of the directives. Sometimes the correspondence appears in an extraordinarily lucid passage. "Those whom God has chosen [saved], therefore, He designates as His children, and determines Himself to be their Father. By calling, He introduces them into His family and unites them to Himself, that they may be one" (John Calvin, *Institutes of the Christian Religion* [2 vols.; 16th American ed.; Philadelphia: Presbyterian Board of Publication, n.d.], II, 179).

28. See Robertson, *Rise of Economic Individualism*. Weber and Tawney would have spared themselves much criticism by confining themselves to religious and capitalist similarities in directives rather than to the end of monetary acquisition. As Troeltsch and as Albert Hyma (*Christianity, Capitalism, and Communism* [Ann Arbor, Mich.: The Author, 1937]) and as Weber himself more or less stated (H. H. Gerth and C. Wright Mills, *From Max Weber* [New York: Oxford University Press, 1946], pp. 331–37), religion has rarely, and then usually ambiguously, claimed that "thou canst serve God and Mammon." The words of any of the great Reformers could be quoted to match the medieval doctrines of *homo mercator vix aut numquam potest Deo placere*, or *nihil inde sperantes*. Thus, Thomas Carlyle, who, as can be seen in the above quotation from *Sartor resartus*, was a believer in the activist directive, was also the one who in *Chartism* (New York: John W. Lovell Co., 1885) stigmatized political economy with the appellation the "dismal science" and despised it for making wealth an object for its own sake.

29. For the attitude of the ancient Greek toward labor see *The Cambridge Ancient History*, ed. J. B. Bury, S. A. Cook, and F. E. Adcock (New York: Macmillan Co., 1927), Vol. V, *Athens 478–401 B.C.;* Werner Jaeger, *Paideia*, trans. Gilbert Highet (3 vols.; Oxford: Basil Blackwell, 1939), Vol. I; and especially Zimmern, *Greek Commonwealth*.

30. One must bear in mind, however, that no religion remains unaffected by cultural influences. May 15, 1891, the date of the encyclical *Rerum novarum* of Pope Leo XIII, has been considered the beginning of a changed attitude on the part of the Catholic church toward the worker.

31. The work ethics of Luther, Calvin, and Wesley were selected for study here because their followers in America make up the overwhelmingly greater part of Protestant denominations. Although ecclesiastical statistics are to be taken cautiously, Thomas Cuming Hall's table of American Protestant church membership, in his *Religious Background of American Culture* (Boston: Little, Brown & Co., 1930), pp. 212–13, proves the point. Hall compiled his table to show that those historians and theologians who claimed that the United States

was a Calvinist nation were in error. However, the procedure of this study—isolating the work ethic from the many varieties of difference among Protestant sects—completely avoids this pointed criticism. It might be said, further, that Hall overlooks the fact that many authors, such as Weber and Troeltsch, who describe this country as Calvinist, generally refer to Calvinism's influence rather than its numerical superiority.

32. André Siegfried, *America Comes of Age*, trans. H. H. and Doris Hemming (New York: Harcourt, Brace & Co., 1927), p. 33. Of course, there were present in America additional factors, such as pioneering and frontier conditions, which have been said to contribute to activism (see Turner, *Frontier in American History;* Sombart, *Quintessence*, pp. 301–7; and especially H. Richard Niebuhr, *Denominationalism*, pp. 135–235). The reciprocal relations of frontier and religion have been carefully investigated by W. W. Sweet (see his article on "The Churches as Moral Courts of the Frontier" in *Church History*, II [1933], 3–21).

33. Alexis de Tocqueville, *The Republic of the United States of America*, trans. H. Reeves (New York: A. S. Barnes & Co., n.d.), II, 144–45. Tocqueville is a worthy choice not only because of his excellent political insight (attested by John Stuart Mill, Lord Bryce, and others) but (for present purposes) because he was French and highborn and therefore well acquainted with the contemplative directive of the Middle Ages and of Catholicism. Moreover, his personal connections and sources of information in the United States and the particular time of his tour enabled him to see with great clarity the effects of a spreading commercialism and an incipient industrialization (see pp. 99–100, above).

34. Psychologists have reported the compulsive character of the work of modern man. See, e.g., Franz Alexander, *Our Age of Unreason* (New York: J. B. Lippincott Co., 1942), p. 310; and Hilde Lewinsky, "Occupation and Obsession," *British Journal of Medical Psychology*, XIX (1941–42), 388–93. For an analysis of "Life as Work" in Germany see P. Kecskemeti and N. Leites, "Some Psychological Hypotheses on Nazi Germany" (Document 60, Experimental Division for the Study of Wartime Communications [Washington, D.C.: Library of Congress, 1945]) (mimeographed), pp. 4–7.

35. Knight in Knight and Merriam, *Economic Order*, p. 71.

36. See, e.g., Sombart, *Quintessence*, pp. 13, 151–52, and "The Age of Record Breaking," p. 178. See, also, Miriam Beard, *A History of the Business Man*, pp. 636–41, 724–26. It is amusing to note that Tocqueville's statement about early nineteenth-century America where "leisure is a vice and temerity a virtue" is nicely matched by the refrain in the Gilbert and Sullivan operetta *Ruddygore*, which is laid in early nineteenth century England.

> If you wish in this world to advance . . .
> You must stir it and stump it,
> And blow your own trumpet,
> Or, trust me, you haven't a chance.

37. Broadly speaking, in the ideologies of family and state the activist directives are (to employ a religious term which can be usefully applied to parts of all systems of beliefs) *adiaphora*, matters of indifference. There is, of course, an un-

deniable prescription of unsparing effort in time of familial or national emergencies, but it is not the same as the directive of continuous and regular work. Finding less opposition, the activist directive can penetrate the household more easily than can the competitive directive, which meets with direct conflict. Much more information, however, is needed. Such guides to family directives as the proportion of mechanical toys (building and tinkering sets, for example) to, say, dramatic toys (dolls, animals, soldiers, etc.) given as gifts; the content of stories read to children at bedtime; or the earliest reading materials —such guides as these would be helpful. On the last item, e.g., it is known that Franklin's *Poor Richard's Almanac* and C. Collodi's *Pinocchio*, both containing firm work ethics, are widely read in American grammar schools, but more information than this is unavailable. (See, however, A. M. Jordan, *Children's Interests in Reading* [Chapel Hill: University of North Carolina Press, 1926], one of the few comprehensive studies of children's reading.) So little is known about the systems of belief of the modern family that one is compelled to use religion as the key factor and to make the assumption that the activist directive will be a larger part of the family belief system in Protestant than in Catholic households.

38. These excerpts have been selected from the lengthy statement of the Middletown credo on the basis of their pertinence to this chapter. See Robert S. and Helen Merrell Lynd, *Middletown in Transition* (New York: Harcourt, Brace & Co., 1937), pp. 406–9, 412, and 415. R. S. Lynd believes that these values "probably apply widely throughout the country" (*Knowledge for What?* [Princeton: Princeton University Press, 1939], p. 62). In attempting to ascertain the directives of belief-systems, the careful community study is preferable to ordinary public opinion polling methods. See, for the limitations of shallowness in polls in this regard, Quinn McNemar, "Opinion-Attitude Methodology," *Psychological Bulletin*, XLIII (July, 1946), 289–374. Occasionally, the polls frame a question which bears on the subject yet leaves many loopholes. As examples see "The Fortune Survey," *Fortune*, XV (January, 1937), 86–87, and "The Fortune Survey," *Fortune*, XXXV (January, 1947), 5–6, 10.

39. These questions, divorced from an initiating event, may seem subjectless. See chap. vi for examples of the context out of which they usually arise. It may happen frequently that the person is so emancipated that whenever he deviates from early training in the norms of behavior he scarcely feels a conflict. But one rarely escapes scot-free from the scrutiny of conscience. Mental conflict is usually present on an unconscious level (see pp. 154–55). This unconscious element is more prominent in discontinuities of the co-operative–competitive attitudes toward fellows, a conflict which troubles Protestant and Catholic alike, though affecting the former in less degree. In the quietist-activist discontinuity with which, generally speaking, the Catholic alone has difficulty, the conflict seems to be more conscious, for work alone violates no previous directive. There is no "Do Not Work" commandment but simply the absence of a premium on labor plus a warning not to let the pursuit of work distract, e.g., from the contemplation of God. The Catholic generally can identify his disturbance in the incessant demands for regularized work characteristic of the

business system of beliefs. For other details of resultant Protestant and Catholic difference see pp. 134–37 and 170, above.

40. On the inability to verbalize the feeling of the danger of helplessness see Freud, *The Problem of Anxiety*, p. 150.

CHAPTER IV

1. And for similar reasons. As soon as a case of contradictory directives develops within one ideology, people begin to split the *ruler* into an old and a new and assign to the new the later addition to the directives (see pp. 45–46, above). In the Reformation, e.g., although both Protestants and Catholics were originally part of one *Corpus Christianum*, the development of new formulas for salvation led to the staunchly held idea on each side that the other was worshiping a false god; similarly, in the 1920's with the fundamentalist-modernist struggle within the body of Protestantism, conflict over matters involving the literalness of the Bible as the source of directives brought a different God to the modernist camp—God as absolute energy, as idealized reality, or (in the words of one New England clergyman) God as "a sort of oblong blur."

2. This example, the following one on kings, and the one in chap. vii on the United States in the late nineteenth century have a common weakness in that they show not the psychological symptoms of acute anomie but the conditions that should lead to it and then show rather surprisingly violent results which can be presumably considered a resentful reaction and attempted solution. Unfortunately, it is only a few extremely recent events that supply helpful psychological observations (see chaps. vii and x).

PART III

CHAPTER V

1. George Herbert Betts, *The Beliefs of 700 Ministers* (New York: Abingdon Press, 1929), pp. 62–66; R. S. and H. M. Lynd, *Middletown in Transition*, p. 416; see also *Middletown*, pp. 313–16.

2. It is possible, of course, for persons to bear other than the filial type of affection, even overtly sexual love, for *rulers*. See, e.g., Gerth and Mills, *From Max Weber*, pp. 343–50, for the conflict of erotic and religious sensations; and Schuman, *International Politics*, pp. 280–81, for examples of other than filial types of love in the political sphere. The love of child for parents, however, is by far the type most frequently found to exist. For an exercise in the ways of expressing filial affection for states one has only to glance through the lyrics of state songs (see George E. Shankle, *State Names, Flags, Seals, Songs, Birds, Flowers, and Other Symbols* [New York: H. W. Wilson, 1934], pp. 385–419).

3. See the discussion of the "Paradise Myth" in W. O. E. Oesterly, *The Evolution of the Messianic Idea* (London: Sir Isaac Pitman & Sons, Ltd., 1908), pp. 123–60. An impression of repetition may result from this brief overview of adult religion and from the following lengthier one on the political ideology. It is not repetition, however, but similarity. In chap. i the belief-systems of the

child transmitted by grownups were considered; in this section the ideologies of adults themselves are discussed.

4. Aristotle, in the *Ethics* and the *Politics*, was one of the earliest to note and emphasize the patterns of resemblance in the state and the household. Among other ways of linking family and state, he was fond of comparing monarchy (the form of government he seemed to favor) with paternal rule over the family. Tyranny, the perversion of monarchy, he considered evil because it deteriorated from a father-son to a master-slave relationship. Carlton Hayes has done the most effective job of analyzing the correspondences in religion and nationalism in his *Essays on Nationalism* (New York: Macmillan Co., 1926), pp. 93–125.

5. See the suggestive studies of H. Clay Trumbull, e.g., *The Blood Covenant* (Philadelphia: J. D. Wattles, 1898); and compare the idea with that expressed in the patriotic song, "America the Beautiful":

> God shed his grace on thee,
> And crown thy good with brotherhood
> From sea to shining sea.

For statements of the way in which communities or nations come to regard themselves as of one blood, distinct by blood, from other communities or nations see M. F. Ashley Montagu, "The Myth of Blood," *Psychiatry*, XXVI (February, 1943), 15–19; and *Nationalism: A Report by a Study Group of Members of the Royal Institute of International Affairs* (New York: Oxford University Press, 1939), pp. 255–57. For the late nineteenth- and early twentieth-century emphasis on race and blood as the integral part of the "nation" or "folk" see the works of the Comte de Gobineau, Stewart Houston Chamberlain, Madison Grant, and Lothrup Stoddard.

6. See Montagu, "The Myth of Blood," Also see p. 220, n. 30, for the relevance of this fact to Lasswell's theory of nationalism. For the precedence of the "race-making period" in the formation of the nation see Walter Bagehot, *Physics and Politics* (New York: D. Appleton & Co., 1920); and the work of William McDougall, which further promoted the thesis, *The Group Mind* (New York: G. P. Putnam's Sons, 1920), pp. 286–336.

7. Madge McKinney, "Certain Characteristics of Citizens" (unpublished Doctor's thesis, Department of Political Science, University of Chicago, 1927).

8. If a man is a traitor to the political or religious community to which people thought he belonged, he has by no means divested himself of his primary, namely, political or religious, beliefs. His disloyalty to the one is his loyalty to another to which he feels he really belongs. The hardened criminal in the United States, for example, usually feels that he belongs to a political community smaller than the nation and to a religious community slightly larger than that conceived by the law-abiding American. He cannot feel that he belongs to none.

9. "Thus the school, the social worker, and the judge assay Johnny on the basis of his repeated delinquencies, his mediocre intelligence, his poverty-stricken and dirt-ridden family, and have only dazed resentment for the mother's insistent cry that 'He's my Johnny.' . . . And this is natural because these family ties are so defiant of rational or reasonable analysis—indeed a

large factor in their strength lies precisely in this inability of reasonable considerations to destroy or materially change them" (Plant, *Personality and the Cultural Pattern*, p. 96).

Of course, communities, primitive and modern, do have naturalization processes, but from the literal exchange of blood in savage practice to the swearing of filial love, faith, and obedience to the *ruler* in modern rites, the ceremonies hold the significance of a brotherly adoption.

10. For these cases, for the psychological cases just above, and for related discussion see Vilfredo Pareto, *The Mind and Society*, trans. Andrew Bongiorno and Arthur Livingston (4 vols.; New York: Harcourt, Brace & Co., 1935), III, 1348–1402; Flugel, *Man, Morals and Society*, pp. 53–55, 136, 151–53; Ranyard West, *Conscience and Society* (New York: Emerson Books, Inc., 1945), pp. 169–70; and Reik, "Unconscious Sense of Guilt."

11. See Jeremy Bentham, *Fragment on Government* (London: Oxford University Press, H. Milford, 1931); and John Austin, *Province of Jurisprudence Determined* (London: J. Murray, 1832).

12. Nevertheless, there are numerous persons in England today who link the weather to the crown. The many people who believed in the "king's weather" which blessed the coronation in 1935 reminded one observer that many others had believed in it when the weather was excellent for the king's jubilee and King George's funeral, forgetting that the weather had not been good "on the day in 1928 when the King caught the cold which began his serious illness from which he never completely recovered his strength" (see Kingsley Martin, *The Magic of Monarchy* [New York: Alfred A. Knopf, 1937], pp. 6–7). See also the letters on similar subjects written by readers to their newspapers, quoted by the same author on pp. 3–4; Hocart, *Kings and Councillors*, p. 143; and the quotation on Hitler's weather, p. 177, above.

13. *Times* (London), November 6, 1930, and October 10, 1933, quoted in Hocart, *Kings and Councillors*, p. 145.

14. G. B. Shaw, *Saint Joan* (New York: Brentano's, 1930), p. 58.

15. See Hocart's illuminating chapter on "idols" in *Kings and Councillors*, pp. 232–43; Edward Gibbon, *The Decline and Fall of the Roman Empire* (2 vols.; New York: Modern Library, n.d.), II, 578–610; and Hayes, *Nationalism*, pp. 108–9. On the enrichment of Protestant worship services and liturgy over the last forty years see Gaius Glenn Atkins, *Religion in Our Times* (New York: Round Table Press, Inc., 1938), pp. 309–12.

16. Drew Pearson and Robert S. Allen, *The Nine Old Men* (New York: Doubleday Doran & Co., 1937), pp. 10–11, 13.

17. For the development of a related idea, the legal personality of the state, see Hans Aufricht, "Personality in International Law," *American Political Science Review*, XXXVII (1943), 217–43.

18. J. Bentham, *Theory of Fictions*, ed. C. K. Ogden (London: Kegan Paul, Trench, Trubner & Co., Ltd., 1932), pp. cxviii–cxix. Actually, some qualities of the concepts Nation and People are superior to "men that live and die" as *rulers*, especially the immortality (thus Kipling: "Who dies if England live?") and the

immensity of a national area or an aggregation of people. On the former quality see, in particular, J. T. MacCurdy, *The Structure of Morale* (New York: Macmillan Co., 1943), pp. 78–109. On these points—in addition to S. Freud, *Group Psychology*—Floyd Henry Allport, *Institutional Behavior*, can be referred to. Mosca had a similar point in mind in his generalization that there is a tendency for men to defer more readily to abstract principles than to individuals (Mosca, *The Ruling Class*, p. 70). It is likely, however, that the strength of this tendency has a cultural variation. One must not forget the influence of Protestant and capitalist rationalism and impersonalism in making men transfer their reverence and devotion from mortal men to institutions or concepts. The constant concern of Protestant leaders to diminish the deference of men to their political leaders can be seen in incessant admonitions to make God the only one worthy of such devotion, in documents as different as the *Vindiciae contra tyrannos* and Richard Baxter's *Christian Directory*.

19. *Nationalism: A Report*, p. 260. Bagehot's opinion is virtually identical. "It is often said that men are ruled by their imaginations; but it would be truer to say they are governed by the weakness of their imaginations. The nature of a constitution, the action of an assembly, the play of parties, the unseen formation of a guiding opinion, are complex facts, difficult to know, and easy to mistake. But the action of a single will, the fiat of a single mind, are easy ideas: anybody can make them out and no one can ever forget them" (Walter Bagehot, *The English Constitution* [New York: D. Appleton–Century Co., 1927], p. 101).

20. "The god People has not a single unbeliever left . . . where is the man who does not feel the need of shouting aloud that everything must be sacrificed to the 'good of the People.' . . . Humanity has its 'Misanthropes' but 'The People' has no 'misodemes.' There is no one bold enough to display hatred or antipathy, or repugnance, or even mere indifference to it" (Pareto, *Mind and Society*, III, 1157; see also, I, 372; and III, 972–73, 1050, 1133, 1157–59, 1526).

21. Augustin Cochin in *La Crise de l'histoire révolutionnaire: Taine et M. Aulard* (Paris: Librairie Ancienne Honoré Champion, 1909), p. 94. See also, e.g, Thurman Arnold, *The Folklore of Capitalism* (New Haven: Yale University Press, 1937), pp. 42–43. Political scientists like Pareto (*Mind and Society*) and, to a lesser extent, Gaetano Mosca (see, e.g., *Ruling Class*, pp. 153–58) and Graham Wallas (see, e.g., *Our Social Heritage* [New Haven: Yale University Press, 1921], p. 81) described the irrational faith in "the People," "the Majority," "Democracy," and "Universal Suffrage." "Who is this new god Universal Suffrage?" demanded Pareto in *Mind and Society* (III, 1526). Others, like Bryce, singled out "public opinion" and "the rule of the majority" (see James Bryce, *The American Commonwealth* [2 vols.; New York: Macmillan Co., 1910], II, 267–73, 347–56; and "The Relations of Political Science to History and Practice," *American Political Science Review*, III [1909], 18). Among other observers of the uncritical faith in "the Jacobin religion" should be mentioned Gustave Le Bon: "The Jacobin is not a rationalist, but a believer," who in his faith in the Jacobin Majority "has replaced the old divinities by new gods" (*The Psychology of Revolution*, trans. Bernard Miall [New York: G. P. Putnam's Sons, 1913], pp.

92–96, 302–10); Herbert Spencer: "The great political superstition of the present" is the "divine right of Parliament [which] means the divine right of majorities" (*The Man versus the State* [Caldwell, Idaho: Caxton Printers, Ltd., 1940]); Augustin Cochin: "L'anthropomorphisme du peuple est plus récent, plus spécieux aussi que celui de la Providence" (*L'Histoire révolutionnaire*, esp. the chapter on "Le Mysticisme du peuple," pp. 91–97); and Alfred Fouillée, *L'Evolutionnisme des idées-forces* (Paris: Félix Alcan, 1906); Louis Rougier, *Les Mystiques politiques contemporaines et leurs incidences internationales* (Paris: Recueil Sirey, 1935), pp. 42–43, 45–46; and M. Ostrogorski, *Democracy and the Party System in the United States* (New York: Macmillan Co., 1926), p. 416.

22. To go into greater description when speaking of persons in all cultures is impossible. To persons in the Western world, it appears that the attributes of the mother characterize the *ruler*, although there is yet some clarification necessary concerning the position of the father (see Sebastian de Grazia, "A Note on the Psychological Position of the Chief Executive," *Psychiatry*, VIII [August, 1945], 267–72; and Trigant Burrow, "Social Images versus Reality," *Journal of Abnormal and Social Psychology*, XIX [1924–25], 230–35), and chap. vii above.

23. Quoted in John Emerich E. Acton, *The History of Freedom and Other Essays* (London: Macmillan & Co., 1907), p. 294.

24. Quoted in the study by E. F. M. Durbin and George E. G. Catlin (eds.), *War and Democracy* (London: Kegan Paul, Trench, Trubner & Co., Ltd., 1938), p. 128.

25. Joseph Barrère quoted in Carlton J. H. Hayes, *The Historical Evolution of Modern Nationalism* (New York: R. R. Smith, Inc., 1931), pp. 69–70. One might object, to be sure, that the French tongue is typically less restrained than the American on such subjects. But compare the quotation in chap. ii, above, from *The Man without a Country* or the speech of Hayes's Congressman in *Essays*, pp. 111–12.

26. Some of the effects in international law and politics of this incapacity are treated in Edward Hallett Carr, *The Twenty Years' Crisis, 1919–1939* (London: Macmillan & Co., Ltd., 1942), pp. 188–210; F. H. Allport, *Institutional Behavior*, pp. 136–54; and, for a nation at war, Caroline E. Playne, *The Prewar Mind in Britain* (London: George Allen & Unwin, Ltd., 1928), and *Society at War* (New York: Houghton Mifflin Co., 1931).

27. For these and other blasphemous incidents see Martin, *Magic of Monarchy*. For a comparable American example see Brooks, *As Others See Us*, pp. 60–61. An excellent description of the political conduct of Englishmen is John Gaus, *Great Britain*.

28. *Nationalism: A Report*, p. 261. It should not be necessary to go into the mystical, juridical, and political theories of sovereignty. For the psychological purpose here envisaged it suffices to note that they all partake of the qualities of supremacy, inaccessibility, immunity, or freedom from interference.

29. Dr. J. G. Zimmerman, physician to His Britannic Majesty at Hanover, writing in 1758, and quoted in Lasswell, *World Politics and Personal Insecurity*, pp. 40–41.

30. See *Nationalism: A Report*, pp. 252–53. The foregoing theory of political loyalty or patriotism differs substantially from that of Lasswell, as presented in his *World Politics and Personal Insecurity*, pp. 29–51. Lasswell's valuable theory may be called the theory of mutual identification, for it attempts to explain nationalism in the individual as a cluster of interlapping identifications with other persons based on the perception of similarities to them. The shortcomings of the theory lie in its inability to account for persons selecting particular similarities with which to identify. Thus Lasswell himself wonders why words about propinquity, tradition, and economic standing have so far outcompeted physical words in the rivalry for human loyalty. He facetiously asks why the curly-haired or dry-skinned or extraverted or leptosomic do not become class conscious and struggle against the straight-haired or oily-skinned or introverted or pyknic. From the domicilial theory presented in this chapter it is evident that the irrelevance of such traits is due to the fact that the members of one family may easily differ in just those characteristics of physique and character, while, on the other hand, the family pattern of relationships includes a locus in which the family members lived together (propinquity), a requirement of due respect for the attendants and their accomplishments (tradition), and an acceptance of similar economic circumstances among all members, with some differential for the attendants (economic standing). In other words, although there is mutual identification among citizens, the similarities on which it is based and from which the sense of oneness is derived are determined by the all-important relationship to the *ruler*, which is not primarily an identificative relationship but a filial relationship of dependence, faith, obedience, and affection. One may better perceive the advantages of this theory by noting that the theory of mutual identification does not help explain the weakness of class systems of beliefs in contrast to national systems. Since, in the latter theory, identification on the basis of any similarity is possible, one kind of ideology should be as attractive as any other. The theory of this chapter, however, would hold that class ideologies suffer from lack of a locus, whereas the territorial boundaries of a nation are tangible and visualizable. In addition, the presumable program of class ideologies to submit all persons, including the rulers, to economic leveling (e.g., Marx and Lenin emphasized "the reduction of the remuneration of *all* servants of the state to 'workingmen's wages' ") does not correspond to the household configuration of unequal economic power in favor of the attendants. As is briefly mentioned in chap. vii, members of a community want to see an economic difference in favor of the *ruler*, just as they want to see that the *ruler* has a great difference in power —a fact noted in chap. v in two separate applications. An excellent study of some of the psychological results of the superior economic position of attendants is contained in Richards, *Hunger and Work*, pp. 36–84, 209–11.

The theory of mutual identification ties in with the theories which have been built around the supposed importance of play groups or relationships of "mutual respect" (rather than the filial relationship of "unilateral respect") in the formation of the pattern of political relationships (see Flugel, *Man, Morals and Society*, for a summary, an advocacy, and an attempted application of the studies;

see also the studies of Kurt Lewin and R. Lippitt, which Flugel did not cover. These theories, however, either ignore or slight the facts that all activities of children, even in the play group or gang, have the protective and directive ceiling of attendants over them and that the one particular in which they all invariably identify is their often unspoken but well understood subordination to parents. The psychological effects of the biological dependence of the young organism cannot be circumvented. Thus, the possibility of providing predominantly "democratic climates" for children and thereby developing some sort of ideal type of self-reliant person who has no need for emotional leadership is highly overestimated (see, for supporting data, Isaacs, *Social Development in Young Children*, pp. 213–43 and *passim;* and, for an extension to adult behavior of loyalty, see West, *Conscience and Society*, pp. 229–30).

31. Other titles include "Lord of Judgment" and "Sun-of-the-Spotless-Law." The lawgiving role of the *ruler* springs from his directive function (see pp. 84–86 and chaps. i and ii, above; for an ethnological approach to "the King's Justice" see Hocart, *Kingship*, pp. 47–57). It may be noted here that, in the psychological sense, Henry Maine (in *Ancient Law* [New York: E. P. Dutton & Co., 1917]) can be considered correct in locating the origin of law in *themis*. Maine appropriated the term *themistes* from Homer, who used it to refer to the judgments laid down by kings under divine inspiration. In refuting Maine's contention that the *themistes* preceded custom, anthropologists have marshaled as evidence primitive societies that have no law but considerable custom (see Robert Redfield, "Maine's *Ancient Law* in the Light of Primitive Societies" [mimeographed lecture, University of Chicago, 1946]). But Maine thought of the *themistes* also as originally issuing from the family patriarchs in archaic society. And it does little good to deride or set aside this theory simply because it is now established that matriarchal societies have existed, too. For one thing, all that needs to be done is the substitution of "attendant" for "patriarch," and the theory then maintains that the judgments of attendants given to the individual preceded the judgments of the community, a fact which cannot be gainsaid. The only defense is a circuitous one, namely, that the judgments of attendants are, after all, mostly determined by the judgments of the community.

32. Bagehot had a clear understanding of the limitations of parliaments as *rulers:*

> When you put before the mass of mankind the question, "Will you be governed by a king, or will you be governed by a constitution?" the inquiry comes out thus— "Will you be governed in a way you understand, or will you be governed in a way you do not understand?" The issue was put to the French people: they were asked, "Will you be governed by Louis Napoleon, or will you be governed by an assembly?" The French people said, "We will be governed by the one man we can imagine, and not by the many people we cannot imagine" [Bagehot, *English Constitution*, p. 102]

33. In the cabinet system this limitation is absent, but its place is taken by the prime minister's dependence for tenure on the parliament.

34. Concomitantly, the nation's significance as the *ruling* entity recedes to

that of the homeland. Psychological aspects of the increase in the chief executive's power during critical periods are discussed in chap. x.

The theory here propounded on the variability of the *ruler* in republics and constitutional monarchies differs essentially from that of M. D. Eder and E. Jones (see E. Jones [ed.], *Social Aspects of Psychoanalysis* [London: Williams & Norgate, 1924]) which maintains that, in a constitutional monarchy, the *ruler* is popularly split into the image of a good attendant (the king) and a bad one (the prime minister). This god-devil dichotomy overlooks the fact that favorable sentiment is usually accorded the prime minister over lengthy spells, and there is little psychological reason to believe that his diabolic role exists simultaneously. It seems more likely that the focus of public attention and emotion shifts with the flux of events and that while kings and nations, over a long span of time, may be the most frequent and deepest repository of popular faith, at intervals they may be temporarily eclipsed. This position does not deny that lesser rulers may be the butt of accumulated antagonisms at set periods, while the crown or the nation most of the time (but not always) escapes unscathed.

CHAPTER VI

1. For these and other passages for comparison see Tocqueville, *Democracy in America*, pp. 42, 136–37, 142–50, 159–60; and Durkheim, *Le Suicide*, pp. 272–88. It is quite probable that Durkheim was familiar with Tocqueville's famous work which, even before it was translated into English, was well known in France among the literati.

2. Georg Simmel, "Die Grossstädte und das Geistesleben," in *Die Grossstadt*, ed. Theodor Petermann (Dresden: Zahn & Jaensch, 1903), p. 194.

3. The first of the six quotations above is from Orvis Collins, Melville Dalton, and Donald Roy, "Restriction of Output and Social Cleavage in Industry," *Applied Anthropology*, V (summer, 1946), 4; the next four quotations are from "Plant Interviews"; and the last is again from Collins *et al.*, "Restriction of Output."

4. C. G. Jung, *Modern Man in Search of a Soul* (New York: Harcourt Brace & Co., 1933), p. 267; see also pp. 226–82.

5. Alexander, *Age of Unreason*, p. 310.

6. Erich Fromm, *Escape from Freedom* (New York: Farrar & Rinehart, Inc. 1941), pp. 250–52, 132–34.

7. Robert E. Park, "Modern Society," *Biological Symposia*, VIII (1942), 234.

8. Horney, *Neurotic Personality*, pp. 286–87.

9. A comparison and evaluation of the methods used in research studies of industrial attitudes can be found in Edward K. Strong, *Psychological Aspects of Business* (New York: McGraw-Hill Book Co., Inc., 1938). The experiments here referred to are described in F. L. Roethlisberger and W. L. Dickson, *Management and the Worker* (Cambridge: Harvard University Press, 1938).

10. A catalogue of the studies done by the Mayo group of the Harvard Graduate School of Business Administration can be consulted in Elton Mayo,

The Social Problems of an Industrial Civilization (Boston: Harvard University Press, 1945).

11. In his early book, *Human Problems of an Industrial Civilization* (New York: Macmillan Co., 1933), p. 172, Elton Mayo, with cómmendable insight, explicitly recognized the possibility that anomie outside the factory may influence behavior within the factory, but he did not conceive of the relation between the need of affection and anomie.

CHAPTER VII

1. Virginia Woolf, *Mrs. Dalloway* (New York: Harcourt, Brace & Co., 1925), pp. 19–28.

2. All except the fourth of these quotations are taken from *Middletown*, p. 327. The fourth appears in *Middletown in Transition*, p. 314.

3. Martin, *Magic of Monarchy*, pp. 13–14, 19.

4. W. R. D. Fairbairn, "The Effect of the King's Death upon Patients under Analysis," *International Journal of Psychoanalysis*, XVII (1936), 278–84.

5. De Grazia, "Psychological Position of the Chief Executive," p. 268. This investigation was followed by an extensive study which exploited the same event and independently corroborated the first study's results. The reactions of 128 college students were ascertained from questionnaires. Though in lesser measure than in the intensive psychiatric work, both the unmanageability of the environment and the attribution of parental resemblance to the chief executive were encountered as responses in the second project (see Dorothea E. Johannsen, "Reactions to the Death of President Roosevelt," *Journal of Social and Abnormal Psychology*, XLI [1946], 218–22).

6. Numerous writers have attested the uniqueness of the struggles in this period. See, e.g., Samuel Eliot Morison and Henry Steele Commager, *The Growth of the American Republic* (2 vols.; New York: Oxford University Press, 1937), II, 160–66, which estimates that in the twenty-five-year period from 1881 to 1906 there occurred thirty-eight thousand strikes and lockouts, involving almost two hundred thousand establishments and over nine and one-half million workers. It is doubtful that the class hatred of the Great Depression ever grew so strong.

7. This Machiavellian proposition is borne out by two recent studies: Paul F. Lazarsfeld, *Die Arbeitslösen von Marienthal* (Leipzig: Hirzel, 1933); and Harold S. Guetzkow and Paul H. Bowman, *Men and Hunger* (Elgin, Ill.: Brethren Publishing House, 1947). The most extensive work on the relationship of economic conditions to political disturbance is P. A. Sorokin, *Social and Cultural Dynamics:* Vol. III, *Fluctuation of Social Relationships, War, and Revolution* (4 vols.; New York: American Book Co., 1937), pp. 383–506; see also Barrington Moore, Jr., "A Comparative Analysis of the Class Struggle," *American Sociological Review*, X (1945), 31–37; Crane Brinton, *The Anatomy of Revolution* (New York: W. W. Norton & Co., Inc., 1938), pp. 39–48; Bohan Zawadski and Paul Lazarsfeld, "The Psychological Consequences of Unemployment," *Journal of Social Psychology*, VI

(1935), 224–50; and, for the French Revolution in particular, G. Le Bon, *Psychology of Revolution*, pp. 63–74, 141–46.

8. A. H. Hansen, "Cycles of Strikes," *American Economic Review*, XI (December, 1921), 616–21.

In confirmation of the inadequacy of the economic theory of revolutions Hansen also found that in a period of long-run rising prices, 1898–1919, strikes correlated directly (+0.49) with business cycles. See, too, Mauritz A. Hallgren, *Seeds of Revolt* (New York: Alfred Knopf Co., 1933), which makes the point, in a historical analysis, that strikes in America are not caused by hunger but are typically recovery phenomena. Pareto's controversial but nonetheless important work on the curve of incomes is also relevant. He found that the shape of the curves of the distribution of income among persons bore little relation to the economic conditions of the country since widely differing periods and economies—England, Ireland, Germany, the Italian cities, and Peru—conformed to the same formula (Vilfredo Pareto, *Cours d'économie politique* [2 vols.; Paris: Pichon, 1896–97], II, 299–345). The basis of the criticisms of "Pareto's Law" is not pertinent here, for it chiefly consists of an attack on his neglect of inherited wealth as a cause of the unequal distribution. What is important for the purpose at hand, and for political science in general, is the remarkable stability of the curves of income despite crises or differences in form of government.

9. See Harry A. Millis and Royal E. Montgomery, *Labor's Progress and Some Basic Labor Problems* (New York: McGraw-Hill Book Co., Inc., 1938), pp. 78–284.

10. M. Beard, *History of the Business Man*, p. 643.

11. On this point see the suggestive chapter, "The Revenue," in Hocart, *Kings and Councillors*, pp. 197–209.

12. Dixon Wecter, *The Saga of American Society* (New York: Charles Scribner's Sons, 1937), p. 390.

13. Associations and mass movements as a consequence of anomie are considered, respectively, in chaps. viii and x.

14. Speech quoted in Solon Buck, *The Agrarian Crusade* (New Haven: Yale University Press, 1920), p. 135.

15. Isabel Simeral Johnson, "Cartoons," *Public Opinion Quarterly*, I (July, 1937), 33. One of the deadliest drawings of the period, achieved by William Balfour Ker, can be seen in Wecter, *American Society*, p. 457.

16. M. Beard, *History of the Business Man*, p. 651.

17. Wecter, *American Society*, p. 368.

18. Theodore Roosevelt, *An Autobiography* (New York: Charles Scribner's Sons, 1913), pp. 470–71.

19. M. Beard, *History of the Business Man*, p. 762.

20. Frederick Townsend Martin, *The Passing of the Idle Rich* (London: Hodder & Stoughton, 1911). Not enough persons have realized that Veblen's *Theory of the Leisure Class* describes a departing way of life.

21. For a summary statement of this psychological progression see Philip

Eisenberg and Paul F. Lazarsfeld, "The Psychological Effects of Unemployment," *Psychological Bulletin*, XXXV (1938), 378.

22. Zawadski and Lazarsfeld, "Psychological Consequences of Unemployment," p. 238.

23. These quotations are taken, respectively, from A. Gatti, "La Disoccupazione come crisi psicologica," *Archivio italiano di psicologia*, XV (1937), 4–28; Eli Ginzberg, *The Unemployed* (New York: Harper & Bros., 1943), pp. 44 and 233; and Zawadski and Lazarsfeld, "Psychological Consequences of Unemployment," p. 237.

24. Anonymous, "Man Out of Work, by His Wife," *Harper's Monthly Magazine*, CLXI (July, 1930), 195–201.

25. See, especially, Zawadski and Lazarsfeld, "Psychological Consequences of Unemployment," pp. 244–45; and E. Wight Bakke, *The Unemployed Man* (London: Nisbet & Co., Ltd., 1933).

26. In a *Fortune* poll of public opinion, 52 per cent of the American population believed that machines take away jobs ("Obsolete Men," *Fortune Magazine*, VI [1932], 24–34). See also Clinch Calkins, *Some Folks Won't Work* (New York: Harcourt, Brace & Co., 1930), pp. 46–58. For the profound psychological effects of machinery see, e.g., Henri de Man, *Joy in Work*, trans. E. and C. Paul (New York: Henry Holt & Co., 1929); Hans Sachs, "The Delay of the Machine Age," *Psychoanalytic Quarterly*, II (1933), 404–24; Lewis Mumford, *Technics and Civilization* (New York: Harcourt, Brace & Co., 1934), pp. 269–73, 364–68; and Victor Tausk, "On the Origin of the 'Influencing Machine' in Schizophrenia," *Psychoanalytic Quarterly*, II (1933), 519.

27. The first of these quotations is from "Plant Interviews"; the second and third are from Bakke, *The Unemployed Man*, p. 3; and the last from De Man's *Joy in Work*, pp. 36–37. The last source contains an excellent account of the workman's animistic belief in machinery (see pp. 26–39).

28. Anon., "Man Out of Work," p. 200.

29. Bakke, *The Unemployed Man*, pp. 67 and 139–40. The breakdown of directives apparently affects related series of norms. Once the set of rules meets with no consistent experience of reward, it becomes clear that all directives are psychologically connected with the commands and prohibitions of the *ruler*. Immorality in other spheres appears (see, e.g., for the increased immorality of the unemployed, J. M. Williams, *Human Aspects of Employment and Relief* [Chapel Hill: University of North Carolina Press, 1933]). The phenomenon of the release of moral restraints is even more clearly present in revolutions, where also the position of the *ruler* deteriorates (see, especially, Pitirim Sorokin, *Sociology of Revolution* [Philadelphia: J. B. Lippincott Co., 1925], pp. 32–192).

The effects on children of the father's unemployment are analogous in several ways to the effects of unemployment on the adult. Children, too, lose the sense of secure leadership and the rationale for conformity to the rules; anxiety and fear color their relationships (see, e.g., H. C. Schumacher, "The Depression and Its Effects on the Mental Health of the Child," *Mental Hygiene*, XVIII [1934], 287–93).

30. Many studies show that the *ruler* in the economic system of beliefs was adversely affected in the depression that followed the "sixteen-million-share day" of October 29, 1929. In addition to the works cited in n. 33 below, see E. A. Rundquist and R. F. Sletto, *Personality in the Depression* (Minneapolis: University of Minnesota Press, 1936); O. Milton Hall, "Attitudes and Unemployment: A Comparison of the Opinions and Attitudes of Employed and Unemployed Men," *Archives of Psychology*, Vol. XXV, No. 165 (1934); and Lilian Brandt, *An Impressionistic View of the Winter of 1930-31 in New York City* (New York: Welfare Council of New York City, 1932), pp. 16-21, a work which, despite the title, is a systematic analysis of the statements of nine hundred social workers.

31. Quoted in Bakke, *The Unemployed Man*, p. 12.

32. This query is by a Pole. See Zawadski and Lazarsfeld, "Psychological Consequences of Unemployment," p. 249.

33. For the belief in the cause-and-effect relationship of businessmen and prosperity in the Coolidge-Mellon-Hoover era see Charles and Mary Beard, *America in Midpassage* (New York: Macmillan Co., 1939), pp. 3-112; James Truslow Adams, "Presidential Prosperity," *Harper's Monthly Magazine*, CLXI (1930), 257-67; F. L. Allen, *Only Yesterday*, pp. 159-85, 290-319; and Wallace Brett Donham, *Business Adrift* (New York: McGraw-Hill Book Co., Inc., 1931), pp. 51-66. For historical location of the time when the business ideology first acquired the idea of "prosperity" see M. Beard, *History of the Business Man*, pp. 735-37.

34. Anon., "Man Out of Work," p. 201.

PART IV

INTRODUCTION

1. In Chart I the peaks are drawn neither numerically nor temporally to scale. They are intended merely to depict a cluster of separation-anxiety or acute anomie points lasting for relatively short intervals within broad life-stages, such as childhood. The heights of the peaks illustrate, in the roughest fashion, psychological observations of the intensities of anxiety in the various periods. Peaks *1-10* represent stages through which all persons pass. The others, *11-13*, are not inevitable and do not necessarily occur in the order given. They might not happen at all in one generation or might even be contemporaneous. "Birth-anxiety," which should mark the first separation of all, has been omitted from the graph because of its problematical occurrence (for the original statement of the theory see Otto Rank, *The Trauma of Birth* [New York: Harcourt, Brace & Co., 1929], and for its criticism, S. Freud, *The Problem of Anxiety*, pp. 121-32).

2. The curves $A'-B'$, $C'-D'$, and $E'-F'$ are discussed on p. 159.

CHAPTER VIII

1. For the overwhelming majority of persons the adaptation of self-sufficiency—one person's attempting to accumulate all the materials for his needs and

thus remove the need for dependence on secular belief-systems—is not only unworkable but inconceivable. Private property in land is sometimes highly prized for such a venture. It appears clearly, e.g., in John Steinbeck's *Of Mice and Men*. A variant of this solution is the hope pinned on the invention of some portable machine that can provide for all one's needs. It is evident in high-flying discussions of the fractional-horsepower motor or portable atomic energy units, as well as in literary efforts like Aldous Huxley's *After Many a Summer Dies the Swan*. The behavior of children also presents clear cases of this kind of "property" motive (see Isaacs, *Social Development in Young Children*, pp. 221–31).

Sociologists might describe the need for affection in terms of a need for primary and sympathetic (as opposed to secondary and categoric) contacts and for personal, intimate, or face-to-face relationships. It seems advisable, however, to retain the word "affection" in an endeavor to keep the psychogenesis of the need in the forefront of its meaning.

The usage of the phrase, an "unusually strong need for affection" may be further clarified by noting that the affection is sought (1) in large quantities, (2) to the exclusion of other relationships with persons, (3) from persons indiscriminately, (4) with an appearance of urgency, (5) with perseverence, or (6) with disregard for the deprivations necessary to obtain it.

2. That simple anomie can be alleviated through fantasy is indisputable. The degree to which it can be relieved, however, is as yet unknown. It is merely known that, except in rare cases, fantasy itself, either intrapersonal or in conjunction with external mediums (e.g., story-tellers, religious symbolism, radio, press, screen, painting, and music), can offer temporary release.

3. Some writers, like Henri de Man (*Joy in Work*), claim that work in present-day factories satisfies man's need for sociability. This is not the case, however, with the vast bulk of modern jobs, as the protests against the competitive directive and the need for affection among most classes of workers have indicated (see chap. vi, above).

4. "Plant Interviews." For numerous illustrations of everyday conflicts in directives see the essay on "The Luxury of Integrity" in Stuart Chase, *The Nemesis of American Business* (New York: Macmillan Co., 1931), esp. pp. 33–50. Chase made an interesting attempt to rank occupations by the amount of moral conflict their ordinary performance incurred. Everett Cherrington Hughes's treatment of "Personality Types and the Division of Labor," *American Journal of Sociology*, XXXIII (1928), 754–68, is similar but not nearly so specific. One might also refer to Charles M. Sheldon, *In His Steps* (New York: J. H. Sears & Co., Inc., n.d.), which attempted to show the conflicts a person would have if he tried unflinchingly to follow Christ's teachings in the modern world.

5. M. Weber, *Protestant Ethic*, p. 35.

6. *Ibid.*, pp. 38, 188–89; for similar evidence see also pp. 35–46. Weber's student, Martin Offenbacher, did the statistical researches. Scarcely anyone has challenged the statistics; critics have sought only to question Weber's interpretation of them.

7. See, e.g., Louis M. Hacker, *The Triumph of American Capitalism* (New York: Simon & Schuster, 1940), pp. 46–50.

8. See, e.g., Siegfried, *America Comes of Age*, pp. 36–40; and Howard Mumford Jones, *America and French Culture, 1750–1848* (Chapel Hill: University of North Carolina Press, 1927).

9. See, e.g., Theodore Maynard, *The Story of American Catholicism* (New York: Macmillan Co., 1942), pp. 420–30; Shailer Mathews, "The Church and the Social Order," in W. C. Bower, *The Church at Work in the Modern World* (Chicago: University of Chicago Press, 1935), pp. 194–95.

10. See, e.g., Liston Pope, *Millhands and Preachers* (New Haven: Yale University Press, 1942); R. S. and H. M. Lynd, *Middletown in Transition*, pp. 85–86; Emily Newbold, "Business and Religion: An Old Partnership Revived," *Harper's Monthly Magazine*, CLXXXI (July, 1940), 148–55.

11. See, e.g., Gabriel, *American Democratic Thought*, pp. 52–66, 143–60; Siegfried, *America Comes of Age*, p. 36.

12. See, e.g., Hans H. Gerth, "A Midwestern Sectarian Community," *Social Research*, XI (1944), 354–62; Pope, *Millhands and Preachers, passim;* and see Robert Hoppock, *Job Satisfaction* (New York: Harper & Bros., 1935), which found that the questionnaire statement "I feel that God called me to do this work" was indorsed by persons in a wide range of occupations, including clerical, secretarial, farming, small proprietorship, accounting, cashiering, dentistry, and laboring vocations (see, esp., pp. 22, 28–29, 78, 87, 102, 112, 116).

13. See, e.g., Gerth and Mills, *From Max Weber*, pp. 302–22.

14. The necessity to adjust to conflicting directives accounts, of course, for a large part of the difficulty in assimilation for these groups (see, in general, Siegfried, *America Comes of Age*, pp. 22–32). For the Lutherans see Heinrich A. Maurer's articles in Vol. XXX (1924–25) of the *American Journal of Sociology.* The greater preference for government jobs among presumably Catholic nationality groups was quantitatively ascertained by L. D. White in *Prestige Value of Public Employment* (Chicago: University of Chicago Press, 1929).

15. Monistic causality is not being claimed for the appearance of any exaggeration in these cultural traits but only that simple anomie contributes to their deviation from other cultural patterns. By "cultural trait" is meant recurring acts which the members of a community expect of other members with a degree of probability.

16. For the handling of love in Shakespeare's plays and sonnets see Lauren J. Mills, *One Soul in Bodies Twain* (Bloomington, Ind.: Principia Press, 1937), pp. 226–374. For the temper of the Elizabethan age see also V. F. Calverton, "Sex and the Social Struggle"; and Storm Jameson, *The Decline of Merry England* (London: Cassell & Co., Ltd., 1930).

17. This is the definition of romantic love of R. M. MacIver in *Society* (New York: Farrar & Rinehart, Inc., 1937), p. 211. For those who understand psychoanalytic terminology the definition in Edmund Bergler, *Unhappy Marriage and Divorce* (New York: International Universities Press, 1946), p. 31, is rec-

ommended. Folsom's entire treatment of the subject, including his stress on "cardiac-respiratory love," is interesting (*Family*, p. 73).

18. Lucretius, *On the Nature of Things*, trans. Cyril Bailey (London: Oxford at the Clarendon Press, 1936), pp. 182, 181. A comprehensive study of Greek love is L. Dugas, *L'Amitié antique* (Paris: Félix Alcan, 1894). See also Zimmern, *Greek Commonwealth*, pp. 327-36, and Albert Galloway Keller, *Homeric Society* (New York: Longmans, Green & Co., 1902).

19. Briffault, *The Mothers*, pp. 151-52. For further evidence of the differences in primitive and also ancient and medieval love see William Graham Sumner and Albert Galloway Keller, *The Science of Society* (3 vols.; New Haven: Yale University Press, 1927), III, 1731-1830; and Edward Westermarck, *The History of Human Marriage* (3 vols.; London: Macmillan & Co., 1925).

20. Ralph Linton, *The Study of Man* (New York: D. Appleton–Century Co., 1936), p. 175. For some studies that consider various aspects of the extraordinary character of modern love see J. Gaultier, *Le Bovarysme* (Paris: Mercure de France, 1921); S. Freud, *Civilization and Its Discontents*, p. 73; André Maurois, *The Seven Faces of Love*, trans. H. M. Chevalier (New York: Didier Publishers, 1944), pp. 49-84, 175-208; Esther Harding, *The Way of All Women* (New York: Longmans, Green & Co., 1933); Martha Wolfenstein and Nathan Leites, "An Analysis of Themes and Plots," *Annals of the American Academy of Political and Social Science*, CCLIV (November, 1947), 41-48; Karen Horney, "The Overevaluation of Love: A Study of a Common Present-Day Feminine Type," *Psychoanalytic Quarterly*, Vol. III (1934); and, of course, the novel which has had such a great influence on modern love, Gustave Flaubert's *Madame Bovary*. In its last nine lines Matthew Arnold's poem "Dover Beach" bears directly on the anomic motivation of romantic love.

21. In addition to pp. 54-55, above, see Mills, *One Soul*, pp. 16-75, 390. The cultural trait of friendship might be said to vary with the presence in the community of simple anomie and the absence of heavy (Puritanical) sexual restrictions. Robert Lowie in *Primitive Society* (New York: Boni & Liveright, 1920), p. 25, made a related generalization in noting that social and sexual restrictions apply to the same categories of persons, so that toward whatever persons one's sexual conduct is circumscribed, custom will also demand special restraints in social intercourse.

22. It will be remembered that the lack of dual male friendship in present times has not been proved but solely assumed in the absence of data. Such friendship as openly exists in adulthood seems to be justified by occupational reasons, or by familial get-togethers ("friends of the family") which are ostensibly cosexual but often quickly divide along sex lines, or by organizational reasons. All these questions have been insufficiently studied; moreover, the few extant studies of an empirical sort have experimented mostly with adolescents. Unquestionably there are strong psychological motives impelling men to make friends of those with whom they work (see S. Freud, *Civilization and Its Discontents*, p. 34, n. 1), but they meet head on with competitive and impersonal pressures.

23. The appreciation of home or family as here considered is to be differentiated from the highly important image of home and family previously discussed. The latter was based on the security of home and family to the child; this section describes the value set upon home life by adults as heads of the family because of its freedom from competitiveness (including impersonalism and rationalism) and activism, namely, because of the escape it may afford from simple anomie.

24. H. V. Routh, *Money, Morals and Manners as Revealed in Modern Literature* (London: Ivor Nicholson & Watson, Ltd., 1935), pp. 142–43.

25. *Ibid.*, pp. 147–48.

26. See, e.g., Bakke, *The Unemployed Man*, pp. 153–76.

27. An interesting discussion of the difficulties adhering to the complex of romantic love, marriage, and home is W. B. Blakemore, Jr., "How Shall the Church Define Marriage?" (mimeographed paper presented to the theological field colloquium, University of Chicago, March 4, 1946). Especially noteworthy in this connection is the continuous rise in the proportion of divorces sought on charges of cruelty, in particular, mental cruelty. Although statistics in this sphere are not reliable for small percentages, the fact remains that approximately one-half of all divorces are granted on cruelty grounds. As W. F. Ogburn said, the data show that "divorces are being sought on less serious grounds than formerly" (President's Research Committee in Social Trends, *Recent Social Trends in the United States* [2 vols.; New York: McGraw-Hill Book Co., Inc., 1933], I, 694–95).

28. See W. L. Warner and A. S. Lunt, *Social Life of a Modern Community* [New Haven: Yale University Press, 1941], p. 113), which finds that a New England city "possesses a larger number of voluntary groupings than any society yet examined by social anthropologists." Perhaps, in order to distinguish the broader usage in this study of the term "voluntary association," it would be preferable to speak of "voluntary groups," keeping in mind the definition given. The meaning of voluntary associations as expanded here intentionally includes the groupings of fads and cults, the groupings in neighborhood "pubs" and taverns, of regularized socials or planned parties, and most sports. Very often for example, the poor man's club is his tavern, where he meets his cronies every night and spends most of his time (with the exception of time at home and work). Even the less trafficked street corner can be the locale at night for an informal association in the poor sections of a city. This kind of association, however, is generally the inexpensive resort of adolescents. Information about voluntary associations as thus broadly conceived can be found treated usually as "leisure activities," although the latter term is obviously more inclusive. The usual quantitative studies of leisure, however, cannot be used because neither do they fit closely enough the definition given of voluntary association nor do they contain cross-cultural data. But for two studies which almost meet the first objection see Pitirim A. Sorokin and Clarence Q. Berger, *Time-Budgets of Human Behavior* (Cambridge: Harvard University Press, 1939), and Edward L.

Thorndike, "How We Spend Our Time and What We Spend It For," *Scientific Monthly*, XLIV (1937), 464–69.

29. For data on memberships and expenditures see *Recent Social Trends*, II, 912–57; Charles W. Ferguson, *Fifty Million Brothers* (New York: Farrar & Rinehart, Inc., 1937); Herbert Goldhamer, "Some Factors Affecting Participation in Voluntary Associations" (unpublished Ph.D. dissertation, Department of Sociology, University of Chicago, December, 1942, pp. 19–69), and "Social Clubs" in S. Eldredge, *Development of Collective Enterprise* (Lawrence, Kan.: University of Kansas Press, 1942).

30. Sinclair Lewis, *Babbitt* (New York: F. P. Collier & Son, Corp., 1922), pp. 257, 395–97. Outside of Tocqueville's illuminating remarks, there seem to be no close examinations of the motives for the high frequency with which Americans organize themselves into associations. Most investigators accept the declared purpose for organization—economic, religious, recreational, and so forth—without troubling over the fact that it does not explain the propensity for association in America, namely, the cultural trait of high associativeness. For this reason no scientific work was found to equal Lewis' irreproachably accurate, documentary novel. Paul Harris, who in 1905 founded the Rotary Club, explained his motive in this way: "I was lonely myself, so I gathered some other lonely ones around me and we agreed to meet once a week."

31. Charles Madge and Tom Harrisson, *Britain by Mass-Observation* (London: Penguin Books, Ltd., 1939), pp. 139, 144–47, 173, and 183. The description given of the neighborhood of Lambeth Walk fits the area as of 1938.

It may be of interest to note here the fact that in the early Christian movement hymn singing was accompanied by hand clapping and dance rhythms (see Paul Henry Lang, *Music in Western Civilization* [New York: W. W. Norton & Co., Inc., 1942], p. 47). The effect of rhyme or rhythm plus music in creating feelings of unity in an assembled body is a subject which for all its practical political importance has been academically slighted since the times of Plato and Boethius. H. L. Mencken had the cohesive power of music and rhythm in mind when he called the military band "the greatest enemy of mankind."

32. William L. Riordon, *Plunkitt of Tammany Hall* (New York: McClure, Phillips & Co., 1905), pp. 128, 182–83.

33. James Aloysius Farley, *Behind the Ballots* (New York: Harcourt, Brace & Co., 1938), pp. 192–93.

34. Roy V. Peel, *The Political Clubs of New York City* (New York: G. P. Putnam's Sons, 1935), pp. 160–77 and pp. 179–90. On the general point see also J. T. Salter, "Personal Attention in Politics," *American Political Science Review*, XXXIV (1940), 54–66. With the exception of Peel and Salter, the chronicling by political scientists of these aspects of political behavior and the appraising of their effects has been slight. (Salter's limitation for the purpose at hand is that he describes only the individual "favor" type of nonimpersonality in politics.) One can see the importance of political affiliations in the excellent collection of illustrations of politics and voting behavior in Pendleton Herring, *The Politics of Democracy* (New York: W. W. Norton & Co., Inc., 1940).

35. C. E. Merriam and H. F. Gosnell (*American Party System* [New York: Macmillan Co., 1940], p. 111) go further, however, and declare that "here we enter into a field of political psychology thus far unexplored, but rich in its possibilities.

36. For convincing evidence on this point see Paul F. Lazarsfeld, Bernard Berelson, and Hazel Gaudet, *The People's Choice* (New York: Duell, Sloan & Pearce, 1944).

37. Merriam and Gosnell (*American Party System*, pp. 108–9) are correct in believing that very often the new voter's pattern of party voting is set by his early family experiences; for the family and especially the father are instrumental in introducing the young member to political associations. "A boy of ten participates in a Republican parade and is henceforth a Republican. . . . His playmates or friends are mostly Republican, or Democratic; it is not the thing to affiliate with Republicans, or vice versa it is not good form to be a Democrat. . . . Let the average voter ask himself when and why he first became a partisan, and the non-rational character of the process will at once become evident." See also H. H. Remmers and Naomi Weltman, "Attitude Interrelationships of Youth, Their Parents, and Their Teachers," *Journal of Social Psychology*, XXVI (1947), 61–68; and Lazarsfeld, *et al.*, *The People's Choice*, pp. 140–45. Because of the role the family plays in initiating the younger generation into political associations, the highest traditional voting is generally found in areas of low geographical mobility.

38. See Ostrogorski, *Democracy and the Party System*, pp. 408, 409–12. Without doubt much of the allegiance which binds together the association of the political party is due to the potential identity of the party's ideology with the primary system of beliefs of the state. (As mentioned earlier, each lesser association has a petty or secondary system of beliefs.) The readiness with which a party leader can become the political *ruler* has been well described by H. R. G. Greaves:

Having once been chosen, the Prime Minister ceases in gradually increasing measure to be the mere creature of his creators. As leader of the party in the country, and still more as the chief member of the Government and the greatest dispenser of patronage in public life, he takes on a new stature. Power makes him interesting. His personality is "put across" to the public by the Press, the newsreel, the radio, the cartoonist. His features and voice and peculiarities are made familiar to every one in the country. He attains a public personality which, often enough, his friends would find a great difficulty in recognizing as his own. He is converted into something of a symbol and a figurehead. Around him centres a certain amount of hero-worship. Criticism by his own followers is regarded as disloyalty. He has grown not only into a leader but into the chief buttress of party unity, and in time of emergency, of national unity [Harold R. G. Greaves, *The British Constitution* (London: Allen & Unwin, Ltd., 1938), pp. 115–16].

The political party's closeness to the nation is amusingly illustrated in the pledge that one Brooklyn political club leader made part of the club's ritual: "I pledge allegiance to the Democratic party of the United States and to the principle for which it stands, one party indivisible with favors and jobs for all!" (quoted in Peel, *Political Clubs*, p. 103).

39. See H. J. Laski, "Law and the State," *Economica*, XXVII (1924), 283; and *Authority in the Modern State* (New Haven: Yale University Press, 1919), p. 65.

40. The viewpoint here is that each association, for example, a firm, a union, or an army, has a lesser or secondary system of beliefs which is relegated to the primary ideologies of church and state. And many of the principles worked out in this book can be applied to what are generally called the "morale problems" of such associations.

A second criticism of pluralism implicates the statement that other associa_tions may attract deeper allegiances. The writer in an earlier article ("Status as a Political Motive") attempted to show the limitations of the system of beliefs based on economic association (which, if any, can claim a competing allegiance) when contrasted to the powerful ideologies of state and religion.

41. Worthy of a small note is the fact that the Index to the Lynds's *Middletown in Transition* has an entry entitled "friendliness" but none on "friends" or "friendship." The persistence of the feeling of being used as an instrument is largely due to the fact that first, one's nonwork hours are often put to occupational purposes. Thus:

> Friendship is one of the few compensations for a complex life. To shower upon strangers and upon people who never could be one's friends all the earnests of comradeship is to debase rare metal. The dismal panorama passes before us: . . . Rotary club luncheons with members roaring songs, embracing one another, "Jim" calling to "Joe" (and Jim hates Joe)—all in the hope of more business. . . . The hearty dinner at home to the chief buyer for the National Widget Corporation with one's wife in a new and alluring frock and carefully coached in the art of drawing out Mr. Blatterfein on his favorite topic—the postage stamps of the Hawaiian Islands. . . . The high and costly strategy employed by publisher B in weaning an author away from publisher A—the agent preferably to be an old college friend. . . . "Contact men" in dinner coats at week-end parties [Stuart Chase, *Nemesis of American Business*, pp. 42–43].

And, second, one's hours outside work are often spent in recreational establishments operated on a profit-and-loss basis by the proprietor who must therefore command a commercial friendliness to customers from his employees (see, e.g., M. Elliott and F. Merrill, *Social Disorganization* [New York: Harper & Bros., 1934], pp. 623–40).

42. Those groups for which the statistical measures of association are acceptable have memberships in many associations (see Goldhamer, "Participation in Voluntary Associations," p. 21). There is some evidence that membership in groups is inversely related to mental disorders (see Anton T. Boisen, "Personality Changes and Upheavals," *American Journal of Psychiatry*, V [1926], 531–51). But the general unsatisfactoriness of leisure activities, which has been largely attributed here to the compulsive search for affectionate relationships, has been noted in many studies.

43. See Henri Pirenne, *Economic and Social History of Medieval Europe*, trans. I. E. Clegg (New York: Harcourt, Brace & Co., n.d.), pp. 14–15, 28–29, 121. See also pp. 45–72, above.

CHAPTER IX

1. Ostrogorski, *Democracy and the Party System*, p. 411.

2. See, e.g., D. W. Harding, *The Impulse To Dominate* (London: George Allen & Unwin, Ltd., 1941), p. 43; and Quincy Wright, *The Causes of War and the Conditions of Peace* (New York: Longmans, Green & Co., 1935), p. 109. Such statements justify treating war here as a voluntary association. In any case, personal *wishes* to go in or go out, if not the actual ability of any single individual to do so, can certainly be thought of as voluntary. Furthermore (and, in this case, unlike the other types of association, there are quantitative measures), war as an association is increasing its membership. "The size of armies, the number of battles, the human and economic expenditures for war are on the increase" (Wright, *Causes of War*, p. 46 and see also pp. 21–49). "The size of armies has tended to increase during the modern period both absolutely and in proportion to the population" (Quincy Wright, *Study of War* [2 vols.; Chicago, University of Chicago Press, 1942], I, 232 and see also 218–48).

3. See pp. 50–51, above. A very small minority which believes that the word "neighbor" refers to all mankind feels a new conflict with the religious directive, "Thou shalt not kill"; but, for the most part, war shows the deep affiliation of the political and religious belief-systems and the lack of any provision for war in the economic system of beliefs.

4. Quoted by J. B. Priestley in *Postscripts* (London: W. Heineman, 1940), p. 43.

5. Quoted in Therese Benedek, *Insight and Personality Adjustment: A Study of the Psychological Effects of War* (New York: Ronald Press Co., 1946), p. 273.

6. *Ibid.*, pp. 269–92.

7. The pioneering and still unexcelled analysis of the military system of beliefs is Sigmund Freud, *Group Psychology and the Analysis of the Ego*, trans. James Strachey (London: International Psychoanalytical Press, 1922), pp. 41–51. It is used today in the best accounts of World War II psychology, e.g., Grinker and Spiegel (see n. 10, below) and Benedek.

The leader of the army group has many similarities to the father of the family: the members of the groups, as if they were children, rely upon his ideals, his purposes, and upon him as the individual capable of fulfilling his responsibilities toward his followers. The members of the group, like siblings within a family, identify with each other in willingness to help him to achieve a task, which thus becomes a common goal for the group. The function of the emotional relationship between leaders and members on the one hand and among the members of the group on the other, is manifold. The leader enlists the help and loyalty of the members to achieve the goal. The members not only give their work but they also relinquish much of their individual freedom for the sake of the common goal—but in return they are relieved from the responsibility which they would carry were they standing alone. While they give each other mutual help, they are rewarded by mutual protection and the prestige of the group [Benedek, *Insight and Personality Adjustment*, p. 45].

One writer has attributed the great superiority of the Roman legion as a fighting invention to a psychological insight: the reinforcing bravery of self-sacrificing comrades (see Michael Anitchkow, *War and Labour* [New York: Longmans, Green & Co., 1900], pp. 17–18). Modern psychiatric evidence supports this hypothesis. For the higher mental casualty rates in modern war among men fighting separated from their comrades, see John Rawlings Rees, *The Shaping of Psychiatry by War* (New York: W. W. Norton, Inc., 1945), p. 113.

8. Erich Maria Remarque, *All Quiet on the Western Front* (Boston: Little, Brown & Co., 1930); and Siegfried L. Sassoon, *Memoirs of an Infantry Officer* (London: Faber & Faber, Ltd., 1930). See also John Brophy and Eric Partridge (eds.), *Songs and Slang of the British Soldier: 1914–1918* (London: E. Partridge, Ltd., 1930).

9. Sassoon, *Memoirs of an Infantry Officer*, p. 202.

10. Roy R. Grinker and John P. Spiegel, *Men under Stress* (Philadelphia: Blakiston, 1945), p. 25 and *passim*. This volume deals exclusively with air force personnel. For the similar beliefs of ground force personnel see the same authors, *War Neuroses in North Africa: The Tunisian Campaign: January–May 1943* (New York: Josiah Macy, Jr., Foundation, 1943), pp. 242–45, 295–96, and *passim*.

11. Quincy Wright notes a certain readiness to resort to war in the modern era:

> The speed with which war spreads, especially among the great powers, indicates the interest in war as well as the working of the balance of power. I find that in only 3 of the 14 war periods of the last three centuries which involved one or more great powers on each side and lasted more than two years, did a single great power avoid being drawn into war. If a great-power war breaks out we may expect all the great powers to get in unless the war ends very rapidly. A belligerent disposition naturally evolves from continuous whetting of the natural war interest. Interest gives familiarity and familiarity gradually brings acceptance. An American population with a tradition of neutrality rapidly became war minded and eventually a belligerent in both the Napoleonic and the World War periods [*Causes of War*, p. 114; see also his *Study of War*, I, 237–42].

12. D. W. Harding, *The Impulse To Dominate*, pp. 127–28, draws a similar conclusion: "Ironically, this very dread of war is one of the most potent means of releasing the impulse to friendly companionship, and so of enhancing that social compactness on which a modern war depends. . . . People can yield to friendliness with each other far more securely than at any other time."

13. Remarque, *All Quiet on the Western Front*, p. 141. Further substantiation of the proposition that men have favorable recollections of war's camaraderie may eliminate Spengler's explanation for the fifty-year periodicity of battle concentration in the last two centuries. Spengler thought that the ex-combatant learned to hate war and therefore trained his sons to dislike it, but the influence of the ex-combatant could not extend in sufficient strength to turn the grandsons away from war's allures (see Oswald Spengler, *The Decline of the West*, trans. Charles F. Atkinson [New York: Alfred A. Knopf, 1934], I, 109–10). For a presentation both of data on the periodicity and of Spengler's proposition

(though with no defense of the latter) see Wright, *Study of War*, I, 229–31. R. S. Lynd touched on the point, too, when he noted:

> It is a commentary upon the dearth of positive designs for living other than the design of personal money-making that the veterans of each great war tend to look back on their war "service" as the greatest experience of their lives; and that the American Legion—the very men who know most intimately the insane horrors of war—unconsciously . . . [prepares] us, through the cherishing of their vanished high moment, for the "glories" of the next war [in H. C. Engelbrecht, *Revolt against War* (New York: Dodd, Mead & Co., 1937), p. x].

See n. 38, p. 241, below, for the relation of war camaraderie to National Socialism. In particular, on the far-reaching effects of the comradeship-in-arms, see Arnold J. Toynbee, *A Study of History*, abridgment of Vols. I–VI by D. C. Somervell (New York: Oxford University Press, 1947), pp. 457–58.

14. Playne, *Society at War*, p. 373 and also pp. 352–60. The role of women was prominent. "The bare mention of an approach to peace caused the women war workers to blaspheme." See also Charles Edward Montague, *Disenchantment* (New York: Brentano's, 1923); Remarque, *All Quiet on the Western Front*, p. 170; and "Peace—It's Lonely, Wac Vets Agree," *Chicago Daily News*, August 23, 1947.

15. See esp. Robert D. Gillespie, *Psychological Effects of War on Citizen and Soldier* (New York: W. W. Norton & Co., Inc., 1942), and the works of A. Freud and D. T. Burlingham previously cited.

16. The source for this impression (which was given in 1946) of England in a post bellum mood is the Dutch psychiatrist, A. M. Meerloo. Major Meerloo divided his war years between occupied Holland and England. The information is as yet unpublished. Some of his observations on occupied Holland can be found in his *Total War and the Human Mind* (New York: International Universities Press, Inc., 1945), pp. 10–26. And see esp. p. 170, above, for the steep drops in suicide rates during wars.

17. At this point a technical statement might be given concerning the relationship of this theory to some of the other social psychological explanations of war. In the first place, it bears some relation to the crowd, herd instinct, and group theories of G. Le Bon, *The Crowd* (London: T. Fisher Unwin, 1896); W. Trotter, *Instincts of the Herd in Peace and War* (London: T. Fisher Unwin, 1916); and McDougall, *The Group Mind*. But the relationship extends only to providing more definite reasons for the trait of extreme associativeness in modern civilization. The approach here owes much more (as it does throughout the entire study) to S. Freud, *Group Psychology*. In the second place, the theory does nothing to dispute the relevance or importance of the more recent group of theories which follow the aggressive instinct or drive aspect of Freud's other works. The present theory and this group are supplementary.

In expatiation of this supplementary relationship it may be reiterated that the threat of war, however brought, is a threat to the entire system of beliefs of the members of the community (see pp. 93–98, 112–15, above). Indeed, for some persons the threat of war alone will bring on the anxiety attacks of acute anomie. See, e.g., the cases of diarrhea, nervous indigestion, fainting, heart attack, and "jitters" reported in Madge and Harrison, *Britain by Mass Observation*, pp. 89–90, for the September, 1938, crisis. This tension, this fear, then leads to hatred of the presumable agent (see, e.g., *ibid.*, pp. 90–91), according to the frustration-aggression theory. And here the aggressive-drive theory of war should take over. All this is but one phase of the relationship of the two theories of war, the anomic and the aggressive. Anomie as a cause of aggression, however, has been considered only in the vaguest manner by the aggressive-drive theorists. They seem not to realize that every war is ideological. Instead, they emphasize almost to exclusion another aspect of aggression, which leads to a second and less intimate phase of relationship between the two theories. They say, to speak *in grosso modo*, that man is inevitably frustrated (Freud later insisted on an instinct of aggression), therefore he is aggressive, yet his conscience tells him that aggression is wrong. At this juncture they make their use (and at times it appears unjustified) of the psychoanalytic mechanism of projection: Man, rather than admit his aggressiveness, attributes ("projects") it to other nations; therefore he sees threats where there are none. The anomic theory does not deny this possibility; it points out an additional possibility. Because of his simple anomie the average person is sensitive to any event that promises to rid him of it. War with its obvious readjustment of beliefs and resulting co-operativeness is such an event.

In short, the anomic theory in relation to war does three things: (1) it supplies the aggressive-drive theorists with specific knowledge of a deprivation in modern life which they had not sufficiently considered and which is serious enough to cause strong aggressive impulses; (2) it emphasizes not the emotion of aggression in men but, rather, their need to retain an ideology (to the point of dying for it) which describes a reality in which they know how to gain security (i.e., freedom from separation-anxiety or acute anomie), a reality for which they know the directives; and (3) it proposes that if men have ideologies with conflicting directives (i.e., have simple anomie), they may foresee that war will remove the conflict.

18. Quincy Wright's statement should also be recalled in this connection. "Even the United States, which has perhaps somewhat unjustifiably prided itself on its peacefulness, has had only twenty years during its entire history of 158 years when it has not had the army or navy in active operations during some days, somewhere" (quoted in Lasswell, *Politics*, p. 53).

CHAPTER X

1. See Goldhamer, "Voluntary Associations," pp. 70–86. Unfortunately, the Thurstone Neurotic Inventory, through which the evidence was drawn, could be administered only to the leaders in associations and not to the general membership.

2. Alcoholism in its dozens of forms is one of the most difficult solutions to disentangle. It can be used in both simple and acute anomie; it is a cultural trait, a psychosis, and even a form of slow suicide (see, e.g., J. P. Shalloo, "Some

Cultural Factors in the Etiology of Alcoholism," *Quarterly Journal for the Study of Alcoholism*, II [1941], 464–78). See, also, for an excellent example of the use of alcohol (by American Indians) for the banishment of acute anomie, Oliver La Farge, *As Long as the Grass Shall Grow* (New York: Longmans, Green & Co., 1940), pp. 34–36.

3. They are the most frequent if one excludes the senile disorders, cerebral arteriosclerosis, and mental deficiency.

4. Fenichel, *Psychoanalytic Theory*, p. 408.

5. Walter A. Lunden, "Suicides in France, 1910–43," *American Journal of Sociology*, LII (1947), 331.

6. Woolf, *Mrs. Dalloway*, pp. 33–37, 139–40, 224–26. The narrative style which weaves continuously from one character to another within minute intervals of time necessitated a juxtaposition of passages. This is excusable only because the book cannot be quoted in full. It should be read from cover to cover to feel the full impact of the psychological drama within the mind of Septimus Smith.

7. Wilhelm Reich, *The Function of the Orgasm* (New York: Orgone Institute Press, 1944), pp. 55–56.

8. The last economic depression brought a few attempts to classify mental disorders in this fashion (see William C. Menninger and Leona Chidester, "The Role of Financial Losses in the Precipitation of Mental Illness," *Journal of the American Medical Association*, C [1933], 1398–1400; and J. H. Travis, "Precipitating Factors in Manic-Depressive Psychoses," *Psychiatric Quarterly*, VII [1933], 411–18). And, of course, the designation "traumatic" makes the "traumatic neuroses" a category of precipitating factors.

9. The coefficient of correlation between the monthly business index and the monthly suicide index during the period of years 1910–31 in the United States is fairly high, namely, -0.47 ± 0.05. It is even higher when calculated on the basis of annual data: -0.55 ± 0.15 (see L. Dublin and B. Bunzel, *To Be or Not To Be* [New York: Harrison Smith & Robert Haas, 1933], pp. 93–109). In 1932 the rate rose to 21.3 per 100,000, the highest figure the country ever had, with the exclusion of the postpanic year of 1908, when the rate was 21.5 (see Frederick L. Hoffman, "The Suicide Record for 1932," *Spectator* [New York] CXXX [1933], 23; and Ernest R. Mowrer, "A Study of Personal Disorganization," *American Sociological Review*, IV [1939], 475–87; see also Maurice Halbwachs, *Les Causes du suicide* [Paris: Félix Alcan, 1930], pp. 355–74; and Walter C. Hurlburt, "Prosperity, Depression and the Suicide Rate," *American Journal of Sociology*, XXXVII [1932], 714–19).

10. See Dublin and Bunzel, *To Be or Not To Be*, pp. 115–24; Durkheim, *Le Suicide*, pp. 149–73; Halbwachs, *Les Causes du suicide*, pp. 241–93; H. Morselli, *Suicide* (New York: D. Appleton & Co., 1882), pp. 122–23; and R. S. Cavan, *Suicide* (Chicago: University of Chicago Press, 1928), pp. 38–39.

11. Data on religious differentials in mental disorder are scarce. Jung, interestingly enough, said that in thirty years the largest number of his patients were Protestants, a smaller number Jews, "and not more than five or six believing

NOTES TO PAGES 170-75

Catholics" (see Jung, *Modern Man*, p. 264; and also Murray, *Explorations in Personality*, p. 739).

12. On suicide and war see especially Morselli, *Suicide*, pp. 159–60; Dublin and Bunzel, *To Be or Not To Be*, pp. 110–14; and Halbwachs, *Les Causes du suicide*, pp. 319–29.

13. Hallgren, *Seeds of Revolt*, p. 47.

14. A similar generalization with many examples can be found in Toynbee, *A Study of History*, pp. 432, 505–30.

15. It is recognized that what is here called an ideological movement or a new ideology would be called a utopia in Mannheim's usage (see Karl Mannheim, *Ideology and Utopia* [New York: Harcourt, Brace & Co., 1936], pp. 173–84). The word "utopia" was not employed in his sense here because it still contains negative connotations of unrealizable community projects.

16. It is estimated that "there are probably three or four million persons [in America] who accept the millenarian scheme in utter disregard of Biblical scholarship, the evidence of history, the findings of science, or the influence of 'modern thought'" (for this and the other factual statements on sects see Elmer T. Clark, *The Small Sects in America* (Nashville, Tenn.: Cokesbury Press, 1937], pp. 43, 273–78).

17. Professor Gieger, as quoted in Svend Ranulf, "Scholarly Forerunners of Fascism," *Ethics*, L (1939), 17. F. Tönnies' *Gemeinschaft und Gesellschaft* (Leipzig: Fues's Verlag, 1887) preceded Durkheim's *De la division* by six years and is in many ways similar to it. The likenesses, however, went unnoticed by Tönnies himself, who reviewed Durkheim's book. Tönnies may have been influenced by Auguste Comte, who was Durkheim's master. Together the two schools of Durkheim and Tönnies form the core of twentieth-century Continental sociology.

18. Bernard Barber, "Acculturation and Messianic Movements," *American Sociological Review*, VI (1941), 663. See, in addition, Arnold J. Toynbee, *A Study of History* (unabridged ed., 6 vols.; London: Oxford University Press, 1934), III, 462–65, for the psychological setting of the conception of the Second Coming.

19. Modern psychological tests were used to verify the existence of the fantasies. "Stories of the good life on the plains before the coming of the white man . . . constantly reappear in the responses to the Thematic Apperception Test" (Gordon Macgregor, *Warriors without Weapons* [Chicago: University of Chicago Press, 1946], p. 207).

20. Theodore Abel, *Why Hitler Came into Power* (New York: Prentice-Hall, Inc., 1938), p. 93.

21. See pp. 39–40, above. The relation between the concept "status" and primary systems of belief was formulated by the author in "Status as a Political Motive," pp. 91–93. Briefly stated, the *ruler* by his presumed regulation of the environment is held responsible for the provision of status positions, namely, the approved occupations in a community. Without one of these occupations the person is without status, namely, the approval of the community for his activ-

ities. The loss of primary status is equated with the loss of the affection of attendants and brings on anomic anxiety.

In Germany swift industrialization did not completely destroy military and bureaucratic status. Unlike the situation in the United States, e.g., the Wehrmacht could offer status positions to the lowly soldier even in peacetime. Nevertheless, for the great majority of the population the business job was the status position. This is evident in the direct relationship between the number of unemployed and the number of votes polled for the N.S.D.A.P. (see, e.g., the tables given in Abel, *Why Hitler Came into Power*, p. 311). More detailed German electoral statistics can be seen in H. Tingsten, *Political Behavior* (London: P. S. King & Son, Ltd., 1937), pp. 27–64; and Rudolf Heberle, *From Democracy to Nazism* (Baton Rouge, La.: Louisiana State University Press, 1945).

It should be noted here that the depression had not yet brought Germany a semistarvation diet. "Its consumption of beer, cigars, and *Konditorwaren* declined appreciably, but it is doubtful whether the ample waistline of the average burgher or the generous proportions of his wife shrank by very much" (F. S. Schuman, *Nazi Dictatorship* [New York: Alfred A. Knopf, 1936], p. 108).

22. Peter F. Drucker, *The End of Economic Man* (New York: John Day & Co., 1939), pp. 22–23, 55, 60–61, 66–67. These remarks should be compared with the mental attitudes and behavior of the unemployed as shown in pp. 122–26, above.

23. For the one attempt to relate Fascist movements to the incidence of anomie see Talcott Parsons, "Some Sociological Aspects of the Fascist Movements," *Social Forces*, XXI (1942–43), 138–47. It is remarkable that apparently no others have done this. However, a penetrating analysis of naziism from the standpoint of anomie (even though the term is not used) is Kurt Riezler, "The Social Psychology of Fear," *American Journal of Sociology*, XLIX (1944), 489–98. One should also see Siegfried Kracauer, *From Caligari to Hitler: A Psychological History of the German Film* (Princeton: Princeton University Press, 1947), which traces the theme of chaos from 1919 to 1933 in such German films as *The Cabinet of Dr. Caligari, M*, and *Dr. Mabuse the Gambler;* and the novel by Hans Fallada (pseud. for Rudolf Ditzen), *Little Man, What Now?* trans. Eric Sutton (New York: Simon & Schuster, 1933).

24. Abel, *Why Hitler Came into Power*, p. 151.

25. *Ibid.*, pp. 152–53.

26. See pp. 25–26, above.

27. Peter Drucker, "End of Economic Man in Europe," *Harper's Magazine*, CLXXVIII (1939), 562. Kracauer, *From Caligari to Hitler*, also finds hopelessness and the wish for a miracle worker expressed in German films between World Wars I and II.

28. In a vague way this is the contention, too, of such books as Eric Russell Bentley, *A Century of Hero Worship* (New York: Lippincott & Co., 1944).

29. Hermann Göring, *Germany Reborn* (London: Mathews & Marrot, Ltd., 1934), p. 80. Whether Göring himself believed this or not (and he most likely

did not) is immaterial. The relevant point is that he could say it to Germans while maintaining a humorless face.

30. H. T. Kane, *Louisiana Hayride* (New York: William Morrow & Co., 1941), facing p. 72.

31. The question, philosophy or no philosophy, hinges naturally on the definition employed. Hitler's *Mein Kampf* or Alfred Rosenberg's *Der Mythos des 20. Jahrhundert* can be thought of, if one wishes, as the philosophical fount of the movement. If a comprehensive philosophical system predating naziism is wanted, Othmar Spann of Vienna will do, as Karl Polanyi has proposed in "Dies irae," in *Christianity and the Social Revolution*, ed. John Lewis, Karl Polanyi, and Donald K. Kitchin (New York: Charles Scribner's Sons, 1936), pp. 359–94. Unless one's meaning is clear, points of similarity can be found with innumerable earlier thinkers—Treitschke a forerunner of Hitlerism, Nietzsche a prophet of dictatorship, etc.

32. Abel also noticed the reversal (*Why Hitler Came into Power*, p. 149). This large-scale protest against the component parts of the economic system of beliefs reveals both the instabilities and the politically serious potentialities of the mixed and conflicting systems of beliefs in contemporary democracies. The author has elsewhere attempted to analyze specific points of survival weakness of the economic ideology in critical situations (see "Status as a Political Motive," pp. 97–101).

33. John Gloag, *Word Warfare, Some Aspects of German Propaganda and English Liberty* (London: Nicholson & Watson, Ltd., 1939), pp. 95, 56, 58–59, 61–62.

34. H. D. Lasswell, "Psychology of Hitlerism," *Political Quarterly*, IV (1933), 379. See also Erik Homburger Erikson, "Hitler's Imagery and German Youth," *Psychiatry*, V (1942), 475–93.

35. Gloag, *Word Warfare*, pp. 98–99.

36. Derrick Sington and Arthur Weidenfeld, *The Goebbels Experiment* (London: John Murray, 1942), p. 220.

37. Robert Ley, *Report and Programme of Work*, quoted in Gloag, *Word Warfare*, p. 75.

38. Quoted in Fritz Morstein Marx, "Totalitarian Politics," in *Symposium on the Totalitarian State* ("Proceedings of the American Philosophical Society," Vol. LXXXII, No. 1 [Philadelphia: American Philosophical Society, 1940]), p. 7. The number and eloquence of those who found in the National Socialist movement a welcomed renewal of the comradely associativeness of World War I life are remarkable. They interpreted the idea of *Gemeinschaft* in terms of their experiences in the great community of the front (see Abel's collection of autobiographies, *Why Hitler Came into Power*, pp. 142–43; and pp. 157–60, above). Kracauer's study, *From Caligari to Hitler*, also found that companionship was a leitmotiv in German films up to 1933.

39. See esp. Joachim Schumacher, *Die Angst vor dem Chaos* (Paris: Éditions Asra, 1937), which describes the exploitation of this fear.

40. The statement of Wesley C. Mitchell in *Economic Reconstructions: Report*

of the Columbia University Commission, R. M. MacIver (ed.) (New York: Columbia University Press, 1934), p. 82. "American history is replete with panics and depressions—1819, 1837, 1843, 1857, 1873, 1893, 1904, 1907, 1921, and 1929—manmade it would seem, for there never was a time when the riches of our natural resources and manpower were not available in abundance" (*ibid.*).

41. Sherwood Anderson, *Puzzled America* (New York: Charles Scribner's Sons, 1935).

42. The precise percentage of the population which must be without status before collective rather than individual solutions are sought has not, of course, been determined here. The incidence of simple anomie, for one thing, must be taken into consideration in the calculation of any such percentage, for its encouragement of associative behavior may lower the necessary proportion much below a majority. It should also be noted that the age limits for adulthood, defined as the community's consensus concerning the age for political participation, will vary from community to community, and this variation too will affect the calculation of the pivotal percentage.

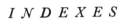

INDEX OF NAMES